How to restore

Kawasaki Z1, Z/KZ900 & Z/KZ1000

YOUR step-by-step colour illustrated guide to complete restoration

Chris Rooke

More from Veloce:

Enthusiast's Restoration Manual Series
Ducati Bevel Twins 1971 to 1986 (Falloon)
How to restore Honda CX500 & CX650 – YOUR step-by-step colour illustrated guide to complete restoration (Burns)
How to restore Honda Fours – YOUR step-by-step colour illustrated guide to complete restoration (Burns)
Triumph Trident T150/T160 & BSA Rocket III, How to Restore (Rooke)

Essential Buyer's Guide Series
BMW Boxer Twins (Henshaw)
BMW GS (Henshaw)
BSA 350, 441 & 500 Singles (Henshaw)
BSA 500 & 650 Twins (Henshaw)
BSA Bantam (Henshaw)
Ducati Bevel Twins (Falloon)
Ducati Desmodue Twins (Falloon)
Ducati Desmoquattro Twins – 851, 888, 916, 996, 998, ST4 1988 to 2004 (Falloon)
Hinckley Triumph triples & fours 750, 900, 955, 1000, 1050, 1200 – 1991-2009 (Henshaw)
Honda CBR FireBlade (Henshaw)
Honda CBR600 Hurricane (Henshaw)
Honda SOHC Fours 1969-1984 (Henshaw)
Kawasaki Z1 & Z900 (Orritt)
Moto Guzzi 2-valve big twins (Falloon)
Norton Commando (Henshaw)
Triumph 350 & 500 Twins (Henshaw)
Triumph Bonneville (Henshaw)
Triumph Thunderbird, Trophy & Tiger (Henshaw)
Velocette 350 & 500 Singles 1946 to 1970 (Henshaw)

Biographies
Chris Carter at Large – Stories from a lifetime in motorcycle racing (Carter & Skelton)
Jim Redman – 6 Times World Motorcycle Champion: The Autobiography (Redman)
'Sox' – Gary Hocking – the forgotten World Motorcycle Champion (Hughes)

Motorcycles & scooters
BMW Boxer Twins 1970-1995 Bible, The (Falloon)
BMW Cafe Racers (Cloesen)
BMW Custom Motorcycles – Choppers, Cruisers, Bobbers, Trikes & Quads (Cloesen)
British Café Racers (Cloesen)
British Custom Motorcycles – The Brit Chop – choppers, cruisers, bobbers & trikes (Cloesen)
Bonjour – Is this Italy? (Turner)
British 250cc Racing Motorcycles (Pereira)
BSA Bantam Bible, The (Henshaw)
BSA Motorcycles – the final evolution (Jones)
Ducati 750 Bible, The (Falloon)
Ducati 750 SS 'round-case' 1974, The Book of the (Falloon)
Ducati 860, 900 and Mille Bible, The (Falloon)
Ducati Monster Bible (New Updated & Revised Edition), The (Falloon)
Ducati Story, The – 6th Edition (Falloon)
Ducati 916 (updated edition) (Falloon)
Fine Art of the Motorcycle Engine, The (Peirce)
Franklin's Indians (Sucher/Pickering/Diamond/Havelin)
From Crystal Palace to Red Square – A Hapless Biker's Road to Russia (Turner)
Funky Mopeds (Skelton)
India - The Shimmering Dream (Reisch/Falls (translator))
Italian Cafe Racers (Cloesen)
Italian Custom Motorcycles (Cloesen)
Japanese Custom Motorcycles – The Nippon Chop – Chopper, Cruiser, Bobber, Trikes and Quads (Cloesen)
Kawasaki Triples Bible, The (Walker)
Kawasaki W, H1 & Z – The Big Air-cooled Machines (Long)
Kawasaki Z1 Story, The (Sheehan)
Lambretta Bible, The (Davies)
Laverda Twins & Triples Bible 1968-1986 (Falloon)
Little book of trikes, the (Quellin)
Moto Guzzi Sport & Le Mans Bible, The (Falloon)
Moto Guzzi Story, The – 3rd Edition (Falloon)
Motorcycle Apprentice (Cakebread)
Motorcycle GP Racing in the 1960s (Pereira)
Motorcycle Racing with the Continental Circus 1920-1970 (Pereira)
Motorcycle Road & Racing Chassis Designs (Noakes)
Motorcycles and Motorcycling in the USSR from 1939 (Turbett)
Motorcycling in the '50s (Clew)
MV Agusta Fours, The book of the classic (Falloon)
MV Agusta since 1945 (Falloon)
Norton Commando Bible – All models 1968 to 1978 (Henshaw)
Off-Road Giants! (Volume 1) – Heroes of 1960s Motorcycle Sport (Westlake)
Off-Road Giants! (Volume 2) – Heroes of 1960s Motorcycle Sport (Westlake)
Off-Road Giants! (Volume 3) – Heroes of 1960s Motorcycle Sport (Westlake)
Peking to Paris 2007 (Young)
Racing Classic Motorcycles (Reynolds)
Racing Line – British motorcycle racing in the golden age of the big single (Guntrip)
The Red Baron's Ultimate Ducati Desmo Manual (Cabrera Choclán)
Scooters & Microcars, The A-Z of Popular (Dan)
Scooter Lifestyle (Grainger)
Scooter Mania! – Recollections of the Isle of Man International Scooter Rally (Jackson)
Slow Burn - The growth of Superbikes & Superbike racing 1970 to 1988 (Guntrip)
Suzuki Motorcycles - The Classic Two-stroke Era (Long)
Triumph Bonneville Bible (59-83) (Henshaw)
Triumph Bonneville!, Save the – The inside story of the Meriden Workers' Co-op (Rosamond)
Triumph Motorcycles & the Meriden Factory (Hancox)
Triumph Speed Twin & Thunderbird Bible (Woolridge)
Triumph Tiger Cub Bible (Estall)
Triumph Trophy Bible (Woolridge)
TT Talking – The TT's most exciting era – As seen by Manx Radio TT's lead commentator 2004-2012 (Lambert)
Velocette Motorcycles – MSS to Thruxton – Third Edition (Burris)
Vespa – The Story of a Cult Classic in Pictures (Uhlig)
Vincent Motorcycles: The Untold Story since 1946 (Guyony & Parker)

www.veloce.co.uk

First published in July 2018, reprinted February 2023 and 2025 by an imprint of David and Charles Limited. Tel +44 (0)1305 260068 / e-mail info@veloce.co.uk / web www.veloce.co.uk. ISBN: 978-1-787111-58-5
© 2018, 2023 & 2025 Chris Rooke and David and Charles. All rights reserved. With the exception of quoting brief passages for the purpose of review, no part of this publication may be recorded, reproduced or transmitted by any means, including photocopying, without the written permission of David and Charles Limited.
Throughout this book logos, model names and designations, etc, have been used for the purposes of identification, illustration and decoration. Such names are the property of the trademark holder as this is not an official publication. Readers with ideas for automotive books, or books on other transport or related hobby subjects, are invited to write to the editorial director of Veloce at the above email address. British Library Cataloguing in Publication Data – A catalogue record for this book is available from the British Library. Design and DTP by Veloce.

ENTHUSIAST'S RESTORATION MANUAL™

How to restore

Kawasaki Z1, Z/KZ900 & Z/KZ1000

YOUR step-by-step colour illustrated guide to complete restoration

Chris Rooke

VELOCE
FINE AUTOMOTIVE BOOKS

Contents

Foreword 6

1. Which model? 7

2. Buying a bike to restore 12

3. Ten golden rules for a successful rebuild 17

4. Preparing to dismantle 20

5. Removing the bodywork & rear mudguard 23

6. Removing headlamp, clocks & carbs 25

7. Removing the wiring loom & other electrics 29

8. Removing the exhaust & rear wheel 32

9. Dismantling the points & generator 37

10. Dismantling the clutch & kick-start assembly 42

11. Removing the gearbox sprocket & casing 45

12. Removing the oil filter, sump & oil pump 48

13. Removing the cylinder head & barrels 51

14. Removing & dismantling the crankcases 55

15. Stripping the crankcases 58

16. Removing & dismantling the front forks 61

17. Dismantling the front & rear wheels 66

18. Vapour blasting, chroming & powder coating 69

19. Polishing engine casings & other alloy parts 74

20. Crankshaft, transmission & oil pump 78

21. Assembling the crankcases 83

22. Reassembling the front forks .. 89

23. Rebuilding the wheels, brake discs & shoes 92

24. Fitting the head races, forks & front wheel 97

25. Replacing the engine in the frame 101

26. Refitting the pistons & cylinder barrels 103

27. Reassembling & refitting the cylinder head 108

28. Camshafts, tappets & oil pressure switch 113

29. Reassembling the gear change & gearbox cover 119

30. Fitting the generator & starter motor 122

31. Dismantling the carburettors 127

32. Rebuilding the carburettors ... 131

33. Carburettor tuning 137

34. Refitting the clutch 140

35. Refitting the swinging arm & shock absorbers 143

CONTENTS

36. Refitting the rear wheel 148

37. Fitting the gearbox outer cover 153

38. Refurbishing & refitting the front brakes 157

39. Fitting the battery box & junction board 163

40. Fitting the carburettors & airbox 167

41. Fitting the rear light, mudguard & indicators 172

42. Fitting the instrument panel 176

43. Assembling & wiring the headlamp 180

44. Ignition, handlebar & rear brake wiring 183

45. Fitting the exhaust system 188

46. Preparing the tank for painting 191

47. Painting & refitting the tank & bodywork 196

48. Teething troubles: no oil pressure & misfiring 201

49. Teething troubles II: the misfire continues 205

50. Tools & equipment 208

51. Summing it all up 212

52. Parts, services, clubs & UK registration 218

Index 223

www.velocebooks.com
New book news • Special offers • Newsletter • Details of all Veloce books • Gift Vouchers

Foreword

Based on the complete ground-up restoration of my 1976 Kawasaki KZ900 A4 (manufactured in America), this book covers the dismantling, restoring and rebuilding of the Z900 engine, electrics, frame, forks, tank, wheels, suspension etc, in detail, complete with a comprehensive set of colour photos. I am an amateur enthusiast with generally good mechanical skills but limited workshop facilities, and I had never rebuilt a 4-cylinder Kawasaki before. In fact, as something of a die-hard British biker, this is the first Japanese machine I have ever restored. This book should therefore allow you to complete your own restoration from the point of view of someone tackling the job for the first time, and encountering various problems that you might also experience, which a more experienced restorer with better equipment might not think to address. There are a few caveats, however, that I'd like to make clear from the start.

First and foremost, this book should be read in conjunction with the two existing workshop manuals – the *Haynes Manual* and the *Kawasaki Workshop Manual* – along with another essential text, the *Kawasaki Parts Catalogue* (see chapter on tools and equipment for full details). These manuals give good instructions and explanations of how to complete tasks, but are not always clear, and there are quite often omissions and assumptions that can confuse the unwary and novice restorer – like me! This book aims to address these omissions and confusion, and help the amateur restorer make sense of the sometimes clinical and technical instructions in the manuals that often lack thorough explanations, and take for granted that some steps will be known. This book is not intended to replace the manuals but supplement them. (What's the point in reinventing the wheel?)

Please note that both the *Haynes Manual* and the *Kawasaki Workshop Manual* contain details of the torque wrench settings, and it's definitely worth book-marking these when it comes to reassembly. Also, the *Kawasaki Parts Catalogue*, apart from being essential for ordering spare parts (ALWAYS try to quote part numbers when ordering; it saves much time and confusion. If you order 'the thingummyjig that goes on the end of the wotsit,' you thoroughly deserve whatever is eventually delivered!), contain some great diagrams that aren't in the manuals, and can be a godsend when trying to work out the order in which everything goes back. Be aware, though, that the parts catalogues can't always be relied on to give accurate diagrams, as occasionally the order of assembly illustrated is incorrect. Parts catalogues for different models are available to download from the internet from places such as the Z-Power website; you can also download some manuals for free or they can be bought as hard copies. I bought my *Kawasaki Workshop Manual* for the Z900 A4 on eBay, and the *Haynes Manual* from Amazon.

The parts catalogue also serves two major functions: First and foremost it supplies the all-important part number, which you can then Google to find a suppiier and price. Secondly, it helps to identify which parts from different models are interchangeable – if they have the same part number, that's fine – if not, beware: it probably won't fit your model and may even damage it. (One owner apparently fitted the crankshaft from a Z1000A3 to his Z1000A2, not realising that they are different, with the former having more teeth on the cam chain sprocket than his original. When he came to start the engine, bent valves all round. Ouch!) Also, although many parts in the catalogues are listed as NLA (No Longer Available) ignore this as these are old catalogues and most parts are now available.

Note that whilst this book deals specifically with the KZ900, it should be relevant to other 4-cylinder models, including the Z1000s, as the engines and cycle parts are essentially the same, though be aware that every model has slight differences, here and there. For ease of reading I refer to the 'Z900' throughout the book as a generic term, but this includes all the Z1s and Z1000s. If there is a clear difference between models in a certain area, I refer specifically to that model.

Although I'm an experienced motorcycle restorer, I have generally worked on British motorcycles previously, and have therefore undertaken this restoration as a Kawasaki virgin (!), which I believe will be of great benefit to other amateurs who are approaching the work in much the same way. This manual covers every element of the restoration in a very clear, step-by-step way, supported by a very comprehensive set of photos. The other good news is that I have several marque experts on hand who have freely given of their time and expertise to fill in the gaps in my knowledge, and corrected me when necessary. Hopefully, the manual will give you the best of both worlds.

Finally, if you are contemplating a full rebuild it's worthwhile reading the entire book before starting work so you're completely forewarned and forearmed about rebuilding a 4-cylinder Kawasaki.

I really hope you enjoy reading the manual, and find it useful and informative. I've tried to write it in a non-technical way – more as a narrative than a manual – because it's intended to be your friend in the workshop, not only to help out and give advice, but equally ready to share problems and help you overcome them. Good luck!

Chris Rooke

DISCLAIMER

Although all advice is given in good faith, the publisher, author and retailer can accept no responsibility for damage or injury caused by errors or omissions in this book.

Please do not undertake any of the tasks described unless you are fully confident of your ability to carry them out safely and with the correct tools.

Chapter 1
Which model?

Perhaps one of the most important parts of any restoration is buying the right bike to restore, so decide which machine you're looking for.
The range of bikes is as follows –
• Z1 900 1972-3
• Z1A 900 1974
• Z1B 900 1975
• KZ/Z900 1976 (including the KZ900 LTD: a custom cruiser with fat rear tyre and alloy wheels)
• Z1000 1977-80 (a fairly wide range of models beginning with the A1/A2 models, continuing with the A3/A4 MKII models, and including a KZ1000 LTD and a Turbo version, and some with shaft drive (not covered in this manual). See the Z-Power website for full details.)

See photos 1.1-1.7 of many of the various models available.

Your first step should be to buy *The Essential Buyer's Guide. Kawasaki Z1 and Z900 1972-1976*, by Dave Orritt. I'm giving you some basic info here, but more detailed and essential info is contained therein.

Another book you should read is *Original Kawasaki Z1, Z900 & KZ900* by Dave Marsden, which contains detailed information on these models, and Z1000s, too.

I would also peruse the Z-Power website, which contains an amazing range of information about these bikes including parts catalogues, owners clubs, model descriptions, etc, as well as a few parts for sale!

Remember, the more you know about these bikes before you go looking, the better. Read as much as possible before committing to the market place.

Pricewise, as a rough guide, the oldest bikes are the most valuable and the newest the cheapest. The order of value from highest to lowest is therefore from the earliest to the latest, so something like: Z1, Z1A, Z1B, Z900, KZ900, Z1000, and prices are currently rising fast. Be aware that, due to the vagaries of the market/taste/international incidents, etc, vehicle values can change quite dramatically. In the late 1980s, for example, the value of classic cars increased massively, and then crashed and burned, leaving many buyers out of pocket. At present, classic car and bike values are going through the roof – but without a crystal ball I can't say whether this trend will continue, or for how long if it does. Who knows how things will look with regard to classic vehicle values in 10 or 20 years' time when environmental restrictions on riding classic bikes will begin to bite ...?

Z1
'The first cut is the deepest' is the old saying and, as with many classic vehicles, it generally holds true in this instance too. These are the most desirable models, but their desirability and relative scarcity is reflected in their value. Even bikes requiring full restoration command high prices. Having said that, some of the early Z1s had 'teething problems' – different cylinder blocks and cylinder head gaskets caused oil leaks – that were sorted out later on in production, and these can affect desirability.

Z1A
Almost as desirable as the Z1 ... but not quite. Easily identifiable by not having the iconic black-painted engine, together with different paintwork, especially on the tank. Still very sought-after and valuable. Some problems highlighted on the Z1 (for example, leaking cam covers and peeling black engine paint) were addressed on the Z1A, and so it is, in some ways, a better bike than the Z1. Carburettors were slightly revised halfway through the run, and the

HOW TO RESTORE KAWASAKI Z1, Z/KZ900 & Z/KZ1000

1.1 Kawasaki Z1.

1.2 Kawasaki Z1A.

1.3 Kawasaki Z1B.

1.4 Kawasaki Z900.

1.5 Kawasaki KZ900.

1.6 Kawasaki Z1000.

1.7 Kawasaki Z1000 LTD.

WHICH MODEL?

tacho featured a brake light failure warning indicator.

Z1B
Slightly revised again from the Z1A, but almost as valuable. Now available in a lovely Tahiti blue, but with the mechanical chain oiler (as fitted to Z1 and Z1A models) removed as superior 'O' ring chains were fitted, and a slightly different speedometer.

Note: All Z1 models were fitted with a single front disc with twin discs an option (so the right-hand fork leg has mountings ready to accept a second calliper if required). A factory-fitted steering damper was another option.

KZ/Z900 A4
A very different model to the previous ones with many improved features that made it a much better bike in many ways – and therefore less valuable – such is the classic market! Z900s were made in Japan, and the KZs were generally made in Kawasaki's brand new plant in Nebraska, USA, with the 'K' added to differentiate between the two. They were both known as A4 models. These bikes had stronger frames, revised (smaller) carburettors, and more restrictive exhaust systems (the originals had '76' stamped on them). This reduced power by 2bhp to 80bhp but improved mid-range response. They also had a revised tank with a locking petrol cap and a revised (vertical) instrument binnacle. The tail lamps were squarer, and Z900 models for the UK market had twin discs as standard.

KZ900 A5
When production of the KZ/Z900 ended in 1977, the USA factory still had quite a few parts left over, so continued to produce them until all the parts were used up. Virtually identical to the A4, the bikes were nevertheless given their own model number of A5.

Z1000
(Four main models produced: A1, A2 (MKI), A3, and A4 (MKII). Very similar to the Z900 models they replaced, the obvious visual difference was the new, 4-into-2 exhaust system rather than the iconic 4-into-4 of the Z1/Z900 bikes. Kawasaki did this to save money on warranty claims: the original 4-into-4 exhaust system was prone to rust, and many owners claimed replacements under warranty. To avoid this Kawasaki decided to ditch the system and replace it with the 4-into-2. I think that, although this saved money initially, it was a very short-sighted move, as this simple change affected the desirability of the bikes as much then as it does now. Not only that, but, unlike the previous models, the exhaust system is currently unavailable. The good news is that the 4-into-4 system from Z1/Z900/KZ900 will fit, with just the fabrication of only a couple of small hanging brackets. Another alternative is to fit a 4-into-1 system which is much cheaper and sounds good, but, whatever the case, if you want to restore a Z1000 to original spec then the exhaust is a major stumbling block.

Z1000s were mainly fitted with twin discs at the front as standard, and used a disc brake at the rear as well instead of the previous drum brake. KZ1000-B3 LTD models were also produced as a custom cruiser for the American market only, with alloy wheels and a fat back tyre: quite a few have now been imported into the UK.

Z1000P
The Z1000 continued to be made as a police bike in the USA long after standard production ceased (up to 2005), and these are desirable in their own way. They came fully loaded with a Windjammer fairing, siren, panniers and Motorola top box, foot boards and flashing lights, etc. Almost unbelievably, they were sold off complete with all these accessories and police decals, so anyone can quite legally ride round on a bike in full police spec and live the CHiPS dream! (I've nearly bought one on several occasions …).

UNOBTAINABLE PARTS
Having decided which model or models you're interested in, you need to know whether any of the parts are unobtainable, as the presence or otherwise of these on a prospective purchase can make all the difference. Some parts cannot be bought new as original stock has run out, and no-one is currently manufacturing replacements, which means that the only way to obtain them is through the second-hand market: prices can be astronomic for some – if you can find them in the first place.

Z1/Z1A/Z1B
The good news with these bikes is that most parts are available as new, and, as they share their DNA with later machines, they are often interchangeable. The bad news is that as relatively few examples of each were made, and as they're very sought-after, second-hand parts aren't that easy to come by, unlike for later bikes; so if it's not available new it can be hard to find that elusive part. For example, choke levers for Z1A models are no longer available. A simple thing like a little black knob with the word 'CHOKE' written on it can become a nightmare. They are completely unavailable (I've been looking for one for about a year now, without success), and if the bike you buy doesn't have one – well, good luck! If you're planning a concours restoration this will be your nemesis.

The mechanical rear chain oiling system is also no longer available, although this doesn't affect prices too much. The oil reservoir itself, situated behind the left-hand side panel, is available, though. At the time of writing right-hand discs for a twin disc conversion aren't available, but I'm reliably informed that they're in the pipeline. Original carburettors are also no longer available.

Z/KZ900
The original carburettor airbox is practically unobtainable. This differs from that on Z1 models and, as no-one is remanufacturing it, examples are increasingly difficult to find. Back in the day, many owners removed them, as the associated air filters were restrictive, and instead fitted aftermarket individual filters on the back of the carbs, with the airboxes inevitably becoming lost/separated from the bike along the way. If the bike you are planning to buy hasn't got an airbox and you want to restore the bike to original, this is a major headache. I've just paid nearly £300 for the only one I could find in the UK. Some people are even buying wrecks

HOW TO RESTORE KAWASAKI Z1, Z/KZ900 & Z/KZ1000

just for the airbox, and selling off the remaining parts for spares.

Brake callipers aren't currently available (unlike for earlier Z1s), which means that, if you've got an American spec KZ model (like mine) with only one disc, then the only way to convert it to twin disc is to find a second-hand calliper. (Callipers will fit on either side of the bike, but only with the correct mounting bracket – which are handed and are now available.)

Z1000

The 4-into-2 exhaust system is unobtainable, and no-one is currently making copies. As exhausts naturally rust out over time, second-hand replacements are very hard to come by. Unless you can find someone to make you a bespoke stainless system, the only other options are to fit a 4-into-1 system or a 4-into-4 from a Z1/Z900. The exhausts on ex-police bikes tend to be better, as they are newer, but they do need the original system to look the part. The earlier MkI models use the same callipers as the Z900, with the same problems of availability. The later MkII models use slightly different callipers that fit behind the fork legs rather than in front, and these callipers are both unobtainable and handed – so not easy to source.

ENGINE PARTS

Virtually all engine parts are still freely available (as well as lots of parts to upgrade the engine). At the time of writing, the only engine parts I can think of that aren't available are the main engine cases, and the little damper rubber that sits behind the rotor in the alternator (but these don't often need replacing, anyway).

NB: All of the above parts are currently unavailable at the time of writing, but may well become available in future. As restoring Japanese bikes becomes more popular, manufacturers are naturally encouraged to begin making replacement parts due to their increasing value, so it's always worth checking with suppliers. It's also worth checking the pinned post on the Facebook page that accompanies this book (Kawasaki Z1/Z900/Z1000 Restoration Manual Updates), as this carries information about parts availability, etc, together with a host of new information.

ORIGINALITY

If you are planning to restore your bike to concours condition there are several things to watch out for –

DATE STAMPS

Various parts of all models carry date stamps, including: wheel rims, original exhaust systems, swinging arms, torque arms, carburettors, and switch gear. Unfortunately, Kawasaki used a variety of dating codes, sometimes based on the Gregorian calendar and sometimes on the Showa calendar (based on the reign of Emperor Hirohito), so they're not that easy to follow. Most Kawasaki parts are generally stamped with two numbers showing the year and then the month of manufacture based on the Gregorian calendar – so, 5 8 stamped on my brake stay shows it was manufactured in 1975 (5) August (8). Other date codes sometimes show the day as well as the month and year. The earlier the bike the more date stamps, and vice-versa.

Wheel rims use a slightly different code with a number followed by a letter: the number being the year and the letter the month. So, 4D is 1974 (4) and April (D).

Brake disc date stamps are a law unto themselves, and use the Showa calendar which starts from when Emperor Hirohito began his reign in 1926. So, 1972 is the year 47 (not 46 for some reason). Date codes only show the last number of the year, so the date code for 1972 is 7. Months are then shown by letters and not numbers (just to confuse us even more!) and are, in fact, not months but 13 groups of 4 weeks: the letters chosen to represent them aren't even sequential! The 4 week groups are as follows: A, B, C, D, F, H, K, L, N, R, S, T, V, with A being the first 4 weeks of the year (January) and V being the last 4 weeks (December). So, for example, the code 8V on my Z1A brake disc indicates that it was manufactured in December 1973. (Phew – now go for a little lie-down!)

Further info on date codes can be found on John Brookes' Z2 website: http://www.freewebs.com/750rs/ (Note that the Z2 was a 750cc version of the Z1 made for the Japanese market as, ironically, only machines no bigger than 750cc were permitted in Japan, so they couldn't ride Z1s!)

If you want a totally original bike look for one that has the correct stamps on it as, without these, it will never be 100 per cent original. You can buy second-hand original parts but, not only are these rare and expensive, you will need to find ones that are stamped with a date that fits with the date of manufacture of the rest of the bike, and this really is difficult to achieve. The main stumbling block tends to be the exhausts, as most were replaced and the replacements don't have date stamps. Personally, this 'totally original' thing doesn't matter to me: as long as the bike is not massively customised and looks pretty standard, that'll do for me – but each to their own.

CARBURETTORS

I think I'm correct in saying that ribless carburettors for the earlier (Z1) models aren't available*, and the earlier versions (as fitted to Z1s and early Z1As) are particularly hard to find. Due to this, some owners have fitted later carbs to earlier machines. Just be aware that changes like these will massively de-value the bike, and replacing them with originals is very difficult. If you're not bothered about originality, that's fine; you should pay a lot less than for a bike in standard trim.

CONCOURS FREAKS

I'm not a complete originality fanatic, but strongly recommend you do read *Original Kawasaki Z1, Z900 and KZ900* by Dave Marsden, as this gives very precise details about originality and what to look for – and, despite its title, does include a chapter on the Z1000s, too. Essential reading for earlier models is John Brookes' *Kawasaki Z1 & Z2. 1972-73 Restorer's Parts Book*, which again, despite its title, covers all Z1 models.

---

* Ribless carbs are so-called as, unlike later carbs, they don't have the little supporting rib on the main body.

WHICH MODEL?

FAKE BIKES

One real problem with these bikes is that all Z1 models are more valuable than later bikes, so many sellers will market their bike as a Z1 when it actually isn't. This often leads to misrepresentation (accidental and deliberate) of some later bikes. I've lost count of the times I've seen a Z900 or a KZ900 advertised as a Z1, or a KZ900 (made in America) advertised as a Z900 (made in Japan), the KZ900 lacking the standard front twin disc brake of the Z900. I've even seen Z1000s advertised as Z1s. Be very careful when considering a potential purchase to be sure of what you're buying (even if the seller isn't). Use Dave Orritt's *Essential Buyer's Guide* (Veloce), check engine and frame numbers and any other available manufacturer's date stamps, and watch out for tell-tale signs such as newer carbs, and vertical instrument binnacle (as opposed to horizontal), etc. You have been warned!

LESSONS LEARNT

- A bike in fairly good condition will cost just as much to restore as one in tatty condition, because although the parts might be okay, they will still need to be restored. It therefore makes better financial sense to buy a bike in poor condition rather than one in reasonable condition as you'll end up doing the same amount of work on both. For example, the paintwork on a decent bike may be in pretty good condition compared to one that is chipped and dented, but you'll still need to have the tank repainted if you want the bike to look top dollar.
- Go for a bike that looks original and relatively untouched rather than one that's been customised over the years with uprated brakes, forks, suspension, etc. You'll pay over the odds for such a bike, and then spend a lot returning it to standard spec – if you can find the parts! An original bike that may be very tired and a bit rusty is a far better option.
- Do as much research as possible before looking at bikes to buy.
- Check those unobtainable parts! If they're on the bike, great; if not, can you get them? Paying that bit more for a complete bike in original condition is always worth it.
- Check that the bike is what it claims to be (see above). Is this really a Z1B with rare twin disc conversion, or a disguised Z900?
- Try to buy from a reputable dealer (often one who specialises in importing bikes from abroad – mainly America). It'll cost a little more but will probably be worth it with several bikes to choose from. (See 'My Buying Experience' later on.)
- Has the bike got all its original parts, such as wheel rims and exhausts? If so, it'll cost a lot more – but even more than that to return to original if it hasn't ... always supposing you can find the parts!

Chapter 2
Buying a bike to restore

Having bought various classic bikes over the years, I know that one of the most important aspects of any restoration is to buy the correct bike in the first place. As a result, I researched as much as possible in advance.

My contacts in the classic bike world eventually put me in touch with Dave Orritt (author of the *Z1 and Z900 Essential Buyer's Guide* by Veloce). His knowledge and experience was essential in helping me find a good bike to restore, and he was able to answer questions and give advice in a way that's hard for a book to do. Having advised on the pros and cons of different models, Dave put me in touch with two businesses he felt may be able to help. He directed me, first of all, to Z-Power, a spares specialist that also restores and sell bikes, and DK Motorcycles, a specialist Kawasaki dealer and major importer of bikes to restore in Newcastle-under-Lyme.

Now, I appreciate that not everyone will have an expert like Dave on-hand, but do try and make contact with someone who knows what they're talking about when it comes to Z1s/Z900s/Z1000s. Failing this, read everything you can – and don't forget the information pages on the Z-Power website.

I already own a very nice Z1A (restored, but not by me. See photo 1.2 again), to which I've fitted a twin disc conversion, so I was looking for something a little different – and considerably cheaper! As a result, I focused on Z900s, KZ900s, and Z1000s.

What I wanted was a largely original bike that could be restored to largely standard spec. I'm not a concours freak so didn't intend to restore it to 100 per cent, rivet-counting original. I did want to build something that looked fairly standard and not 'rodded,' but with a few sensible upgrades and changes where appropriate: the colour scheme, for example.

Initially, I spoke to Z-Power to see if it had a suitable bike for restoration that it might be prepared to part with. Z-Power had a Z1000-A2 scheduled for restoration, but was willing to sell it. The bike had a seized engine, as a PO (previous owner) had fitted a crankshaft from a MkII Z1000-A3, not realising that they were different (there's an extra tooth on the cam chain sprocket on Series 3 and 4s, apparently). As soon as the owner started the engine after rebuilding it, the valve timing went out of sync and bent all of the valves ... It's information like this that is so valuable! I mean, who would have suspected that? Most British bikes didn't have a change of crankshaft for decades, let alone when going from a MkI to a MkII! I considered buying this bike, but realised that I wanted a 900 with the iconic 4-into-4 silencers and rear drum brake.

My main resource of bikes suitable for restoration was, of course, eBay, but the problem with this route is that you are bidding several thousand pounds for a bike without ever actually having seen it in the flesh! Photos are a very poor substitute: if you place photos of a really rough bike and a concours bike side-to-side on eBay, chances are you'll see very little difference, which means that a really rough bike can look great on eBay, making it very easy to buy something that's much worse than it appears – and possibly for a lot of money! Only when you actually see the bike will you know what's it's really like. Failing this, ask for close-up photos of all areas of the bike (poor condition examples on eBay tend to feature long/middle distance shots only, which don't give a true indication of condition).

I spent quite some time looking

BUYING A BIKE TO RESTORE

at possible bikes on eBay but discounted them – mainly because they were considerably altered from new with aftermarket items such as new forks, new swinging arms, alloy wheels, expensive 4-into-1 exhaust systems, new carburettors, rear disc brakes, etc. If you're in the market for a customised street racer then the world's your oyster (there are many around), but I wanted originality, primarily. See photo 2.1 of a bike I didn't buy as it was too customised, and appeared to be a Z1000 badged as a Z900 (twin front discs behind the fork legs and a rear disc brake).

I also really wanted a Z900 rather than a KZ900, as Z900s were fitted with twin discs at the factory and, for reasons known only to my anal inner self, I really didn't like the designation 'KZ' – just 'Z' for me, thank you. Silly, I know, but there it is ... By far the majority of 900s advertised for sale in the UK that were in need of restoration were KZs: that is, US bikes imported to the UK by specialist bike import companies such as DK Motorcycles.

I had heard of DK Motorcycles, and saw that it had for sale a couple of KZs in need of total restoration, which had been imported from the USA. The advantage of such bikes is that they're generally low mileage and not too abused. The downsides are that they are usually non-original, with 4-into-1 exhausts, King and Queen seats, and K&N air filters, for example. They also come with no history whatsoever, so you have no idea what's happened to them in the past, how many owners they've had, etc; they are also, by definition, KZ900s rather than Z900s. However, another advantage of a company like DK is that it imports bikes on a regular basis, so there are usually a couple to choose from, with more on the way. An obvious disadvantage, of course, is that DK is in the business to make a profit, so prices are always slightly on the high side compared to the private market.

Anyway, a potential restoration prospect quickly appeared – a late 1975 KZ900 that seemed in largely original condition. The main upsides were that it was quite low mileage, pretty original, and unmolested. Downsides were the price (naturally), and the fact that it was missing the original airbox and tube silencer/air filter (the former is currently unobtainable and the latter very expensive to replace). It also had a replacement 4-into-1 exhaust system rather than the original 4-into-4, but then just about every bike I'd seen for restoration had a 4-into-1, so I was prepared to buy a complete new pattern system, anyway.

Needless to say, the bike had only one front disc and I wanted twin discs (by modern standards the twin disc setup on a Z1/Z900 gives only marginal braking, and with only a single disc it's downright lethal!). It also had a damaged rear rim which I didn't think could be mended, so the original Takasago stamped rim would be lost. It also had a fairly new seat, but this was from an earlier Z1 model (you can tell from the pattern: see photo 2.2).

I rang DK and it agreed to end the eBay auction early – for the right price. I arranged to go over to the shop in Stoke-on-Trent and view the bike, taking a trailer with me. What a wonderful shop the company has! I would strongly recommend that anyone interested in classic bikes of any description, but especially Japanese examples, to pay a visit. The ground floor is jam-packed with bikes ripe for restoration, all imported from the States: you could spend several hours just looking round them (and I did, see photos 2.3-2.7), as well as the usual assortment of brand new bikes for sale. Upstairs is a little museum of classic bikes – including a Triumph Hurricane – together with a café and large spares counter – ideal. See photos 2.8-2.10.

Anyway, after a good look round the bike and a chat with the staff, it appeared to be as advertised and just about exactly what I was looking for – apart from the fact that it was a KZ900 rather than a Z900. After some negotiation we agreed on a figure of £6000 for me to take away the bike on the trailer I'd hired. I think I probably paid over the odds for this bike. I think that, being a business, the guys at DK can smell when someone is desperate to buy a bike, and knew I'd pay. The fact that I'd arrived with a trailer was a bit of a giveaway – no? What can I say? I was desperate to buy a bike as I wanted to begin the

2.1 I didn't buy this one as it was too customised and would have cost an awful lot to put back to original.

2.2 The KZ900 as advertised.

HOW TO RESTORE KAWASAKI Z1, Z/KZ900 & Z/KZ1000

restoration ASAP, and I didn't want to get involved in a bidding war on eBay. That said, I think I could have probably bought this bike for £4000 on a good day, and no more than £5000 generally, but there you are – I'm good at mechanics and words and totally crap at negotiating! What the hell, I had a bike! If you're reading this a few years down the line I hope you'll be thinking: 'Wow! Only £6000! What a bargain, I wish they were that cheap now!'

In a bit of a rush in a fairly crowded car park on a busy day I loaded the bike onto the hired trailer (which I'd used several times before, often to trailer two bikes at once), strapped it down with the proper ratchet straps and set off home to Sheffield. You might think that paying £6000 for a restoration project was bad, but worse was yet to come ...

Halfway home I was driving through Buxton when, as I rounded a left-hand bend, my worst nightmare happened; the bike fell off the trailer! I saw the whole thing unfold in slow motion in my rear view mirror, but there was nothing I could do to prevent it. The bike went over to the right, disappearing from view and turning over the trailer with it. All I could do was brake as quickly as I dared and swerve to the left to try and prevent the bike falling into incoming traffic. I got out of the car to find the bike on its side in the road, entangled in now useless straps, with debris everywhere and the trailer half lying on top of it.

Luckily (very, very luckily) there'd not been a vehicle coming the other way as it would have been a far more serious incident. The lorry travelling behind me stopped and put on his hazards, preventing traffic coming from behind and, as luck would have it, the very next car coming the other way was a police car! He stopped and put his flashing lights on, stopping traffic from coming forward. Not only this but the accident had happened right opposite a building site, and the men working there downed tools and came to help me recover the bike and trailer.

Eventually, we disentangled the bike from the straps, righted the trailer, and loaded the bike back on. Having carefully strapped down the bike I set off once I'd stopped shaking, admonishing myself over and over again. After a very brief initial inspection it seemed that the bike was less damaged that I thought it must be, but I waited to get it home before thoroughly inspecting it (and the hired trailer) for a complete damage assessment. See photo 2.11 of the aftermath of the accident, with the bike back on the trailer: note the long scratch on the tarmac from the corner of the trailer. I didn't take a photo of the overturned bike and trailer because I was in shock and we were all busy retrieving the bike and getting it back on the trailer and trying to open the road again. Not the best time to stop and take a snap!

So what had happened? Several small things combined, it seems. I'd been in a bit of a rush putting the bike on the trailer to start with; it was a bike I was unfamiliar with when strapping down, so wasn't sure of the best places to position the straps; I'd hired the trailer several times before so was over-confident about knowing what I was doing, and I'd not stopped to check the straps a couple of miles after leaving as I usually did. I really

2.3 Loads of bikes to choose from!

2.4 A couple of Hondas, a nice Triumph and a Kettle.

2.5 A typical American import.

2.6 This one for the brave ...

2.7 ... and this one for the very brave!

BUYING A BIKE TO RESTORE

2.8 750 H2 The Widowmaker.

2.9 Triumph Hurricane.

2.10 The mighty Honda Cub.

don't know why this was, other than not seeing a suitable stopping place – but this is a poor excuse. Anyway, all was not lost and the incident could have been so much worse (I could have killed someone ...), but I was going to have pay for it – literally.

Having made it home I was able to properly assess the damage. As I'd first thought, I'd been very lucky and the damage was mainly superficial. There was no damage to the tank or the engine, or even the exhaust system (which I was going to replace anyway, but was hoping to sell to offset some of the restoration costs), but the exposed parts on the top of the bike weren't so lucky. Suffering terminal damage were –
• the front mudguard
• the headlamp and front indicators
• the instrument cowls
• the right-hand wing mirror and the front brake lever assembly (which was probably already beyond repair so was due to be replaced anyway)

See photos 2.12-2.14 of the damage. I thought I'd been pretty lucky until I noticed that, when the front mudguard had hit the road, the impact was strong enough to burst open the boss on the lower right fork leg where the mudguard bolts to it: a new fork leg was needed – damn! If you look at photo 2.12 again you can see where the mounting bolt has burst through the alloy boss. To add insult to injury, it transpired that the trailer had suffered damage to the front right

2.11 The aftermath of the trailer accident.

HOW TO RESTORE KAWASAKI Z1, Z/KZ900 & Z/KZ1000

corner and mudguard, etc, so I lost most of my £200 deposit. Great.

The good news was that, regardless of the accident, the bike was in generally good condition, and there didn't appear to be any unexpected horrors (although the engine was very much an unknown quantity, of course – but it did turn over). I had been very, very lucky; it could have been so much worse. See photos 2.15-2.18 of the rest of the bike in general.

So, I now had a bike that was ready for restoration – now a darn sight more ready than it had been when I purchased it. Ho-hum ...

LESSONS LEARNT
- Buying the right bike to restore is one of the most important aspects of the entire restoration process.
- Research as much as possible about your chosen model before looking to buy.
- Establish which parts are unobtainable; don't get a nasty shock later.
- Know what you want from your restoration before you begin: a 100 per cent concours machine or a custom street racer? This will determine what bike you're looking for as a basis for your restoration.
- A few bike dealers specialise in importing bikes for restoration, and these are always a good starting point – although the machines tend to be US-spec and are relatively expensive.
- eBay is also a good starting point, although photos can be very deceptive – especially when taken from a distance.
- If you put your bike on a trailer, do not neglect to properly strap it down – and stop to check everything's okay every so often, as straps can loosen!

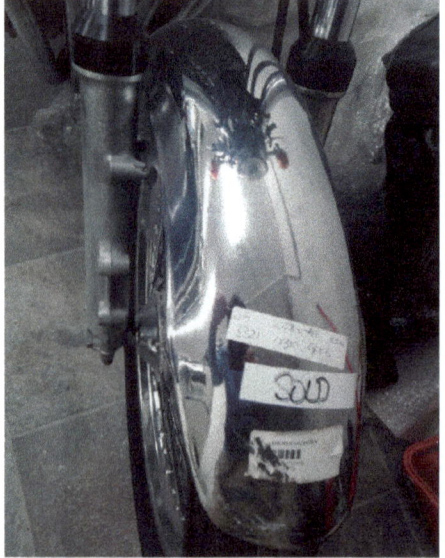
2.12 Badly damaged front mudguard.

2.13 Damage to front headlight, indicators, and instrument cowlings.

2.14 Damage to front brake lever assembly and wing mirror.

2.15 The bike was dirty and rusty but not too molested or damaged.

2.16 No airbox or silencer.

2.17 Leaking and seized front brake.

2.18 Bike looks okay – but remember that long distance shots don't show the faults!

Chapter 3
Ten golden rules for a successful rebuild

RULE 1
When dismantling a bike (or anything mechanical), before beginning, take as many photos as possible of what everything looks like/is located – and then take some more. You simply cannot take too many photos of how things look and where they go. In this day and age of digital photography there's no excuse for not taking copious pictures. I think I took something like 500 during the dismantling process, chronicling the disassembly as thoroughly as possible, and these proved invaluable during the reassembly process when I encountered a part that I wasn't sure how to reassemble, and there was no mention of it in the manuals. Being able to look back at how it was originally is so helpful.

Under NO CIRCUMSTANCES should you be tempted to think 'Oh, I'll remember how this goes together; there's no need to take any photos,' because this will not be the case. I often can't remember how to reassemble parts I dismantled just a few days ago, let alone those that have lain untouched for several months/years, as most parts of a full restoration do. Not taking pictures is just laziness – you tell yourself there's no need as you'll remember, but, in truth, you simply can't be bothered to do so (I know: I've been there!). Do this and you will regret it in a big way (and my words will come back to haunt you!).

RULE 2
Bag and box up all parts as you dismantle the bike, AND LABEL THEM CLEARLY as you do so. I use a selection of different sized freezer bags, into in which most parts can simply be bagged (and sealed) with what they are clearly written on the outside. Being plastic, they can be filled with oily or greasy parts without a problem, and won't rot or split. You can also add oil where necessary to ensure that parts don't go rusty in storage. I have a large plastic storage box for each section of the bike: electrical, cylinders and cylinder head, crankcase internals, electrics, front forks, etc. The only time I don't bag things is if they are too big or are VERY easily identifiable – the swinging arm or rear shock absorbers, say – otherwise I 'bag and tag' everything, regardless. In addition, try and separate parts as much as possible: for instance, you might have one bag for the oil pump, another for the gear selector shaft, and another for the oil bypass valve, etc, rather than putting the entire contents of the crankcase in one huge receptacle! I even have bags with just a single nut in them, as it makes reassembly so much easier when you know exactly what parts and components are.

RULE 3
Briefly assess the condition of each item before bagging and storing it. I tend to examine parts in detail only as I begin to reassemble everything, and restore/replace as necessary then. However, some parts take longer to recondition, so if you have an idea of what is required you can make that a priority. For example, if you discover you need a rebore as you take apart the engine you can obtain pistons, etc, and organise the rebore earlier rather than later, and won't be waiting several days/weeks to get the necessary parts and the machining work completed, potentially delaying reassembly.

An example of this was with the chroming. I knew I needed to rechrome several parts, and wanted to chrome others, so rang my local chrome plater for a chat about how

HOW TO RESTORE KAWASAKI Z1, Z/KZ900 & Z/KZ1000

the parts should be prepared (all paint removed, not shot-blasted – too rough a surface – and old chrome left as is). During the call I was told how long the waiting time was – five months! Yes, the waiting time for chroming was five whole months, as the company in question was so busy. I therefore knew that my first priority following dismantling was to take all of the requisite parts for chroming and get in the queue! I later found another company whose lead time was only six weeks, so used this instead, but even so I had to get the parts to it ASAP so as not to hold up the restoration. I also had a fair idea that this second company wouldn't be as good as the first, which was why its wait time was so much shorter – and my concerns were later confirmed.

RULE 4
Most parts will be oily and/or greasy and pretty horrible. Make liberal use of WD40 on oily/greasy parts to clean them to an acceptable level for storage. Full cleaning/refurbishment can be carried out as necessary at a later date. If absolutely necessary, you can use white spirit to clean parts, although WD40 is a lot more user-friendly, and does a great job. Conversely, if parts are too dry or rusty, also spray them with WD40 to protect from further deterioration. Placing them in freezer bags will protect them from moisture, etc' and so prevent further rusting.

RULE 5
Decide what you want out of your rebuild and plan accordingly. For example, I knew that I wanted to complete a high quality, nut-and-bolt rebuild to create what I think of as a stunning bike, that was largely original but with modern upgrades where appropriate – so not 100 per cent concours. This meant I would have all engine parts blast-cleaned, there would be much additional chromework; custom parts where applicable/available, new bearings throughout, a powder-coated frame, stainless steel wheel rims and spokes with polished hubs and new tyres, stainless fasteners throughout, etc. I therefore had to ensure I had the following in place –
• a chrome plating company
• an engineering firm
• wheel rebuilder
• instrument restorer
• parts suppliers
• a knowledge of where to buy good quality custom/upgraded parts, etc

Plan ahead, and begin scouring the internet for companies that sell upgrades and other parts for your bike so you know what your options are. Companies that I used are listed at the back of this manual.

RULE 6
Make sure you have both time and money for such an undertaking. Rebuilds always take far longer than expected, and, as time goes by, other jobs that also demand your time (and money!) begin to mount, so make sure you are able to stay focused and get the job completed, even when it takes twice or three times longer than you'd anticipated.

Ensure that your life is fundamentally stable enough to support a rebuild. As well as time, money, space, tools, etc, problems can arise from unrelated aspects such as divorce, children, moving house/job/city, holidays, home improvements, illness, etc. Life sometimes gets in the way ...

Always remember the golden rule: rebuilds have an inversely proportional time to completion ratio – the closer you get to finishing the restoration, the slower the rate of progress. The first few days are spent happily pulling apart the bike, with you thinking how easy this is and you'll have it finished in no time. Then things begin to slow down as you have to source new parts, and get old ones repaired, etc ... then the spare room needs redecorating, your partner insists you go on holiday, and your job suddenly changes. Before you know it, your rate of progress has slowed to a crawl, and becomes steadily slower as the rebuild continues. Therefore according to the law of inversely proportional time, 20 per cent of the rebuild is completed in a week, 30 per cent in one month, 40 per cent in three months, 50 per cent in six months, 70 per cent in a year, 80 per cent in 18 months, and so on. Be advised: this is a mathematical certainty and cannot be avoided! (Note that by definition this also means that no restoration is ever 100 per cent complete!)

RULE 7
Know your limitations. Make sure you have the necessary expertise, temperament, and patience to complete a project like this, and, if you haven't, find suitable specialists to complete the work for you. I'm lucky in that I've always had some mechanical/practical ability (inherited from my father), and having learnt the hard way as a teenager pulling apart bikes, and then not being able to put them back together, I now know I'm old enough and experienced enough to get things finished. However, there are still things that I know I'm no good at (like paintwork and seats), so, if necessary, I give these jobs to others. Know your strengths and weaknesses, and use professionals/friends and contacts as necessary.

RULE 8
Ensure you have enough tools, equipment, and space to complete a restoration. I've built up a large collection of tools over the years, and am in the fortunate position of being able to buy anything I haven't already got, especially in terms of special tools. This is a big bonus. A list of the special tools and general tools I used during the rebuild can be found at the end of the book.

I have a basement-cum-garage that gives me sufficient room – room to work, room to assemble the bike, room to store all the parts of the bike, room for tools, etc. Remember that a bike in bits takes up at least three times the room of a complete bike. I have a good workbench that is solid, and has a decent vice: a recent acquisition has been a bike lift. Fantastic! If you can afford one then definitely go for it – by far the best tool I've bought in years. How I ever managed to crawl around on the floor rebuilding bikes I'll never know; my knees are still recovering. With a bike lift you can either sit or stand and work on the bike at the perfect height – it makes the job so much easier and enjoyable.

RULE 9
Make sure you really love your bike and want to rebuild it – it simply won't

TEN GOLDEN RULES FOR A SUCCESSFUL REBUILD

get finished otherwise. Want to go down the pub every night or follow other interests? Forget it. If you don't really want it, it won't happen. When things go wrong with the rebuild (and they will), you need to have the desire and commitment to face the problem, possibly take it all apart, and start again.

RULE 10

If working on the bike and it's not going right – that nut that's hard to reach simply won't go on, or a part won't fit, say – STOP WORK! Go for a breather and a cuppa (or, even better, leave it overnight), and come back to it refreshed and relaxed. I guarantee that the nut will suddenly screw on, and those parts will suddenly come together. If you don't have that break and continue working, chances aren you will cross-thread the nut and break the parts – and the same applies if you need the loo!

LESSONS LEARNT

- Ignore these ten rules at your peril. You can complete a rebuild without following some or any of the above – but it will be a whole lot harder!
- Never forget the fundamental law of inversely proportional time to completion, and go with the flow.
- You will make mistakes – but accept them, learn from them, move on, and your understanding of mechanics and the bike itself will increase.
- If you've read the rules and are unable to adhere to them, either pay someone else to rebuild the bike for you or buy a bike that's already been restored – there's always work to be done on any classic bike, no matter how well (or not) it's been restored, and there is much joy to be had from tinkering with a bike rather than fully restoring it.
- Keep the faith!

RULES OF THE WORKSHOP

- Proportion of time spent working on bike in the workshop: 10 per cent. Proportion of time spent looking for that flipping tool you had in your hand just a few seconds ago: 90 per cent.
- Any nut, screw or washer that is dropped onto the garage floor immediately transports into a third dimension, and will only return after many hours of fruitless searching, and when a replacement has been ordered ...
- Proportion of time spent sleeping in bed: 10 per cent. Proportion of time spent wide awake in bed trying to work out why something's wrong: 90 per cent.
- Ability to listen to someone for longer than five minutes without your mind wandering off onto the rebuild: nil.
- Time waiting for parts to be delivered, and waiting in not wanting to miss the parcel: infinite.
- Ability to enjoy holidays when you know they're taking up valuable rebuild time and money: low.
- Having to explain why all the other essential and urgent jobs that need doing round the house should be put on hold until after the rebuild: relentless.
- Worrying that when parts suppliers ring up and leave a message with 'someone else' they say how much it will cost: constant.
- Going out to a posh do with oil under your fingernails and cuts on your hands: normal.
- And, of course, your greatest fear: that when you die your wife will sell your bikes for what you told her you paid for them!

And, finally, never forget this mathematical equation –
It has been scientifically proven that the formula for the number of bikes you need is $X + 1$ (where X equals the number of bikes you already own!)

Chapter 4
Preparing to dismantle

Before starting work my first task was to decide what kind of restoration I wanted. Did I want a 100 per cent original bike with only original parts built to concours standard? Or a modern street bike with all the modern custom upgrades I could think of? Or a semi-original restoration with the odd upgrade and aftermarket part? In my case it was the last of these. Remember, it's your bike so restore it as you see fit, but try to decide what you want at the beginning so that you know where you're headed, and don't have to make major changes halfway through the rebuild.

If you've a good idea of what bike you want to have at the end of the restoration you can plan accordingly, and begin assembling the necessary parts at the earliest opportunity, especially if you require hard to find parts such as the air box for the Z900 model specifically (original air boxes are available for other models). If you know you're building a streetfighter-type bike then you'll probably be using some kind of aftermarket air filters or bellmouths or whatever, but if you're planning on going back to original then you need to start looking for a replacement air box ASAP if you're rebuilding a Z900 and the one on your bike is missing.

In my case I wanted to build a bike that was largely original but which had a few tweaks and changes to make it look good and be a bit special. This is what I planned at the start in terms of changes/upgrades –
• Polish the hubs and fit stainless steel spokes to the wheels – and possibly change to alloy rims as the rear rim on my bike is probably unsalvageable.
• Paint the tank, etc, in yellow and green in Z1A style – not to make a Z1A copy but because that's my favourite colour scheme and style.
• Fit new badges to the side panels that say 'Z900' rather than 'KZ900' – the KZ moniker irks me for some reason.
• Fit stainless steel fasteners.
• Re-fit standard-looking rear shocks, but try to use ones that have been upgraded internally (which I think are available). The original Kawasaki shocks look right but don't work too well.
• Polish engine outer casings and clean engine casings and carburettors. (You have to be careful with this so as not to overdo it, but a little extra bling is always a good thing in my book.)

• Fit a twin disc conversion – these were standard on Z900s and an option on KZs so the bike is already designed to take twin discs: the only problem being that callipers are NLA (No Longer Available), but I managed to source a second-hand one. All other parts are available new. I was also considering fitting uprated callipers and floating/vented discs to the front because they work better and look really good, but I eventually decided against this because they were outside my budget (I'd recently retired and my pension pot had already shrunk faster than the polar ice caps!). I also liked the look of the originals on a fairly standard bike.
• Fit LED bulbs where possible (I knew there was a slight problem with fitting a stop/tail LED bulb inasmuch as the bulb failure warning light in the tacho needs to be re-wired in some way to work with an LED bulb), but almost certainly an LED headlight upgrade. (This turned out not to be possible as the Z900s use sealed beam units, not separate bulbs, and there's no LED replacement for a sealed beam unit.)
• I also wanted to fit a combined modern rectifier/regulator unit to the electrics as the originals were a bit of

PREPARING TO DISMANTLE

a weak spot on the original bikes. I would have also converted the bike to electronic ignition but this had already been done on my bike. I was also considering fitting uprated ignition coils, though, in the end, decided to just fit new standard ones.
• Other than that everything was to be cleaned, restored, replaced, re-chromed or polished as necessary to make the bike look good and run as sweetly as possible.
• I'd already decided against such things as fitting an hydraulic clutch conversion or increasing engine capacity, or fitting bigger carburettors, etc, as I didn't think it necessary for what I wanted: a classic bike that looked pretty original which I could use for Sunday ride outs (I'm not planning on racing!). I'm also not a big concours/originality freak, which is why I was happy to change things like the colour and badges, and use stainless steel fasteners, etc, and stick with the newish seat that came with the bike. It's a seat for a Z1 rather than a Z900, so the pattern and fitting is slightly different to the original – but that's fine by me as long as it looks okay – and it does.
• You should also waste no time sourcing the following services –
• A list of very reputable spare parts suppliers. You will almost certainly be buying a whole host of parts for your bike during the restoration, so identify reliable and efficient parts suppliers who only sell either original parts (NOS: New Old Stock) or quality replacement parts, and who deliver quickly. For a list of recommended suppliers see the back of the book. In my case I tended to use Z-Power as it is in the UK, on the end of the phone, and has a comprehensive supply of spare parts for Z900s. I tend to find a good supplier and stick with them, but always remember that, in this day and age, putting a part number into Google can work wonders!
• Try to build a list of enthusiasts and contacts who can offer advice and help when needed (and it will be!). The best place to start is by joining one of the owners' clubs (see back of book for details), and looking on the web and Facebook for pages and forums (again, see the back of book for details). Good parts suppliers are also a great source of knowledge and expertise.
• A good metal finisher (chroming and polishing) to chrome parts as necessary and buff any alloy parts you want shiny unless, you're polishing them yourself, as I did.
• A decent machine shop to carry out any necessary work on the engine – a re-bore or head skim, say – as well as being able to properly mend broken fins, etc, on the cylinder block where necessary (a decent company will make an almost invisible repair).
• A painter for the tank and panels, who should be VERY familiar with painting tanks to ensure painted correctly, as Kawasaki used a rather unique system to paint their tanks, and to ensure that they're ethanol-resistant, and won't peel or bubble round the vulnerable tank filler cap area.
• Unless building the wheels yourself, a recommended wheel builder which can either refurbish your existing wheels to original or carry out additional work such as polishing the hubs, fitting stainless steel spokes and/or rims, and fitting new tyres (to save you the hassle of trying to find a good motorcycle tyre fitter later on).
• Somewhere to take your parts for blast cleaning. Be aware that some parts are softer than others, and can be badly damaged by blast cleaning if the wrong process is used. For example, the carburettors are made of much softer aluminium alloy than the crankcases, and can only be cleaned using a gentle method such as vapour/aqua blasting.
• Somewhere to powder coat your frame and other parts as required, if that's a route you wish to go down – some restorers choose to paint the frame, and either do it themselves or have it done at a local paint shop.
• A large wad of cash to spend on your bike – the restoration is clearly a top priority and takes precedence over all other household expenditure such as holidays (clearly unnecessary), and the purchase of such fripperies as soft furnishings and other household items – although generous (or at least regular) gifts to your other half should be maintained at all times to ensure that the restoration continues smoothly, and without interruption (flowers and chocolates go a long way!).
• Finally, don't forget the two Golden Rules of dismantling –
• Take copious photos of EVERY aspect of the dismantling procedure so that you have full reference when trying to put it back together. For instance, does the washer go in front or behind the bracket? Which way round does the battery box go? How does the rear light assembly fit together? These may seem like simple things but, when you come to reassemble everything a few months later, it's suddenly not quite so straightforward.
• As you dismantle parts put them in plastic freezer bags and label them with a permanent marker. Keep the parts as separate as possible by using multiple bags rather than one large one containing a large number of parts.
• I know I've mentioned these points before, but make no apologies for doing so, because they are so important. If you only take two things from this book, take these.

THE PLANNED TIMELINE FOR MY RESTORATION
• Completely dismantle the bike, briefly inspecting each part as it came off to check for any that were badly damaged or missing which may be hard to source, so I could begin my search for them straight away or make a note of any parts that required specialist attention.
• Take the relevant parts (mainly engine cases and carburettors and forks) to the specialist vapour/aqua blast cleaner for cleaning.
• Assess cycle parts as to need for and suitability/cost for re-chroming. If in very poor condition it might be better to replace them with aftermarket parts. Similarly, due to the high cost of chroming, it may be cheaper to buy replacements than to pay for re-chroming.
• Take the relevant parts to the chrome plater for chroming or polishing ASAP.
• Send bodywork parts (tank, side panels and rear moulding) for re-painting.
• Send the wheels to a specialist wheel builder – not sure, yet, exactly what finish to have: stainless steel spokes, alloy rims (rear rim is dented probably beyond repair)? Decision to

HOW TO RESTORE KAWASAKI Z1, Z/KZ900 & Z/KZ1000

be made later.
- Send the frame for powder coating.
- Having assessed the various parts of the engine/gearbox assembly, decide what work is required (re-bore, etc), what parts need replacing, and have the necessary work completed and replacement parts ordered accordingly. I intend to use only recommended specialists for machining work. I used to use my local machine shop but decided its work really isn't top quality. If you're going to have work done, have it done properly. I'm also going to use only specialist parts suppliers to source parts where possible as there are just too many cheap and poorly-made replacement parts available on the internet from unknown suppliers of unknown provenance. Always worth looking on the internet, but beware of cheap parts that are poor quality.
- Begin engine reassembly whilst waiting for other parts to arrive.
- Retrieve frame.
- Mount half-completed in frame to hold engine in place and ensure engine is light enough to easily re-fit into frame (not sure if the front forks and wheel will be ready by this time, which causes a bit of a problem in terms of holding up the frame – might need a temporary support).
- Recondition and reassemble parts such as the carburettors, and complete engine rebuild as parts return from the chrome plater.
- Rewire bike using new or reconditioned parts where appropriate. In my case I ended up re-using the existing wiring loom, as it was in generally good condition.
- Buy replacement cycle parts where necessary, including a complete new 4-into-4 exhaust system, unless I've found a second-hand set in VGC (Very Good Condition) in the meantime.
- Assemble cycle parts.
- Fill bike with requisite fluids and start engine. Check all is well.
- Insure bike using existing documentation.
- MoT bike
- Apply to register bike in UK and receive an age-related number plate.
- Give bike a full road test and sort out teething problems as necessary.
- Sit back and enjoy the completed restoration (bearing in mind Rule 6 of the Ten Golden Rules!).

LESSONS LEARNT
- Make a plan for the restoration, but be prepared to amend it as work progresses,
- Find parts suppliers and service providers ASAP.
- Join clubs and/or Facebook groups to source advice and support when necessary.
- Make sure everything's ready before starting to dismantle.
- Find a regular supplier of flowers and chocolates!

Chapter 5
Removing the bodywork & rear mudguard

Armed with my trusty smartphone camera and a vast array of freezer bags (small, medium, and large), I began disassembly. First off, I wheeled the bike onto the bike lift and sat it on its centre stand. I can't emphasise enough how much easier restoration is with a bike lift. For years I managed without one (lack of space and cost being the main reasons), and, as a result, suffered with very painful knees, aches and pains, and a permanently damaged muscle in my back caused by bending and twisting at odd angles. I can honestly say that if I had my time again, I'd buy one for the sake of my knees and back. Prices have reduced considerably in recent years, with cheaper products aimed more at the DIY market, and as I finally have a workshop with more space, it was an easy decision to buy one. If you're wondering whether or not to buy one, I'd say definitely go for it.

Anyway, I was finally ready to take apart the bike. My plan was fairly simple – start at the top with the various pieces of bodywork. Next, tackle the electrics and handlebars, etc, and work my way down to the rear wheel and swinging arm. I planned to leave the front forks and front wheel in place so that the frame would stay upright and enable me to dismantle the engine in situ without the need for an engine stand. (This seemed to work out well, the only downside being that I couldn't send the wheels, etc, for rebuilding/chroming before the engine was completely stripped.)

I pumped up the lift to its lowest position so that I could easily reach everything near the top of the bike, and then removed the side panels by simply pulling them off their rubber mounting lugs and safely storing them. After this, I removed the seat by removing the two long pins from the two hinges on the right of the bike.

Next, came the tank, the removal of which is a little more challenging than the panels and seat. To loosen it, simply unhook the rubber strap and pull it backwards off the rubber mounts at the front – easy. However, before you can pull it off completely, you have also to remove the petrol pipes that are attached to the petrol tap ... and these are a total pain; held on by fiddly little clips which are hard to remove and even harder to replace. Not only that, but the pipes tend to be a very tight fit on the petrol tap, having hardened over time, and refuse to come off. After a lot of fiddling, the pipes finally came off the tap (in hindsight I should have just cut the pipes off as they were due to be replaced, anyway), and I was able to remove the tank and carefully place it in a protective box.

A note here is that, in my experience, most damage to a petrol tank occurs not when it's on the bike, but when it is in storage. Tanks are dropped or fall off shelves, or heavy and sharp things fall on them, so I always immediately put my tank in a plastic box to protect it from the infinite dangers of the average workshop. See photo 5.1.

I then took a full can of WD40

5.1 Tank stored safely in a plastic box.

HOW TO RESTORE KAWASAKI Z1, Z/KZ900 & Z/KZ1000

5.2 Removing the rear cowling.

5.4 Rear mudguard removed.

5.6 The full extent of damage to the wiring revealed.

5.3 Removing the rear mudguard.

5.5 Very dodgy wiring under the mudguard.

5.7 Rear cowling and mudguard removed.

and liberally sprayed every nut, bolt and screw on the entire bike in the hope that it might help in the removal of rusted fasteners as I went along. To be honest, I'm never quite sure how effective at penetrating rusted nuts any kind of lubricant is (although I'm a very big fan of WD40, generally), but I think it's worth a shot.

With the spraying completed I turned my attention to the rear cowling and mudguard – best to remove all delicate and easily-damaged parts first. Having removed the two bolts under the rear lip of the cowling, and the two on the top of the cowling 'arms,' it simply lifted away. See photo 5.2. To remove the rear mudguard I unscrewed the four bolts on the bracket holding it to the rear frame (see photo 5.3), along with the two at the front and the mudguard came free. See photo 5.4.

I also tried to remove the rear light unit but was foiled by the wiring harness that needed to be split before the wiring could be pulled through: there were a bunch of connectors under the mudguard on my bike which shouldn't have been there. I had a quick look at these, and discovered a host of damaged wires that, no doubt, caused many electrical faults. See photo 5.5. I then undid the connectors to enable me to pull the wiring from either end, and this revealed the extent of wiring damage caused by chafing on the rear mudguard. See photo 5.6.

The bike was now minus tank, side panels, rear cowling, seat and rear mudguard, and already looking like a pile of scrap. See photo 5.7. I always think it's amazing how bad you can make a bike look just by removing a few basic parts.

I then removed the rear grab rail by removing the mounting bolts to the frame, and loosening the two bolts at the top of the rear shock absorbers, enabling the grab rail to slide out.

LESSONS LEARNT
• Bike lift – the best tool I have ever bought – honestly!
• Z900 tank removal is a bit of a paradox: they're incredibly easy to release, but a nightmare to get off the petrol pipes.
• Place your tank out of harm's way in a plastic box – the only way to virtually guarantee it won't get damaged in the workshop.
• The wiring to the rear light underneath the rear mudguard can suffer from chafing.

www.velocebooks.com
New book news • Special offers • Newsletter • Details of all Veloce books • Gift Vouchers

Chapter 6
Removing headlamp, clocks & carbs

The very first thing I did before starting on the electrics was to disconnect and remove the battery from the bike. I have had many accidents over the years when I've been working on a bike's electrics without bothering to disconnect the battery ('it's only a small job, no need to disconnect the battery') which usually results in a short puff of smoke and a string of swear words and self-recrimination, followed by a previously unnecessary phone call to the spares supplier. As a result I now always ensure that the battery is fully disconnected before starting work. See photo 6.1 of the battery before removal. (When I put the battery on charge it actually took and held a charge, much to my amazement – but I was planning to change it to an Absorbed Glass Mat (AGM) battery anyway as these are so much better at holding a charge, and don't require any attention at all after fitting.)

Turning to the front end of the bike, I began to remove the handlebars, headlamp, and instruments. To begin with, I drained the remainder of the brake fluid from the front disc brake. Having loosened the bleed screw in the calliper, I pumped what was left from the reservoir, and then undid the hose from the master cylinder to ensure that all fluid was out of the system by allowing air in at the top. See photo 6.2.

6.1 The battery ready to be removed.

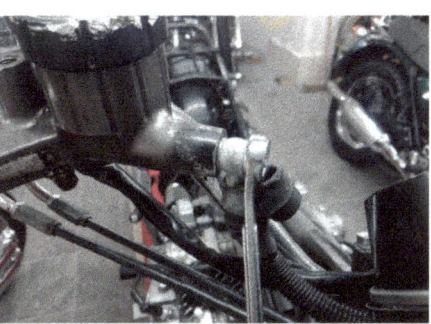

6.2 Removing the hose from the master cylinder.

Having removed the headlamp lens and rims by unscrewing the two screws at 5 o'clock and 7 o'clock on the shell, I removed the indicator stems, having first taken copious photos of the wiring. One of my indicators was already off, courtesy of my little mishap with the trailer. See photo 6.3. With the indicators removed, the headlamp simply pulls away from the front fork shrouds (although, on earlier models, the headlamp also has a securing nut underneath, which was blamed for causing premature headlamp bulb failure due to the vibration it transmits, so was omitted on later bikes). See photo 6.4. On the bottom

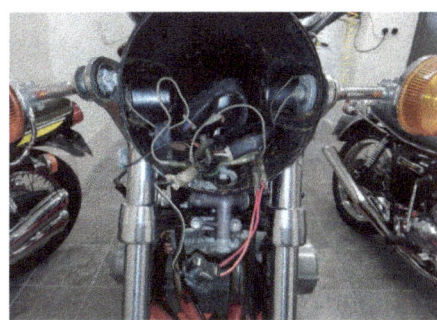

6.3 Removing indicators to remove headlamp shell.

of my headlamp shell was also the indicator warning buzzer fitted to these models See photo 6.5).

I then had good access to the underside of the instrument binnacle. Having removed the speedo and tacho cables, and disconnected the wiring, the binnacle could be

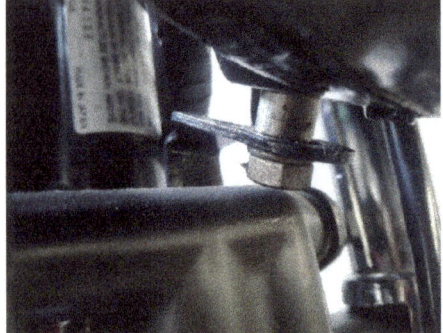

6.4 The locking nut under the headlight of earlier models.

6.5 Headlamp shell removed with indicator warning buzzer attached.

removed by undoing the two nuts underneath it. See photo 6.6. Once I had the instrument binnacle on the bench it was clear that the instrument bracket had been fractured by the trailer incident (see photo 6.7), but I checked and the bracket's still available, so no major problem.

What was more of a problem was the damage to the chrome trim between the speedo and the cup.

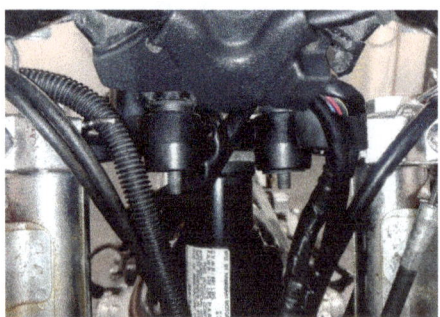

6.6 Removing the instrument binnacle.

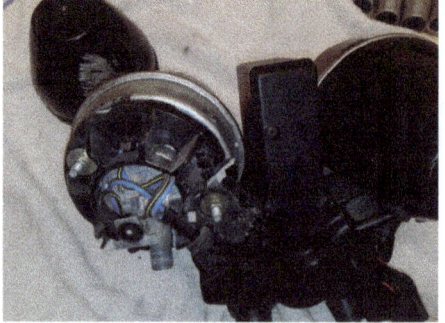

6.7 Instrument binnacle damaged in trailer incident.

The cups are available (in black or chrome), but I wasn't so sure about the chrome rings. See photo 6.8.

Once the instruments were removed, I took off the handlebars, together with the brake and clutch levers, by loosening the switch gear at each side, and sliding them off the bars. Removing the four mounting bolts from the two brackets on the top yoke meant that the bars were free to come away. See photo 6.9.

I now had to deal with the throttle and clutch cables, which were left dangling in mid-air. First off, I removed the two throttle cables from the top of the carburettors (don't forget that these bikes have push and pull cables to open AND close the throttle). To do this, I loosened the two locknuts on the end of the cables just enough so that they cleared the ears on the throttle mechanisms, and the cables wrestled free of the guides. See photo 6.10. Having said that, they were more fiddly to remove than I expected, and took a bit of 'persuasion' to come out of their guides. With the cables now loose, I was able to unclamp the right-hand switch gear and remove

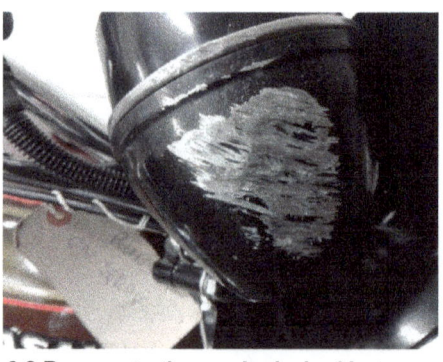

6.8 Damage to the cup looks bad but new ones are readily available – not so sure about the chrome ring.

6.9 Handlebars, headlamp and clocks removed, clutch and throttle hang free.

6.10 Removing the throttle cable from the carbs.

the cables from the throttle. See photo 6.11. The cables themselves could now be removed from the switch gear by simultaneously unscrewing the chromed right-angled guides from the bottom of the switchgear. They need to be unscrewed together as otherwise they get in each other's way.

To remove the clutch cable I loosened off all of the adjusters (don't forget the one in the middle of the cable, halfway down the frame down tube), which allowed me to remove the clutch lever. To completely remove the clutch cable I had to then take off the left-hand outer gearbox cover by unscrewing the cover bolts.

6.11 Removing the throttle and cables from the switch gear.

REMOVING HEADLAMP, CLOCKS & CARBS

See photo 6.12. Having removed the bolts and the gear lever, the casing was free to come away, with clutch cable still attached. See photo 6.13. The cable could then be withdrawn by pulling the little retaining split pin from the end of the cable, and freeing it from the actuating mechanism.

With the throttle and clutch cable out of the way, I could now remove the left- and right-hand switch gear. See photo 6.14 of the switch gear waiting to be unplugged from the loom. Note the damage to the right-hand switch unit from leaking brake fluid. Unplugging the multi-pin connectors on top of the frame revealed that one connector had quite bad corrosion on one of the terminals.

See photo 6.15. Hidden away under the fuel tank I'm sure such connections can cause problems if water manages to get in.

I also took the opportunity to remove the carburettors, which was easy now that the throttle cables had been removed. I simply took the aftermarket K&N filters off the back of the carbs and then loosened the clamps on the rubber manifolds, and off the carbs came as one complete unit. See photo 6.16. It became clear that the previous owner had suspected an air leak through the rubber manifolds, and had liberally coated a couple of them in brown sealant! See photo 6.17. However, I think that the cracks which often appear in the rubber inlet manifolds are actually only superficial, and not usually the cause of air leakage. Also note the two take-offs on the oil pressure switch unit under the

6.16 The carbs come off as a complete unit.

6.12 Removing the left-hand gearbox cover.

6.15 One of the multi-pin connectors for the handlebar switches showing corrosion.

6.17 A previous owner had suspected air leaks and taken (in)appropriate action!

6.13 Left-hand gearbox cover removed.

6.14 Switchgear ready to be unplugged. Left-hand side damaged by leaking brake fluid.

6.18 Removing the inlet manifolds with the help of an impact screwdriver.

HOW TO RESTORE KAWASAKI Z1, Z/KZ900 & Z/KZ1000

manifolds, for the after-market oil cooler fitted to my bike. I planned to replace this with a standard unit without the take-offs and remove the oil cooler altogether.

I then removed the inlet manifolds from the head with the aid of an impact driver (as I was to do many times over with stubborn cross-head screws on the engine). See photo 6.18.

I also removed the remaining brake pipes and hydraulic junction box with the brake light switch attached. Note that its spacers and two cable guides are attached. See photo 6.19. This junction box will be replaced later on with a double one for twin discs.

The dismantling process continued with the bike slowly coming apart – see photo 6.20. I also removed the after-market oil cooler from the front of the frame which had been poorly fitted and was damaged.

I had already decided not to refit it or replace it but remove it completely. All that was required to convert it back to original was a new oil pressure switch unit to replace the existing one with two take-offs for the cooler. See photo 6.17.

LESSONS LEARNT
• Always completely disconnect the battery before working on electrics ... or live to regret it!
• Early models had a third headlamp mounting screw, which can, apparently, cause bulb failure.
• Brake fluid is highly corrosive and can cause havoc (but remember it's also hygroscopic so can easily be washed away with water if spilt).
• Drain the brake system as fully as possible before dismantling it.
• The Z series uses a double throttle cable which works well but is a bit of a bugger to remove/replace.
• Over time, water can get into multi-pin connectors and cause havoc with the electrics, giving rise to problems that are hard to track down.

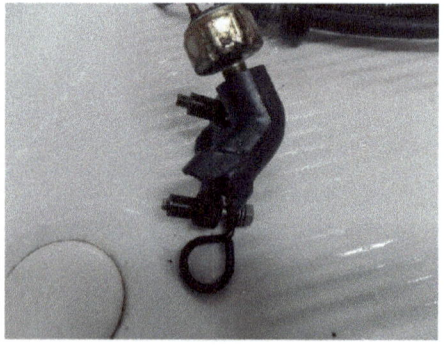

6.19 Front brake hose connector showing spacers and cable guides.

6.20 Bike slowly disappearing.

Chapter 7
Removing the wiring loom & other electrics

With the bodywork and headlamp/instrument assembly out of the way, it was time to remove the rats' nest that was the old wiring harness.

To begin with, I noticed that the loom had been cut open near the headstock, and then repaired with insulating tape. See photo 7.1. I wasn't sure why this had been done, so had a quick look by peeling off the already loose insulating tape (note that insulating tape is, at best, only a temporary repair as it will invariably come unstuck over time, leaving a horrible gooey mess). I couldn't find any reason why the plastic covering had been cut off as all the wiring looked to be in good condition – see photo 7.2 – and can only surmise that the corroded multi-pin connector as found previously may have been causing electrical problems, which the owner possibly thought were caused by a fault in the loom itself, so cut it open to check. Close, but no banana.

I then began to strip off the wiring, taking copious photos of every single connection before doing so. I've found over the years that wiring diagrams never seem to exactly match your model, and, often, new looms don't come with

7.1 Wiring loom cut open and then mended with tape.

7.2 No evidence of why the loom was cut open found.

a wiring diagram, and frequently have different colour coding for the wires (unless they're NOS – New Old Stock). So, the more photos and info

7.3 Photos of every connection were taken before disconnecting – in this case showing the added wiring for electronic ignition.

you have about how the wiring was originally, the better. See photo 7.3 as an example, showing the new wiring added into the loom by the previous owner, who converted it to electronic ignition.

When it came to the main electrical components behind the left-hand panel (right-hand panel on a Z1). I took special care to take photos. Components include the main junction box, regulator, rectifier, starter solenoid, and indicator flasher unit. See photo 7.4. There are more details on these components in the chapter covering electrical refitting.

29

HOW TO RESTORE KAWASAKI Z1, Z/KZ900 & Z/KZ1000

See photo 7.5 of the main units being stripped out. This mess of spaghetti gives a good indication of why taking lots of dismantling photos is so important!

With the main loom and associated components stripped off the bike I then removed the ignition coils. These are bolted to the top rails under the petrol tank (see photo 7.6), which can apparently give rise to them cracking due to vibration, resulting in strange ignition problems. Mine looked to be okay, however, and I removed them from the bike, labelled them, and stored them with the other components. See photo 7.7. At this stage I was unsure whether or not to replace them with new or uprated units, but, in the end, replaced them with new, as closer inspection showed the originals to be unserviceable.

Alongside the coils I also discovered a small component that had clearly been disconnected in the past and just left hanging (thankfully), though I had no idea what it was. I later discovered that this was the rear brake light failure switch, which is currently unobtainable, but without which the brake light failure warning light on the instrument panel won't work, so I was very glad it was still there! See photo 7.8.

This now left a Meccano set of bracketry between the rear of the engine and the back wheel. See photos 7.9 and 7.10. This assembly is held together with the usual assortment of cross-headed screws and 10mm bolts, and came apart quite easily, although the whole thing seemed over-elaborate.

After much removing of screws and bolts, the battery carrier came away, with the rectifier screwed to the bottom of it. See photo 7.11. The battery carrier assembly was now

7.4 Junction box in place for reference.

7.5 Main electrics being stripped out.

7.6 Ignition coils in situ under the tank.

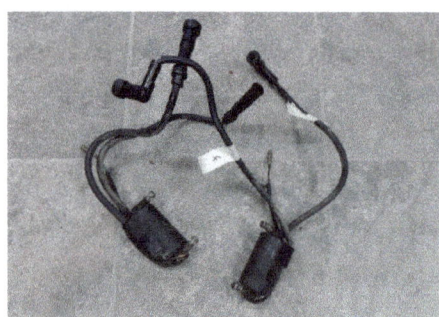
7.7 Ignition coils removed and labelled.

7.8 This strange unit had been disconnected and left hanging – but what was it? (The rear brake light failure switch, it turns out).

7.9 Left-hand side of battery carrier assembly before dismantling.

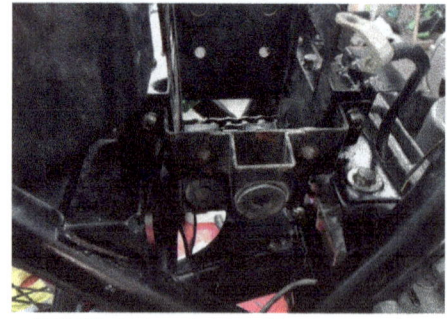
7.10 Right-hand side of battery carrier assembly.

7.11 Rectifier bolted to bottom of battery carrier.

7.12 Battery carrier assembly removed.

REMOVING THE WIRING LOOM & OTHER ELECTRICS

removed from the bike and placed out of the way. See photo 7.12. After this I was able to lift the main wiring harness away from the bike, together with the hazard light relay and its regulator, from the right-hand side of the battery box. See photo 7.13. Note that the hazard warning light switch had already been removed from the bike by a previous owner and wired out.

The bike was slowly being stripped. See photo 7.14.

LESSONS LEARNT
• Insulating tape will always come loose after a time and leave a horrible, sticky mess. Where necessary, use as a short term fix only.
• New wiring looms don't necessarily come with a wiring diagram – or even the correct colour coding.
• Ignition coils can crack due to engine vibration and cause ignition problems that are hard to track down (and the HT leads can disintegrate over time, as mine had done).
• The battery box assembly on a Z900 conceals the rectifier underneath it.
• Electrics on various models are much the same, but Kawasaki tended to reposition these, model to model.

7.13 Hazard light relay and its regulator removed from battery box.

7.14 Bike slowly being stripped down.

www.velocebooks.com
New book news • Special offers • Newsletter • Details of all Veloce books • Gift Vouchers

Chapter 8
Removing the exhaust & rear wheel

Now that I was working on the lower section of the bike I raised the bike lift to its highest setting, which I regarded as a significant step in the dismantling process. I decided next to remove the exhaust, then the rear brake pedal, followed by the rear wheel and swinging arm.

Removing the aftermarket 4-into-1 Kerker exhaust system was simple (see photo 8.1A). Removing the 4 chrome mounting collars bolted to the cylinder head revealed the two collets holding each downpipe in position. See photo 8.1B. These were then tapped out (see photo 8.1C), and, when the single rear silencer mounting was also removed, the entire system simply lifted away. See photo 8.1D.

Possibly a big mistake here was not removing the silencer from the downpipes while the system was still on the bike because, when I tried to remove the silencer afterwards, it was almost impossible to hold the downpipes firmly whilst twisting and pulling off the silencer. With the downpipes held firm in the cylinder head this would have been much easier, although there was the danger of actually cracking the cylinder head if too much force was applied

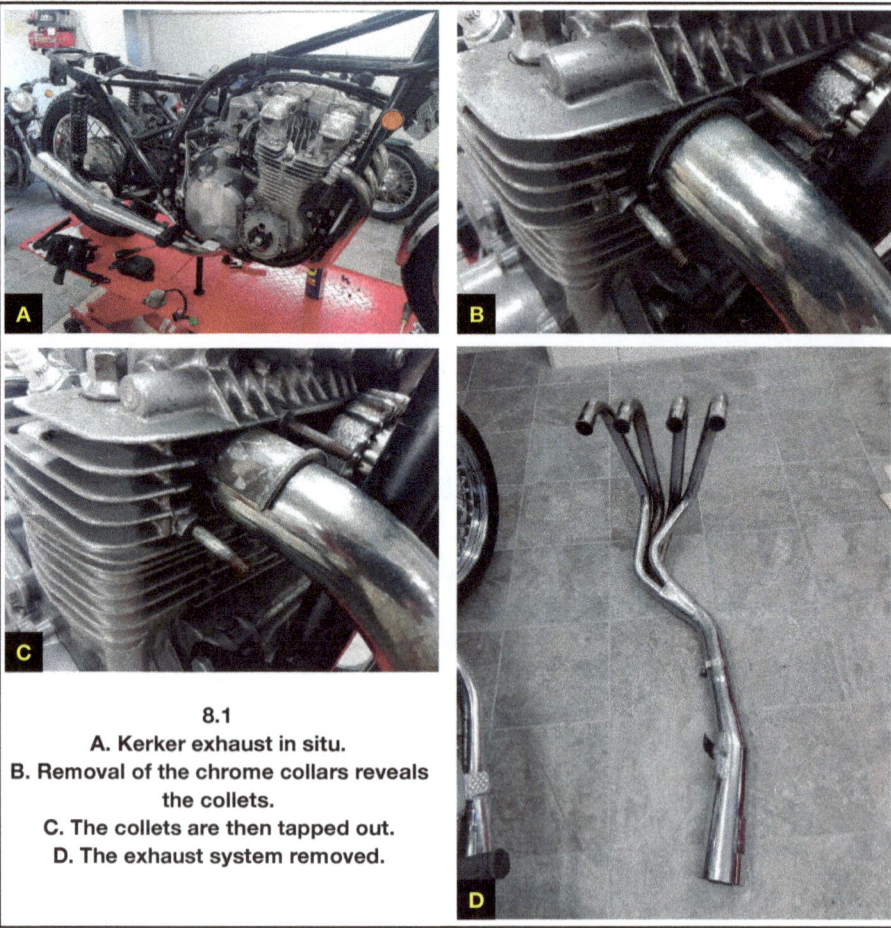

8.1
A. Kerker exhaust in situ.
B. Removal of the chrome collars reveals the collets.
C. The collets are then tapped out.
D. The exhaust system removed.

REMOVING THE EXHAUST & REAR WHEEL

to the downpipes whilst wrestling with the silencer. Anyway, I finally got the silencer off (much heat, much penetrating oil, and much brute force), and sold the system on eBay to help fund the rebuild (and offset the not-inconsiderable cost of a new standard exhaust system).

Before tackling the rear brake lever I removed the kick-start lever to get it out of the way. To do this, I fully removed the bolt from the bottom of the lever as this sits in a groove in the kick-start shaft, and the lever won't come off unless the bolt is completely removed. The lever still didn't want to come off, even so, so I inserted a flat-bladed screwdriver into the jaws of the clamp to force them further open, and then the lever slid off. See photo 8.2. I then removed the domed nut from the end of the brake pedal, and removed the brake rod by unscrewing it from the clevis pin at the top of the brake pedal. See photo 8.3.

Having done this I realised that I couldn't remove the pedal without first removing the right side footpeg, as the brake lever is under tension from its return spring, and the lever has to be able to swing upward to relieve the tension, but the footpeg is in the way. I therefore removed the footpeg by undoing the two domed nuts that hold it in position and pulled it away. However, I immediately realised I also needed to remove the lower of the two shafts that the footpeg mounts on, as well as the footpeg itself, so removed the locking nut from the back of the shaft (see photo 8.4), and then unscrewed the shaft from the frame. See photo 8.5.

Having removed the lower of the two spigots for the footpeg, I realised I also needed to remove the upper one as it, too, was in the way, so did so, along with the small arm that operates the brake switch. See photo 8.6. With the footpeg and its mounting spigots out of the way, I was able to lift the brake pedal sufficiently to relieve pressure on the return spring, and pull off the lever. See photo 8.7.

With the brake pedal removed I turned my attention to the rear wheel, first of all removing the long chromed brake stay that mounts between the brake drum and the frame. I'm sure many owners have cursed many times whilst wondering why their rear wheel wouldn't come off because they forgot to remove the brake stay first. See photos 8.8 and 8.9 of brake stay removal. Note the date stamp on the back of the stay which uses a different dating system to the brake discs, in that the year is shown in the more usual Gregorian format, with the year shown first and the month afterward. In my case, the stamp reads 5 8, which means that it was manufactured in August (8) 1975 (5).

8.2 Removing the kickstart lever.

8.4 Undoing the footpeg mounting shaft nut.

8.6 Removing the rear brake switch operating arm.

8.3 Brake pedal retaining nut removed and brake rod being unscrewed.

8.5 Withdrawing the footpeg mounting shaft.

8.7 Raising the brake lever to relieve tension on the return spring and enable easy removal.

HOW TO RESTORE KAWASAKI Z1, Z/KZ900 & Z/KZ1000

8.8 Loosening the brake stay.

8.11 Loosening the chain adjuster and wheel spindle.

8.14 Driving the spindle out – almost!

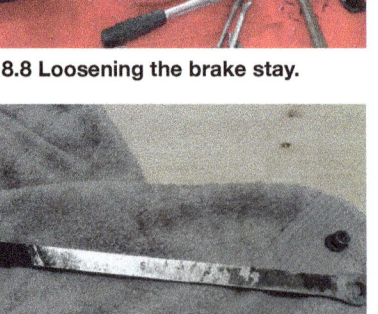

8.9 Brake stay removed. Note date stamp.

8.12 Loosening up the left side.

8.15 Rear wheel starts to come apart when removing it.

8.10 Locating and removing the horseshoe link on the rear chain.

8.13 Withdrawing the wheel spindle.

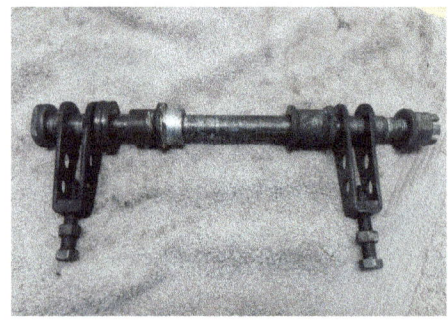

8.16 Order of assembly of rear wheel spindle for reference.

I then removed the rear wheel. Having loosened the chain tensioning adjusters on the ends of the swinging arm, and also the wheel spindle to allow the wheel to be knocked forward slightly to relieve tension in the chain, I rotated the back wheel until I came to the split link with its horseshoe clip, which had been fitted backwards in my case, to enable me to remove the chain. I find the easiest way to remove horseshoe clips is to press on the ends of the clip with a pair of pliers and push it forward, rather than trying to prise out the clip, which usually leads to it being twisted and damaged, and no longer fit for use. See photo 8.10.

I then fully undid the wheel spindle to enable its removal. See photos 8.11 & 8.12. I started to knock out the wheel spindle (see photo 8.13), but this was very stiff, so I used one of my longest flat-bladed screwdrivers as a drift to knock it fully out ... big mistake. Halfway through, the tip of the screwdriver slid off the end of the wheel spindle somewhere in the middle of the hub, and jammed itself between the spindle and the hub – a situation then exacerbated by my continuing to clout it, not realising it was jammed. See photo 8.14. By this time, the screwdriver was seriously jammed between the spindle and the hub, and I couldn't move the spindle or the screwdriver in either direction. After much frustrated effort, I was eventually able to release the screwdriver by clamping a pair of mole grips on its shaft, and then hitting the mole grips outward to free the screwdriver. All this just to knock out a wheel spindle! I then took my long drift (an old cylinder head stud from a Jaguar XK engine, which was of such a shape that it couldn't possibly jam), and knocked out the wheel spindle with that, which is what I should have used to begin with.

Even then, things didn't go totally smoothly as the hub began to fall apart as the spindle was withdrawn, although by holding the two together the wheel came off okay. See photo 8.15. With the wheel finally removed, I immediately loosely reassembled the wheel spindle and its associated parts in the correct

REMOVING THE EXHAUST & REAR WHEEL

order, again, for future reference. See photo 8.16. I also had a quick check of the condition of the rear hub, and the rear sprocket was badly worn, as expected (see photo 8.17). You can check for a worn chain by seeing if it will lift off the sprocket when in situ. To check for wear on a sprocket, look at the teeth to see if they are hooked, as is the case here.

I inspected the shock absorbers in the rear hub and, very much to my surprise, they looked to be in very good condition. See photo 8.18. These rubbers can wear badly with age and cause problems such as knocking and a jerky ride. Mine looked nearly new – perhaps they were?! However, the grease round the rear wheel bearing certainly looked past its sell-by date – discoloured and hard. The rear drum looked okay but I would inspect it more closely later on. See photo 8.19. Both wheel bearings and the rear brake shoes would be replaced as a matter of course – together with the rear chain and sprockets.

My next job was to remove the swinging arm. I removed the rear shock absorbers by undoing the mountings at top and bottom, which left the swinging arm free. All I had to do then was undo the nut holding the swinging arm spindle in place on the left side of the bike. However, two problems quickly arose. First of all the nut had been previously damaged (see photo 8.20), and it was difficult to get a socket onto it; secondly, it had been over-tightened – and I mean *way* over-tightened! I managed to hammer a socket onto the nut and then tried to undo it with my ratchet – no chance. I reached for my long socket extension, which usually gives enough leverage to loosen the tightest of nuts (see photo 8.21), but the nut wasn't having any of it. I therefore fitted a standard tommy bar (see photo 8.22), and belted it with a lump hammer – the nut came loose! (NB: You have to lock the nut on the other end of the spindle to stop it turning). With the nut removed, the spindle pulled out easily, and the swinging arm with it. An initial inspection revealed a complete absence of grease and rather worn bushes and bearings.

I've always found that, with a nut that won't shift, the most effective way to do so is to use a short extension and a lump hammer, rather than a long extension and muscle. The 'short, sharp shock' approach seems to do the trick, usually. Having said that, I think a powered impact wrench would be easier!

The main item of note with the swinging arm removed was the damage done to it by a worn or loose rear chain. See photo 8.23.

8.17 One very worn out rear sprocket – note the bent and worn teeth.

8.18 Shock absorbers appear to be in surprisingly good condition – but bearing grease is old and hard.

8.19 Brake drum looks okay. Will inspect more closely later.

8.20 The damaged swinging arm nut.

8.21 Trying to undo the nut with an extended bar.

HOW TO RESTORE KAWASAKI Z1, Z/KZ900 & Z/KZ1000

Finally, I removed the side stand by removing the lock nut underneath, then unscrewing the retaining bolt from the top (see photo 8.24), which allowed the stand to slide, so relieving tension from the spring and facilitating easy removal.

The bike was now fully dismantled, apart from the engine and front forks/wheels (which were being used to hold the bike in position on the lift). See photo 8.25.

LESSONS LEARNT
- Removing a 4-into-1 exhaust system is easy – getting the silencer off the downpipes afterwards is a nightmare!
- Fully remove the kick-start lever clamping bolt before trying to pull off the lever.
- Remove the right-hand footpeg and its mounting shafts before removing the brake pedal.
- Don't forget to remove the brake stay before trying to remove the back wheel!
- When knocking out the rear wheel spindle use a proper drift that won't jam in the hub (like a flat-bladed screwdriver might!).
- If a nut is totally jammed or rusted on, the most effective way to remove it is by fitting a socket with a short tommy bar attached, and giving the tommy a good blow with a lump hammer. Having said that, I think the absolute best way to remove one is with an electric (or air-powered if you're lucky enough to have a good compressor) impact wrench. I kept meaning to buy one but still hadn't at the time.

8.22 Removing the nut with a short T-bar and a lump hammer.

8.23 Chain damage to the swinging arm.

8.24 Sidestand removal.

8.25 Just the engine and front wheel and forks to go.

www.velocebooks.com
New book news • Special offers • Newsletter • Details of all Veloce books • Gift Vouchers

Chapter 9
Dismantling the points & generator

At last, it was time to begin dismantling the engine. I had deliberately left the front forks and front wheel in situ so that the frame made its own engine stand, which I hoped would make disassembly easy and negate the use of a proper engine stand, as well as meaning that I didn't have to struggle to get the engine in or out of the frame in one lump.

My first job was to drain the engine/gearbox oil (these are all-in-one). Looking underneath the engine revealed the large oil filter housing, with its own small drain plug next to it and the engine drain plug in front of it. Needless to say, the drain plug had been burred and rounded by previous owners (I was just as guilty of this when I was younger, back in the day): see photo 9.1 showing the rounded drain plug, the oil filter, and the oil filter drain plug. The oil filter sits in its own housing, and has its own drain plug for draining the oil before removing the oil filter itself.

Despite the drain plug being rounded, it was still serviceable and, having managed to get a socket on it, I unscrewed this and drained the oil into my bespoke engine oil drain tank. (I bought this years ago, but

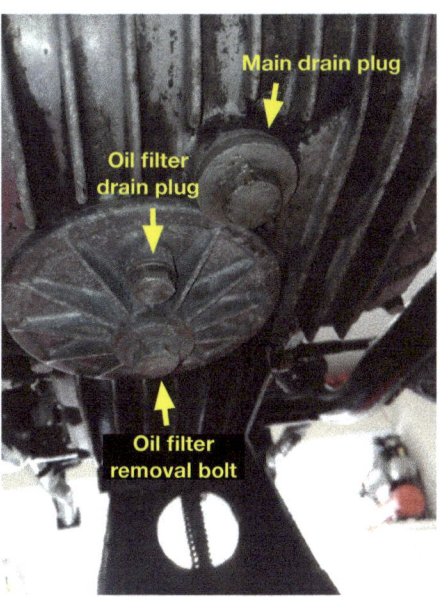

9.1 The damaged drain plug with oil filter housing behind.

9.2 Draining the oil.

I'm not sure if they're available any more – a drain tank that becomes a sealable can that you can take to the recycling centre without too much mess). See photo 9.2. Much to my surprise the engine oil looked almost new. (I am beginning to think that the last owner had some problems with the bike that he spent time trying to fix, but, having failed to do so, he sold it as a non-runner.)

Next up was the oil cooler that had been added at some point, and was very much the worse for wear. This was easily removed by unbolting it from the frame. See photo 9.3. The oil cooler was in bad shape, but even worse was that to get it to fit, the bracket on the frame that holds the

37

HOW TO RESTORE KAWASAKI Z1, Z/KZ900 & Z/KZ1000

9.3 Oil cooler as removed.

9.6 Oil pressure switch assembly removed.

9.9 Cam cover is removed by undoing 16 bolts.

9.4 Reflector mounting bent inwards to facilitate oil cooler fitting.

9.7 Removing the engine breather cover.

9.10 Ready to remove the electronic ignition and advance and retard mechanism.

9.5 Removing the cam chain tensioner.

9.8 Removing the breather plate.

9.11 Checking the valve timing before dismantling.

reflector had been hammered flat. See photo 9.4. This will require repair, although, hopefully, it should just bend back into shape (I'm glad to report that it did). I then removed the cam chain tensioner from the rear of the barrels by removing the two mounting screws. See photo 9.5. I also removed the bespoke oil pressure switch fitting adapted to fit the oil feed and return pipes. This was a bit awkward to remove as the cross-head screws/bolts were tight (replacement bolt heads would take either a spanner or a cross-head screwdriver), and I couldn't get a spanner or an impact driver on them. Eventually, I managed to force a mini socket onto them without damaging the crankcases, and loosened them enough to fully remove them with a screwdriver. See photo 9.6. I had already decided to remove the oil cooler, so began looking for an original oil pressure switch mounting. These aren't available new but I found a secondhand one on the internet without too much trouble.

Next, I removed the engine breather cover (see photo 9.7) by undoing the central bolt, before removing the plate underneath it, held on by two cross-head screws. See photo 9.8.

I finally turned my attention to the cam cover (which I'd been itching to do for ages), and removed it by unscrewing the 16 bolts that hold it down. See photo 9.9. Note the HT lead guides on the 4 bolts on the inlet side of the cover.

I removed the cam cover at this point because I wanted check the valve timing, to both ensure it had been correct before, and give me a guide to how it should look when reassembled.

First of all I rotated the engine by loosely refitting the kick-start lever until the 'T' mark next to the 1 and 4 marks on the advance and retard mechanism under the electronic ignition plate aligned with the mark on the points cover. See photos 9.10 and 9.11. Then I looked at the exhaust camwheel to check that the little arrow on the metal part of the camwheel aligned with the top

DISMANTLING THE POINTS & GENERATOR

of the cylinder head. If you look at photo 9.12 you can just about see the very small arrow in line with the bolt, pointing at the top edge of the cylinder head – although this arrow is very hard to see in the photos (It's clearer in the photos covering reassembly). Then, looking at the cam chain I counted 28 pins on the chain, beginning from the one directly above the arrow until I came to the top of the inlet camwheel, where there is a clear arrow that has '28' on it. My chain was indeed exactly 28 pins round and therefore correctly timed! Look again at photo 9.12, and then 9.13 for clarification.

Having checked the valve timing, I removed the electronic ignition by undoing the 3 screws that hold it in position, and then removed the advance and retard mechanism by undoing the central bolt that holds it to the end of the crankshaft. I then began to remove the inner cover by undoing the set screws that hold it on. However, having undone this it wouldn't budge, and there's no way to lever it off as it sits flush with the crankcases. I therefore tried my trusted No 1 method of heating the cover with a blowtorch, which is often effective as it softens the gasket cement, allowing the cover to come away. See photo 9.14. In this case, it made no difference at all. Hmmm ...

In this situation, whatever you do, resist the temptation to try and loosen the cover by inserting a screwdriver between the two cases. You WILL damage the cases if you try this – they are very soft aluminium, and are much more easily damaged than you might think. I can't tell you the number of times I've been sorely tempted to reach for that screwdriver, but you have to resist – or be ready for considerable damage that's hard to put right.

In this case I used a method that had worked previously for removing my screwdriver jammed in the rear hub (see chapter 8). I replaced the two long screws that held the outer casing in position by just a few turns. They were long enough to allow me to gently clamp a pair of mole grips behind their heads, and then hammer the mole grips outward with a soft-faced hammer (soft in case you accidentally hit the casings – easily done). This worked a treat (see photo 9.15) and, once the seal was broken, the cover came away easily enough to reveal the end of the crankshaft. See photo 9.16.

Flushed with success I then started to remove the generator/

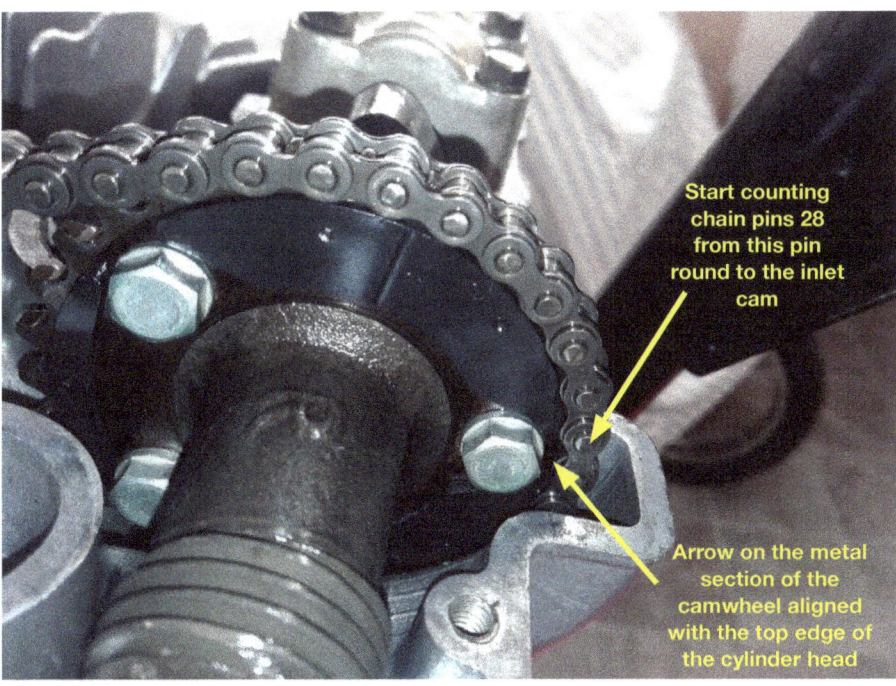

9.12 Exhaust cam in correct position with arrow on cam lining-up with top of cylinder head.

9.13 Inlet cam in correct position – 28 pins round on the chain.

9.15 Removing the inner cover with a set of mole grips.

9.14 Trying (and failing) to remove the inner points cover with heat.

9.16 Inner cover removed to reveal end of crankshaft.

HOW TO RESTORE KAWASAKI Z1, Z/KZ900 & Z/KZ1000

alternator cover from the left-hand side of the bike. Having removed the screws around the outside, however, I was faced with the same problem of the casing not moving. In this case, I couldn't repeat the screw trick as there was no outer casing with associated screws to hold onto. Hmmm, again.

I soon realised that part of the cover stood slightly proud of the crankcases, providing a lip to work on (towards the rear of the casing). I held a small block of wood against the lip and tapped this carefully with a lump hammer: after a little while the gasket gave way and the cover was loose. See photo 9.17. I used a block of wood (drift) rather than a soft-faced hammer as it gave me a more accurate point of contact. After a little more wiggling the cover came off to reveal the alternator, rotor, primary drive gear, and starter motor gear. See photo 9.18. The cover itself was left hanging by the wiring that runs under the starter motor. Having removed this, the cover came fully away.

I then removed the two screws that held the rear of the starter motor in position (see photo 9.19) and, with these gone, the starter motor simply pushed out from the chain case. See photo 9.20. All seemed to be in good condition, and the starter motor was set aside for further examination and refurbishment later on.

One item to note, though, was that there was clearly a small but persistent oil leak from the generator/alternator cover where the wiring came out (about the 5 o'clock position). I know that this is a recognised problem, and it's one that I wanted to ensure was fully addressed when I rebuilt the engine.

Next up was rotor removal. Having removed the nut holding the rotor in place (see photo 9.21), it was time to pull the rotor from the end of the crankshaft. I had read in the Haynes manual that you could screw the rear wheel spindle into the rotor and use this as an extractor, but actually discovered that it was the swinging arm spindle that fitted the thread in the end of the rotor. I duly screwed in the spindle and tried to tighten it, which effectively pushed the rotor off the crankshaft, but I couldn't seem to get the spindle tight enough to force the rotor free. I therefore tried clamping my mole grips on the shaft, and used these to try and free the rotor (similar to removing the inner timing cover), but again to no avail. See photo 9.22. I therefore decided to buy the bespoke removal tool from Z-Power – which arrived promptly, as ever – and, when screwed into the end of the rotor, forced it off in no time. Job done. See photo 9.23.

I carefully put aside the rotor, noting the three rollers and springs in the rear of it (the starter motor clutch) that could easily be lost (see photo 9.24), and then slid off the drive sprocket for the electric start, as well as prising out the Woodruff key of the crankshaft. See photo 9.25. (I don't think there is one on later models; the rotor is simply held by the taper). Note that the damper rubber that sits behind the sprocket was misshapen and distorted, and would require replacement; although unfortunately it's one of the few engine parts that currently aren't available. The idler gear then slid out with its shaft (see photo 9.26), leaving the generator casing satisfyingly empty. See photo 9.27. Job done.

LESSONS LEARNT

- Dismantling the engine whilst it's still in the frame with front forks and wheel attached seems to work.
- Engine casings are made from soft aluminium alloy, and they WILL be

9.17 Removing the generator (alternator) cover with a block of wood and a lump hammer.

9.19 Removing the two bolts from the rear of the starter motor.

9.18 Generator cover off revealing rotor and starter motor mechanism.

9.20 Starter motor simply pushes out from the inside.

9.21 Removing the nut that retains the rotor on the crankshaft.

DISMANTLING THE POINTS & GENERATOR

9.22 With the swinging arm spindle screwed in I also tried to hammer the rotor off by hitting a pair of mole grips – without success.

badly damaged by trying to separate them with screwdrivers, etc, or if hit with hammers, so NEVER be tempted to do this. If you can't get the cases apart, go away, think about an alternative plan, and come back refreshed.
• It's prudent to check the engine valve timing before dismantling, to both determine whether it was set correctly before, and also to get an idea of what it should look like for when you reassemble it. Note that when I checked the valve timing on the Z1A I found that it was way out! This helped me understand why the bike hadn't been running at all well.
• The starter motor simply slides out when the two mounting screws to the rear are removed.
• One weakness of these engines is their tendency to weep oil from where the alternator leads exit the casing through a grommet that is hard to replace (as you need to remove the wiring to do so).
• Apparently, you can remove the generator from the crankshaft with the aid of the swinging arm spindle ... but I couldn't.
• Removing the generator with the proper bespoke tool is easy.
• Don't lose the roller bearings in the back of the rotor (the clutch for the starter motor) or the Woodruff key in the crankshaft if one's fitted.
• Watch out for any parts that don't look right, and make a note to investigate further before reassembly.
• Happiness is an empty casing.

9.23 Using the special tool to remove the rotor – success!

9.25 Rotor assembly and starter sprocket removed – note the misshapen damper rubber, and don't forget to remove the Woodruff key from the crankshaft if it has one.

9.24 Rotor removed – don't lose the springs and rollers at the back.

9.26 The idler gear for the starter motor then simply pulls off.

9.27 The generator casing now satisfyingly empty.

Chapter 10
Dismantling the clutch & kick-start assembly

It was time to dismantle the clutch and kick-start mechanism. I removed the large clutch outer casing using my impact driver and a soft-faced hammer to start the screws, which tended to be locked solid with mild corrosion (this seemed to be the best method of removing most of the engine casing screws). The clutch screws were easy to reach, and came undone with a few taps on the impact driver (as ever, a short, sharp shock worked better than applying continuous pressure). See photo 10.1. I also placed a small oil tray under the engine to catch any engine oil drips, but there were hardly any.

I then removed the clutch pressure plate by unscrewing the five bolts with springs under them, which exposed the clutch plates that I teased out using two small screwdrivers. See photo 10.2. I think that, possibly, a magnet would have worked equally well to pull them from the clutch basket. After much fiddling, the plates were out and the clutch basket empty. See photo 10.3.

I then pulled the mushroom-shaped clutch pusher out of the mainshaft, followed by the ball bearing that sits behind it (see photos 10.4 and 10.5) by gently tilting the bike toward me and it rolled out – don't lose it!

My next job was a seemingly easy one that turned into a bit of an ordeal – trying to remove the clutch hub nut. The problem with these

10.1 Clutch cover removed.

10.2 Removing the clutch plates with two small screwdrivers.

DISMANTLING THE CLUTCH & KICK-START ASSEMBLY

10.3 Clutch pressure plate and friction plates removed.

10.4 The mushroom-headed clutch pusher just pulls out.

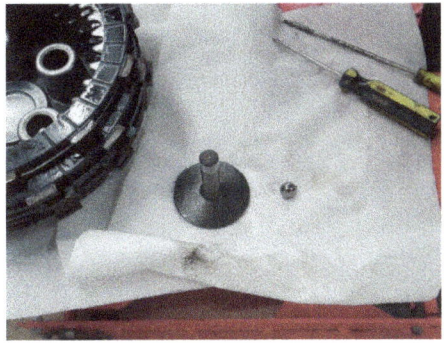

10.5 Followed by the ball bearing that sits behind it.

10.6 Attempting to lock the clutch with the universal tool, to enable the clutch centre nut to be undone.

10.7 The arms of the tool weren't quite wide enough to engage with the grooves in the clutch basket.

10.8 Look at this bad boy! A cordless impact driver with variable settings. Garage porn!

are that they are tightened to a very high torque, and there is nothing to prevent the clutch hub from spinning when you try to undo the nut: two factors that, combined, spell trouble.

I decided to invest in a clutch hub locking tool, and duly ordered one from a Kawasaki supplier. When the tool arrived, I fitted it in position ready to remove the hub nut (see photo 10.6), and tried to undo the nut. As soon as any real pressure was applied on the nut, the new tool slipped out of position, allowing the hub to turn freely again. Having tried several times, it became clear that the tool simply wasn't up to the job, being a universal clutch locking tool rather than one specifically for the Kawasaki Z900, and, as such, almost guaranteed not to fit perfectly. See photo 10.7. (On reassembling the bike I found I *was* able to use the locking tool effectively – I'd obviously been using it incorrectly! See chapter on clutch assembly.)

Time for a different approach. I'd had similar problems on previous bikes, and various people had recommended using a powered impact driver. I'd never bought one as I always thought of them as air-driven tools (which I have no facility for), or as rather cumbersome electric ones. However, technology has moved on! Cordless impact drivers that are relatively cheap and very powerful are now available. Time to invest in one (opportunity to buy a new tool? I didn't need much persuading!). I went for a good make rather than a cheap one (always worth it), and was soon the proud owner of a DeWalt 18 volt ½in drive, variable power cordless impact driver. See photo 10.8.

I knew that I needed to just hold the clutch basket still, rather than lock it solid in order to remove the nut with the impact driver (the main advantage of using this), so dispensed with my new locking tool and, instead, jammed an old cold chisel between the gearbox sprocket and its casing to lock everything. See photo 10.9 (with the bike in gear). I hadn't tried this method of locking the clutch before because I knew from bitter experience that trying to undo the clutch hub nut using this method of locking the engine can result in damaging the gearbox sprocket casing. If you look again at photo 10.9, you will see that the casing round the gearbox sprocket is thin, and not designed to take the extreme force required to lock the engine: it would be very easy to break an engine casing like this, and really be in trouble (plus you'd never forgive yourself).

However, using this locking method with the powered impact driver was fine, as little stress was put on the casing. With the sprocket locked, I put the socket on the impact driver and set it to maximum power (phasers set to stun!). 30 seconds later the nut came off as if it had been only finger-tight: one of my better purchases without a doubt! See photo 10.10.

Since then, I have used the cordless impact driver on numerous occasions to remove nuts and bolts which otherwise would have been a

43

HOW TO RESTORE KAWASAKI Z1, Z/KZ900 & Z/KZ1000

10.9 Rear sprocket locked with a cold chisel.

10.10 Thirty seconds later the stubborn nut is easily removed!

10.11 The clutch hub then slides off the mainshaft splines.

10.12 The sprung locking washer behind the clutch hub nut is helpfully labelled.

10.13 Kickstart cover removed.

major problem (eg: some of the bolts holding together the crankcases). Expensive, yes (£160 at the time of writing), but worth every penny!

I removed the nut and clutch hub from the mainshaft, and the clutch was then as fully dismantled as it could be without splitting the crankcases. See photo 10.11. Note that the locking spring washer that sits behind the nut is clearly marked as to which way round it should be refitted. See photo 10.12.

I then removed the kick-start cover casing (see photo 10.13) to reveal the kick-start shaft and return spring. Removing the kick-start cover was difficult as there's nothing to tap on to ease it off. In the end I used heat and a small block of wood to tap on an edge that stood slightly proud of the crankcases.

With the cover removed, I employed a pair of mini mole grips to remove the kick-start return spring (see photo 10.14) by unhooking it from its retainer, so that the spring and retainer slid off the shaft. See photo 10.15. As with the clutch, this

10.14 Unhooking the kickstart return spring with a pair of mini mole grips.

10.15 The kickstart cover, return spring and spring guide removed from shaft.

was as far as the kick-start could be dismantled without splitting the crankcases.

LESSONS LEARNT

• My preferred method of removing seized casing screws is with a manual impact driver and lump hammer, as this easily frees off locked screws. A short, sharp shock (impact driver) is better than sustained force (screwdriver). An alternative method is to gently heat the casings first to loosen the screws via expansion of the casings – this can be used together with an impact driver on really stubborn screws.

• Don't forget about or lose the ball bearing that sits inside the mainshaft behind the mushroom-headed clutch pusher.

• Trying to lock the clutch hub to remove the clutch hub nut has been a pain on every bike I've worked on, and I've tried many removal methods over the years. By far the easiest and most hassle-free method has to be using a cordless powered impact driver – brilliant! Wish I'd bought one years ago.

• I have since discovered that bespoke clutch locking tools are available for different Z900 models, which I didn't know about before, and these are supposed to do the trick. I've seen them advertised on eBay (but there are different ones for virtually every model, so make sure you get the correct one for your bike), but can't vouch for their effectiveness. (A cordless impact driver is still tops for me as it can be used on any engine, with minimal locking, and also on any other stubborn nuts and bolts, too.)

• Tools are only as good as the person using them, of course ... especially when it comes to clutch hub locking tools!

• Be very careful if locking the gearbox by jamming the gearbox sprocket as it's easy to cause major damage to the casings.

• You can't fully dismantle the clutch or kick-start mechanism without first splitting the crankcases.

• Cordless impact drivers – the business.

Chapter 11
Removing the gearbox sprocket & casing

Next up was the gearbox sprocket and outer gearbox casing.

The gearbox sprocket casing was in its usual very greasy state, with chewed heads to the mounting screws where previous owners had removed the casing to fit a new chain and gearbox sprocket, as these wear relatively quickly. See photo 11.1.

NB: Later chains fitted to Z1Bs on are stronger than earlier Z1 chains in that they are a wider 'O' ring chain, though still wear. You can convert earlier models to the later chain but have to put spacers behind the sprockets to provide sufficient clearance for the wider chain.

With the sprocket cover removed, the sprocket and gear change shaft are revealed. See photo 11.2. As ever, I was then faced with the tricky job of undoing the gearbox sprocket nut. This is always a faff as you need to find a way to lock the shaft so it doesn't turn whilst trying to undo the nut. I was thinking of using my cold chisel jammed

11.1 Gearbox sprocket cover – with chewed screw heads.

11.2 Outer cover removed to reveal the gearbox sprocket together with the clutch pushrod on the left and the gear change shaft bottom right.

HOW TO RESTORE KAWASAKI Z1, Z/KZ900 & Z/KZ1000

11.3 Gearbox sprocket removed with ease using my cordless impact driver.

11.6 Inner cover removed to reveal the gear change mechanism.

11.4 I used a pair of mole grips to help remove the cover as the casing is hidden so any damage caused by the jaws would be unseen …

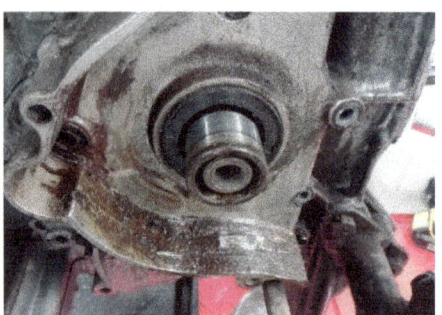

11.5 … but I found that removing the spacer first made the job easier.

under the sprocket again, but was worried that I might break the casing, especially now that the sprocket cover was removed, thus leaving the casing less supported and easier to break. However, I had been told that cordless impact drivers can be useful in such situations, putting little strain on any locking tools, and so it proved. I used the impact driver and the nut came off straight away. See photo 11.3. Just one of my best tools ever.

With the sprocket removed, I tackled the outer gearbox cover, which, as expected, was held fast with gasket sealant, and didn't want to come off. I used a pair of mole grips to grab the side of the casing and give me something to pull/wiggle in order to remove the casing. See photo 11.4. I thought this method was okay as this casing is completely hidden with the engine assembled, so a couple of jaw marks on the casing wouldn't hurt. Even with the moles attached, the cover resisted my attempts to dislodge it, so I removed the spacer from the main shaft and pulled out the clutch pull rod as well, and this gave a little bit more freedom to wiggle the casing in order to get it to let go. See photo 11.5.

Eventually, the casing came away to reveal the gear change mechanism behind it. See photo 11.6. It was at this point that I also noticed a hole for a pin in the main shaft; a pin that was clearly missing on my bike. See photo 11.7. Should there be a pin in the gearbox main shaft? More investigation required.

After taking the usual copious number of 'before' photos to aid with

11.7 Unused hole for a split pin in the gearbox mainshaft and 'O' ring seal behind spacer.

REMOVING THE GEARBOX SPROCKET & CASING

reassembly (see photo 11.8), I then removed the gear change assembly. See photo 11.9. The outer gearbox cover was now stripped. See photo 11.10. Note that there are six pins in the gear change drum, and that one of them is longer than the others. Also note that the longer pin in this photo is in the incorrect position for reassembly. It's in this position because I'd selected first gear to lock the gearbox sprocket and forgot to then return it to neutral.

LESSONS LEARNT
- Cordless impact driver – definitely one of the best tools, ever!
- Earlier Z1s had thinner chains that weren't as strong as the later 'O' ring chains, but they can be converted to take the later chains without too much fuss.
- Always be aware that the order of assembly of mechanical parts as found may not necessarily be right, as a previous owner may have put them together incorrectly.
- After some investigation I found that the missing pin in the mainshaft was used to drive the now obsolete rear chain oiler as fitted to earlier models, so was no longer required.
- Photos: you simply cannot take too many.

11.8 Close up of the gear change mechanism, for reference.

11.9 Gear change mechanism removed.

11.10 Gearbox sprocket housing now stripped.

Chapter 12
Removing the oil filter, sump & oil pump

My next task was to remove the oil filter, sump (oil pan), and oil pump. It is worth noting that there is a separate oil drain plug just for the oil filter, situated in the housing itself. The oil filter holds a surprising amount of oil, even after the main engine oil has been drained, so unless you want to be swimming in oil, drain the filter before removing it. See photo 12.1.

As ever, the oil filter nut had been damaged, but I was able to hammer a socket onto it and remove the whole assembly. See photo 12.2. With the filter removed you can see the component parts of the oil filter assembly in photo 12.3. Note the large 'O' ring inside the filter rim.

With the filter and residual oil out of the way, I began to remove the sump. First off, I removed all of the bolts holding the sump to the bottom of the crankcases. It's really easy to miss one, so check and double-check this before trying to remove the sump. If a bolt has been left in, it's possible to crack the casing trying to get it off. See photo 12.4.

With all bolts removed, the sump sat there and stared at me, refusing to budge: it was well and truly stuck, and there was no obvious way of encouraging it to let go; neither are there any obvious protrusions to knock against. I tried heating the casing but that didn't help. Eventually, I discovered a small ledge of sump protruding beyond the crankcase underneath the kick-start housing, and used a block of wood and lump hammer on that, which, together with more heat from a blowtorch finally did the trick and the sump came away, but it had been a struggle.

What I then realised was that the sump, unlike most other engine casings, had no locating dowels to hold it in position, so could have been tapped sideways in order to loosen it. You live and learn.

As soon as the sump was off I noticed a foreign body lying in the bottom of it – a bit that was definitely not supposed to be there. See photo 12.5. Further inspection revealed it

12.1 Draining the oil from the oil filter housing.

12.2 The oil filter removed.

12.3 The oil filter components.

REMOVING THE OIL FILTER, SUMP & OIL PUMP

12.5 Sump finally removed – but what's that in the middle?

12.4 The sump bolts removed ready to drop the sump (oil pan).

12.6 The front cam chain guide snapped off and lying in the bottom of the sump – a common problem.

12.7 Oil pump removed from lower crankcase. (I bet you noticed that I forgot to take a photo of the oil pump in situ before I removed it!)

was the front cam chain guide, which had snapped off from its two fixing points in the cylinder barrels, and was now lying redundant in the bottom of the sump. See photo 12.6. This is a relatively common fault with Z900s, etc. even though by the time the actual Z900 came along Kawasaki had improved and strengthened the guides from earlier bikes. I bet the engine sounded like a bag of spanners! When I stripped the engine down on my Z1A I also discovered that the same guide was broken in exactly the same way, so a definite weakness.

12.8 Oil pump assembly on the bench.

I then removed the oil pump which sits under the crankshaft in the lower crankcase. Removal was very straightforward, and the whole assembly came off as a unit. See photos 12.7 and 12.8.

LESSONS LEARNT
• Drain the oil filter before attempting to remove it – it holds a fair amount of oil.
• When removing engine casings, and especially large casings like the

HOW TO RESTORE KAWASAKI Z1, Z/KZ900 & Z/KZ1000

sump, check and double-check that you have removed all of the bolts
• There are no dowels holding the sump in place, so it can be tapped sideways to free it if it refuses to come away.
• The cam chain guides/tensioners are a known weakness on Z900 engines, and should be replaced if there's any doubt about their integrity. Note that the same guide was also broken on my Z1A in exactly the same manner. Not good.
• At last I've found something wrong with the bike! I was feeling a bit of a fraud as everything else has been in such good condition: the front cam chain guide is broken – hurrah!

In all honesty I have been stunned by the excellent overall condition of this bike and especially the engine. I've rebuilt many bikes over the years (mainly British), and all have been knackered. This one has been amazing in that it's in such good condition, despite being over 40 years old and having clearly seen better days. It's a real tribute to the engineers at Kawasaki who designed such an amazing machine. Where were the oil leaks, the broken studs, the rounded screw heads, the cracked casings, the worn bearings, the dragging clutch, the worn-out cylinders, and generally knackered bits?

While I'm on the subject, let me say thay Kawasaki did what it set out to do with the Z1, and got it right. The engineering is brilliant – brilliant in its simplicity. The company looked at how to do something, experimented, and then came up with the right way to do it, and, as with any great mechanical triumph, it's stunning in its simplicity and execution. Most British machines have a host of mechanical problems and idiosyncrasies, and owners are continuously trying to improve them with various modifications and upgrades to try and get them to work properly. The Z900 doesn't have any such problems (generally*), and doesn't require exact setting up or modification to work properly: it's simply a great piece of engineering. As a mechanical bod I am really seriously impressed.

---

*Having praised the Z900, I think it does have a slight weakness with the cam chain guides, and maybe some of the electrics – but nothing's perfect!

Chapter 13
Removing the cylinder head & barrels

With most ancillaries removed from the engine, I turned my attention to the cylinder head and barrels. I had already removed the rocker box to check the valve timing before disassembly, and to give me an idea of what it should look like on reassembly.

My first job was to remove the cam chain idler assembly from the top of the head. This was done by simply removing the four bolts that secure it – note that there also four rubber mounting blocks to remove with it. See photos 13.1 and 13.2. (Note that as I was carrying out a complete rebuild it didn't matter if something accidentally fell down the cam chain tunnel and into the sump – but it would have mattered if I'd just been doing a top end overhaul. In this case I would have stuffed the cam chain tunnel with rag to prevent anything accidentally falling down.)

After this I removed the four bearing caps that hold down the camshafts. I tried to remove these carefully to reduce stress on the covers and the camshafts. See photo 13.3. With the bearing caps removed I slid the camshafts out from under the loose cam chain. See photo 13.4.

I prised out the camshaft bearing caps from their seats and gave them an initial inspection: the bearings showed some signs of wear which, as they're plain bearings, didn't surprise me. I had already decided to replace these bearings as any plain bearings on an engine tend to wear quite quickly, and it would be a false economy to not replace them as a matter of course. The good news is that these are the only plain bearings in the entire engine; the bad news is

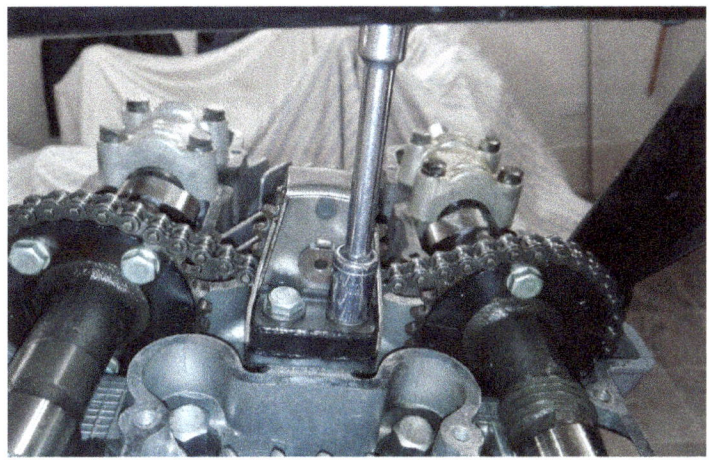

13.1 Removing the cam chain idler assembly.

13.2 Idler assembly removed.

HOW TO RESTORE KAWASAKI Z1, Z/KZ900 & Z/KZ1000

13.3 Removing the camshaft bearing caps.

13.4 With the caps removed the camshafts slide out under the cam chain.

that they're quite expensive at £100 for a non-genuine set (and a whole lot more for a genuine Kawasaki set). Still worth changing them, though, as part of an engine rebuild. See photo 13.5.

Next up I removed the cylinder head nuts and two outer studs. I removed the two outer studs first, to prevent any undue stress in this delicate area of the head (in the cooling fin area). Not strictly necessary, but why take the chance? See photo 13.6.

With all cylinder head nuts removed it was time to remove the head – or rather, for me to try and remove the head, as it just sat there, refusing to budge. The head was clearly well and truly fixed on by the head gasket, and was in no mood to let go. I tried gently tapping it at the front under the cam chain overhang, and at the rear next to the oil pressure switch aperture where there was solid metal, but to no avail.

At times like this you really have to be patient and not resort to whacking it in all the wrong places with a large lump hammer. This may sound obvious, but, after half an hour's struggle with no result, it becomes increasingly tempting. You can tap on the cam chain tunnel, but don't go near the outer fins.

Eventually, I freed the head by using a blowtorch to heat the joint between barrels and head until it was quite hot, as well as replacing the sparkplugs, and turning over the engine to provide cylinder compression (by means of a bolt in the end of the left-hand side of the crankshaft), then tapping the head as before. Eventually, it started to move and then came off. See photo 13.7 of the head on the bench. In retrospect, I could have used a block of wood in the exhaust ports, hit with a lump hammer to aid removal. There are also areas just under exhaust ports 1 and 4 that can be used to prise the head off – but be very careful.

I had a quick look at the head to check that all was okay, and everything looked fairly normal for an engine with 20,000 miles on the clock. I turned the head upside down to check the combustion chambers, see photo 13.8. The only cause for concern was the presence of some oil or similar in the combustion chamber of No 1 cylinder. However, I wasn't sure if this was oil or possibly excess liquid starting spray left over from when the importer had used it to get the engine to run. It needed checking anyway. See photo 13.9.

I also had a quick check of the tops of the pistons and the cylinder bores still on the bike – all seemed okay – see photo 13.10.

13.5 Camshaft bearings showing signs of wear.

13.6 Removing the cylinder head studs, beginning with the outer ones.

REMOVING THE CYLINDER HEAD & BARRELS

13.7 Head removed and on the bench with tappets and shims in place.

13.8 Combustion chambers and valves don't look too bad.

13.9 Number 1 cylinder seems to have had oil leaking into it.

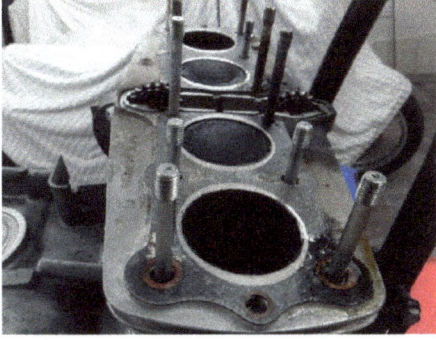

13.10 Cylinder barrels and pistons look okay.

13.11 Tappets with their shims fallen out on the bench – but which is which?

Having checked the combustion chambers I turned the cylinder head back over and immediately realised my mistake: I had forgotten to first remove the tappet buckets from the head, and all the buckets had slid out of their bores and were strewn across the bench. See photo 13.11. The problem with this is that the buckets should really go back into the bores they came out of, but I now had no idea which went where! Twit. I didn't think it mattered too much, to be honest, as the tappets would still work okay, and probably not wear excessively, but I was annoyed with myself for making such a basic error.

The bike was now nearly fully disassembled, with only the bottom half of the engine left, along with the frame and front forks. See photos 13.12 and 13.13.

Next up was removal of the cylinder barrels. These proved as hard to remove as the head, with the added complication that there was no compression to help things along, and even fewer places I could safely whack with a soft-faced hammer. Once again, though, I triumphed by

13.12 Disassembly so far.

HOW TO RESTORE KAWASAKI Z1, Z/KZ900 & Z/KZ1000

13.13 Not far to go now.

13.16 Note, the bottom of the front chain guide had snapped off, and was left sitting in its groove in the top of the crankcases.

13.19 Crankcases and con-rods with pistons removed.

heating the alloy quite a lot with a blowtorch, which seemed to help soften the cylinder base seal. As usual, it was a long, slow process that was quite frustrating, but the barrels eventually let go. When they did lift clear they left behind a considerable amount of crud, principally from the stud holes (photos 13.14 and 13.15). See 'Lessons Learnt' regarding an easier way to remove the barrels.

Inside the barrels were the guides and tensioners for the cam chain, which just slot into place together with their little mounting rubbers. Along with these were also the rest of the remains of the broken front cam chain guide that I'd found in the bottom of the sump. If you look at photo 13.16 you can see the bottom section of the broken guide which was still sitting in its slot in the top of the crankcases when I removed the barrels. In photo 13.17 you can see the screw at the top of the barrels – all that remained of the top section of the guide. Apart from that, the bores of the barrels all looked to be in good condition, and would hopefully only require honing rather than reboring, though would be fully checked later.

I then removed the pistons from the small ends of the con rods by prising out one of the small circlips on the end of the gudgeon pins and, after heating the piston very gently, pushed the gudgeon pins out. I then numbered the pistons to ensure they went back in the same bores. See photos 13.18 and 13.19.

LESSONS LEARNT
• Block the cam chain tunnel to prevent any parts falling into the engine if you're doing just a top-end overhaul.
• It's probably a good idea to replace the plain camshaft bearings as a matter of course.
• The camshafts simply slide out under the cam chain (and can't be mixed up as the exhaust cam has the tacho drive gear on it).
• Remove the outer head studs first.
• Getting the head to actually lift away is always difficult, but don't rush – those fins are easily damaged and a nightmare to mend.
• Don't turn the head upside down before you've removed (and marked) the tappet buckets!
• Removing the cylinder head and barrels requires a very special tool – patience. I was later to discover that there are actually two slots in the tops of the crankcases on later models (Z900 onwards) to allow the barrels to be levered off. See photo 13.20. Although I think these should be used with care.

13.14 Barrels off with crud left behind.

13.17 Where the front cam chain guide should be (not in the sump where it was!).

13.15 More crud on the cylinder head studs.

13.18 Prising out the gudgeon pin circlips.

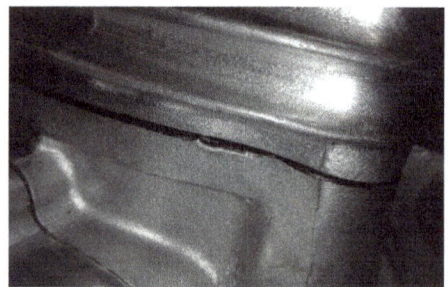

13.20 Later models have slots under the cylinders to aid removal.

Chapter 14
Removing & dismantling the crankcases

With the barrels removed, the engine was stripped down as much as possible whilst still in the frame. I'd decided to strip the engine this way as I thought that the frame (with the front wheel and forks still attached and sitting on a bike lift) made a very good engine stand, as well as making the engine as light as possible in order to remove it. With the engine stripped, it was time to take it out of the frame. See photo 14.1.

I enlisted the help of a neighbour to make sure all went smoothly and safely, and 'just in case something went wrong,' as you never know. I undid all of the remaining engine mounting bolts, and, although I feared the engine would then drop in the frame and jam, all was well. I made a note of order of reassembly of the main engine mounting bolts, as well as marking the two central bolts on each side of the bottom of the crankcases with their unique, pear-shaped brackets that cleverly lock into the crankcases. See photos 14.2 and 14.3.

With the engine mounting bolts removed I lifted the engine out of the frame, which proved easier than I thought it would. The engine was light enough to lift on my own without

14.1 Engine ready for removal from frame.

my neighbour's help, although it was reassuring to know he was there, if needed. Anyway, the engine was now on the bench (see photo 14.4), leaving a very empty frame. See photo 14.5.

It's worth noting that the engine wasn't too heavy to lift as it was stripped down to just the crankcases, and also I was lifting from waist height (not from the floor): these two factors combined to make the job manageable – but be aware that a more complete engine, or one that's sitting on the floor, will be much heavier, and more difficult to lift.

The next job was to split the crankcases, and I set about removing all of the bolts. I found that there were

HOW TO RESTORE KAWASAKI Z1, Z/KZ900 & Z/KZ1000

14.2 Rear engine bolt assembly.

14.3 Bottom engine bolt assembly – note differing length of bolts.

14.4 Engine out and on the bench.

14.5 Now there's something missing here …

far more 6mm bolts than I anticipated, and that the bolts around the crankshaft were 8mm diameter, and very, very tight. Once again I was very thankful that I'd invested in an impact wrench as, without it, I would have struggled. Some of the 8mm bolts round the crankshaft were particularly tight and corroded or Loctited in (as a couple of them should be). See photo 14.6. Make sure you don't miss any of the crankcase bolts, and note that there are a few that are almost hidden away. See photos 14.7 and 14.8.

With all of the crankcase bolts removed (I checked three times), I took three of the 8mm crankcase bolts and inserted them into the three threaded holes in the crankcases (two at the front, and one at the rear), whose purpose is to help separate the crankcases. See photos 14.9 and 14.10. By slowly tightening these three bolts the two halves of the crankcase are forced apart – by far one of the easiest and simplest methods of crankcase splitting I've ever come across. Another thumbs-up to Kawasaki.

In my case, what I didn't realise was that, despite having spent their lives facing downward, these three threaded holes were full of crud, and when I tightened them to the point where I thought they were pushing on to the upper casing, they were, in fact, jammed in their threads. This made the job nerve wracking because although I tightened the bolts more and more, as they weren't actually pushing on the cases they didn't split, and I worried that I might crack them. I checked several times that I had removed ALL of the crankcase bolts as I couldn't work out why the cases wouldn't split. Luckily, I eventually realised what the problem was and removed the bolts, cleaned the threads properly, and started again (of course, it's essential to evenly tighten the three bolts to avoid damage to

REMOVING & DISMANTLING THE CRANKCASES

14.6 Larger crankcase bolts were corroded and Loctited in.

14.9 Use two larger bolts to split the cases at the front …

14.10 … and one bolt at the rear.

14.7 Don't forget the two bolts inside the crankcase …

the cases). This time, all went well and the cases soon came apart. See photo 14.11.

LESSONS LEARNT
• Partially dismantling the engine in the frame before removing it worked well for me.
• Having someone around 'just in case' when lifting a heavy and irreplaceable component is highly recommended.
• Crankcase bolt removal: another reason to buy an impact driver.
• Remove ALL of the crankcase bolts (there are an awful lot of them), and then check three times that you have.
• Clean out the three threads used for forcing apart the crankcases – they've been left open all their lives and can be full of crud and corrosion.
• Tighten the three separating bolts evenly to avoid possible catastrophic damage to the crankcases.

14.8 … or the two bolts just to the outside.

14.11 Crankcases split!

Chapter 15
Stripping the crankcases

With the crankcases now separated and the bottom half lifted away, it was time to remove the internals.

Rather to my surprise, the mainshaft, layshaft, and kick-start shaft simply lifted out of the upper crankcase without further ado, and the clutch basket then simply slid off the end of the mainshaft. See photo 15.1 of the shafts as removed and awaiting inspection. (Don't lose the two semi-circular locating rings on the end of the gearshafts – which somehow I did!)

With the gearshafts out of the way, I removed the last parts of the gear change mechanism still attached to the crankcases. See photo 15.2, showing the pins being removed from the gear shift drum, although I should have removed them before. The main thing is not to lose any; also note that one of the pins is slightly longer than the others.

After this I removed the selector fork rod and the selector drum. See photo 15.3. I tapped out the selector fork rod which released the two selectors. The selector drum was held in position by the drum retaining bolt and the large selector fork bolt, so I had to remove both of these.

15.1 The kickstart shaft, main shaft, clutch basket, and layshaft removed from the crankcases.

15.2 Preparing to remove the gear selector mechanism.

15.3 Preparing to remove the selector drum (shift drum) and selector forks.

STRIPPING THE CRANKCASES

15.4 Preparing to remove the selector drum bolt.

15.5 The selector drum and positioning bolt removed.

15.6 The centre crankshaft bearing cap.

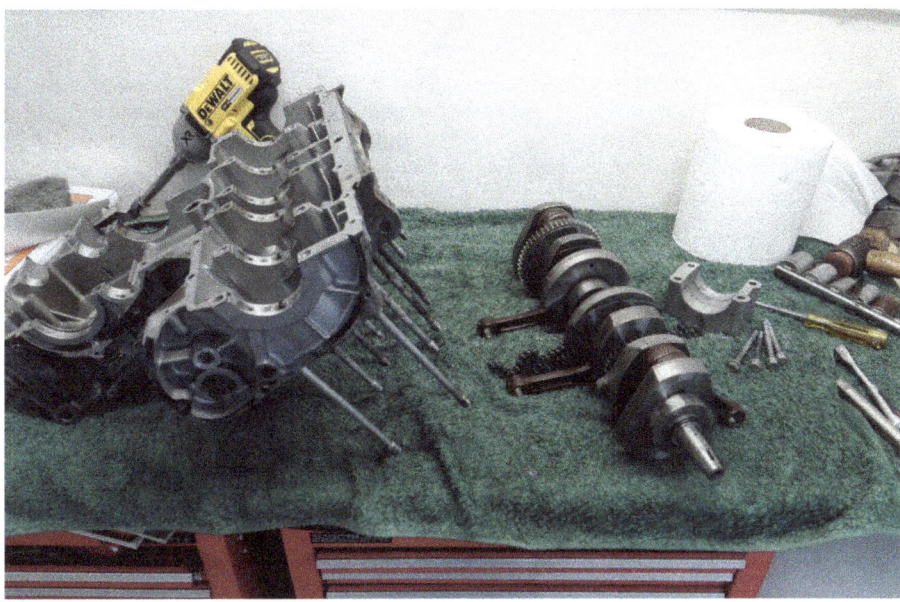
15.7 Crankshaft removed from casings.

15.8 A few bits lying in the casings – including a small stone!

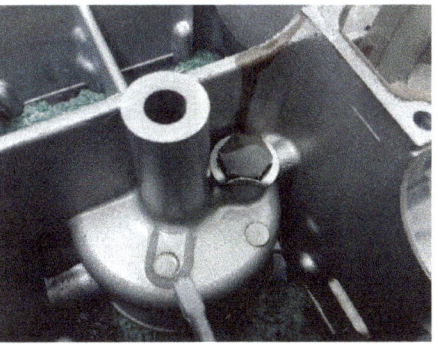
15.9 Last bolt – the oil pressure release valve.

15.10 Oil pressure release valve removed.

15.11 My new stud removal tool – not impressed.

See photo 15.4 of the drum retaining bolt on the left and the selector fork retaining bolt on the right. See photo 15.5 of the selector drum removed together with the selector fork and drum retaining bolt.

Next up was the crankshaft itself. All that was holding this in place was the centre bearing cap retained by 4 bolts. See photo 15.6. With these 4 bolts and the cap removed, the crankshaft simply lifted out as a complete unit. See photo 15.7. I found some detritus underneath the crankshaft – including a small stone! See photo 15.8.

Finally, I removed the oil pressure release valve with its accompanying spring and ball bearing. See photos 15.9 and 15.10.

The crankcases were now fully stripped, apart from the cylinder head bolts. These seemed to be pretty tight in the upper crankcase: I had a go at removing them with a pair of mole grips but they didn't want to budge. In the end, I bought a stud removal tool, which I'd always meant to buy but had never got round to. See photo 15.11 of my new purchase. However, this tool proved worse than useless, and not only failed to remove the studs but also left teethmarks on the shafts where I'd used it. I wasn't at all happy ...

HOW TO RESTORE KAWASAKI Z1, Z/KZ900 & Z/KZ1000

I then tried using the time-honoured method of locking together two nuts on the top thread and unscrewing them that way – but they really didn't want to come out. In the end, I decided that discretion was the better part of valour and left them where they were as they weren't really in the way.

The cases were now ready to be vapour blasted. See photo 15.12.

LESSONS LEARNT
- The mainshaft, layshaft, and kick-start shaft simply lift out when the cases have been split – wonderful!
- Don't lose any of the small pins that fit in the end of the selector drum.
- It's amazing what you can find in the bottom of the crankcases ...
- Don't lose the semi-circular retaining rings that locate in the grooved bearings on the gearshafts and crankcases. I'm usually pretty meticulous, but they still vanished somehow. I think I might have accidentally thrown them out with some oily kitchen towel.
- I still can't get over the amazingly simple yet superb engineering of this engine. It's all so well engineered, and so well thought-out. It's just brilliant. Kawasaki Heavy Industries 1; British engineering 0.

15.12 Crankcases stripped and ready for vapour blasting.

www.velocebooks.com
New book news • Special offers • Newsletter • Details of all Veloce books • Gift Vouchers

Chapter 16
Removing & dismantling the front forks

With the engine now out of the frame and disassembled, it was time to remove the front forks and the front wheel. First of all, I strapped down the rear of the frame in order to lift the front wheel clear of the bench, raising it by a good few inches to allow enough room to drop the wheel out of the forks. See photo 16.1. In retrospect, I could have done this earlier, removing the front wheel before removing the engine by strapping down the rear of the frame so that it wasn't resting on the front wheel. The advantage of this would be that I could have sent off those parts that required blasting, chroming, painting, and wheel building earlier than I did. However, in reality it didn't make much difference in terms of time, and the frame didn't feel too safe on the bench like this, so maybe better to have done it as I did.

I removed the front wheel by undoing the nuts on the studs at the bottom of the fork legs to allow the wheel to come out easily (make sure the wheel is high enough off the bench for the spindle to clear the studs) – see photo 16.2. I was then able to remove the front mudguard (badly damaged in my case) and cable guide: see photo 16.3.

16.1 Raising the front wheel off the bench with the aid of tie-down straps.

With the wheel removed I turned my attention to the forks and loosened the pinch bolts in the top and bottom yokes – see photo 16.4 – which enabled me to start to withdraw the stanchions from the yokes. See photo 16.5. Both stanchions came out quite easily by twisting and pulling on them. However, note that if the fork legs are stuck, you can get them moving by using a hide mallet on the fork top nuts, as the nuts are narrower than the stanchions and don't need to be removed before removing the

HOW TO RESTORE KAWASAKI Z1, Z/KZ900 & Z/KZ1000

16.2 Front wheel removed.

16.3 Front mudguard removed.

16.4 Pinch bolts slackened off on top and bottom yokes.

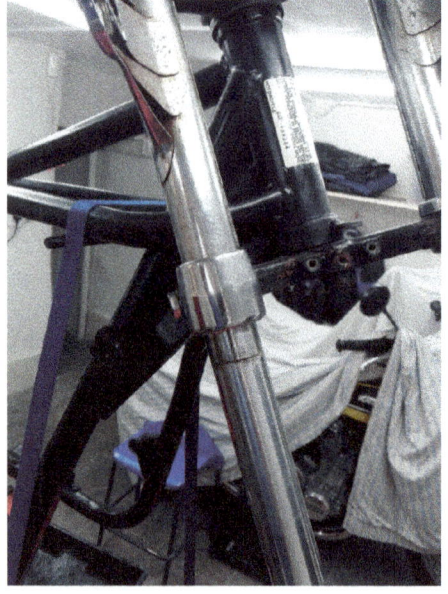

16.5 Beginning to withdraw the fork legs.

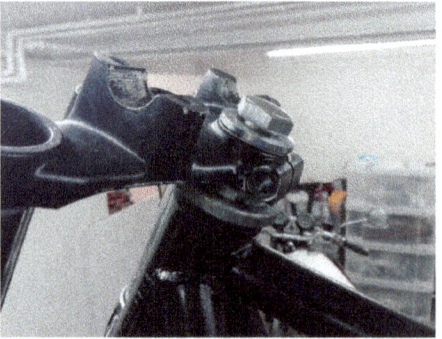

16.6 Removing the stem bolt.

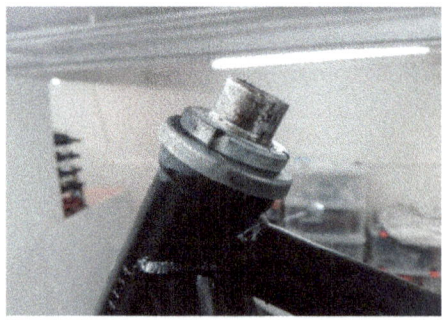

16.7 The stem head nut ready for removal.

stanchions, and provide a handy place to tap on if necessary.

With the fork legs gone I removed the stem bolt from the top of the yokes, which allowed the top yoke to come off. See photo 16.6.

Underneath the top yoke is the stem head nut which holds together the head bearings, and is used to adjust play in the bearings. See photo 16.7. This is a special nut which supposedly requires a special tool to remove it (and adjust the head races). In my case I discovered that my head races were way too tight, and when I moved the yokes round, they were very stiff and jerky – a sure sign of over-tightened bearings. In order to remove the nut I used a shock absorber adjuster, better known as a 'C' spanner, which I found fitted perfectly. See photo 16.8.

Be aware that, as you loosen the stem nut, the yokes will come off and all of the loose ball bearings in the yokes will fall out, so remove the yokes carefully. I was aware of this but still made a hash of it. As I loosened the stem head nut, the bottom yoke didn't move and I forgot about it for a second ... at which point, it suddenly dropped and sent ball bearings flying all over the workshop floor, many disappearing into the fifth dimension, never to be seen again. Bugger. See photo 16.9 of the bottom yoke removed with a few remaining ball bearings sitting in the ball race, and the same for the head race in photo 16.10.

The order of reassembly of the nuts, spacers and washers on the top yoke can be seen in photo 16.11. This is one of many such photos I take as a matter of course during disassembly – if you don't take photos like this then reassembly can be a nightmare: 'Does the washer go

REMOVING & DISMANTLING THE FRONT FORKS

16.8 Using a shock absorber C spanner to remove the stem head nut.

16.11 The order of assembly of the steering stem bolts and washers.

16.9 Bottom yoke out with a few ball bearings left in place!

16.12 The fork top nut and spacers removed.

16.14 Removing the dust cover reveals the seal retaining circlip which is then prised out.

16.10 The top-head race with ball bearings in situ – mostly!

16.13 The fork spring removed and foul oil being drained.

16.15 With the circlip and washer removed (left of photo) the oil seal is revealed.

in front of the spacer or behind it?'

I then began to dismantle the forks. First off, I undid and removed the alloy fork top nuts together with the spacer and cupped washer. See photo 16.12. I then inverted the forks and removed the springs and drained the fork oil. See photo 16.13. One note on this is that, for some reason, the fork oil was really, really smelly! I'm not sure if it had always smelled like that or if it had deteriorated with age, but, whatever the case, it stank – and when your workshop is in the basement, and the stench slowly rises and permeates the whole house, 'you-know-who' isn't best pleased!

With the oil drained I removed the rubber dust covers from the top of the seals, and prised out the wire circlip from its groove. See photo 16.14. I then slid these off the stanchions together with the large washer underneath the circlip to reveal the fork seals. See photo 16.15. On some bikes you have to remove the fork seal before you can remove the stanchions, but the Kawasaki Z900 isn't one of them, luckily.

I therefore turned my attention to the Allen set screw at the bottom of the fork legs which holds in place the damping unit and stanchions. See photo 16.16. These are often a

63

16.16 The Allen screw at the bottom of the fork leg.

16.17 The Allen screw removed (with my impact driver) and remaining oil drained.

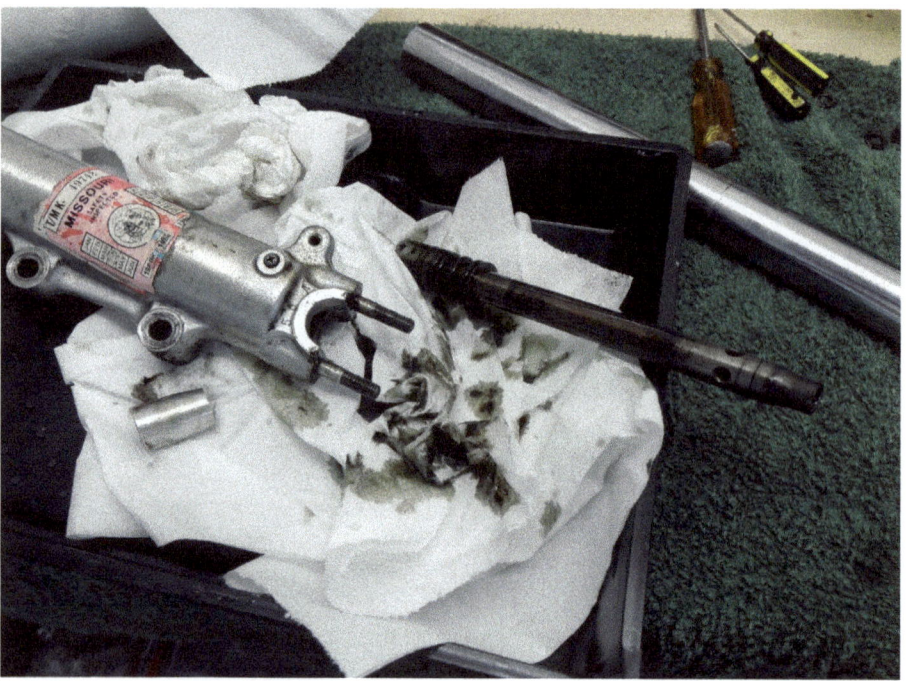

16.18 The stanchion and damper unit removed from the fork leg.

complete pain to remove as they are very tight, and the damper unit they screw into inside the fork stanchions turns with the screw rather than undoing. There are two ways around this: prevent the dampers from turning by using a special tool or whatever to jam the dampers; or use a powered impact driver. Up until this time I had always used the first method; trying to find something very long (I have a couple of very long screwdrivers for just this purpose) to insert down inside the stanchions and jam the dampers, or having to resort to buying the special tool (where available). But, wait! I now had a brand-spanking-new cordless impact driver! Putting this on full power and attaching an Allen key socket (I have a set of Allen keys on ½in socket drives – really useful) on a short extension, 30 seconds later the Allen screw was out and on the bench – result! See photo 16.17 of the Allen screw removed, and the remaining oil being drained from the fork leg.

Next, I slid the stanchion and the damper unit inside it from the lower fork leg – see photo 16.18 – and then removed the damper mechanism from the bottom of the stanchions (an assortment of spacers and springs inside the bottom of the stanchions) by first removing the circlip, and then sliding out the remaining parts. See photo 16.19.

I then faced the final and most dreaded challenge – removing the front fork oil seals. These are often an absolute bugger to remove, and I wasn't looking forward to the job. I bought a bespoke front fork oil seal removal tool, as previously I've always just used screwdrivers and tyre levers, which work okay but aren't great. The main problem is that you need to lever out the old seals without damaging the (very soft alloy) lower fork legs – not easy.

I tried to prise out the old seals with the requisite tool, having protected the leg with cardboard, but to no avail; they wouldn't budge. See photo 16.20. I heated the legs with my blowtorch and then gave the tool a short, sharp blow with a lump hammer, and out they came. See photo 16.21. As is so often the case, the answer to easy dismantling took the form of applying heat and a short, sharp blow rather than sustained pressure: It's amazing the difference it makes – especially with alloy parts that readily expand when heated. Heat is also the only method

REMOVING & DISMANTLING THE FRONT FORKS

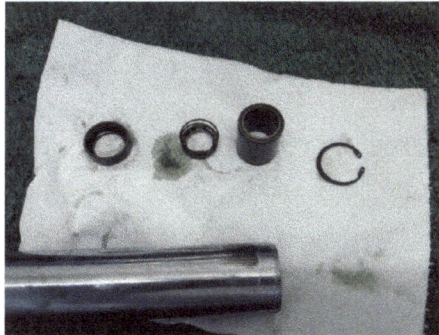

16.19 The damping mechanism removed from the bottom of the stanchion.

I know of undoing something that's been put together with red Hermetite or a similar heavy-duty locking agent: bolts will often shear rather than loosen unless heated to a high temperature in this case.

The wheel, forks and yokes were now removed ready for inspection and refurbishment.

LESSONS LEARNT
- It may be easier to leave the front wheel in situ before removing the engine from the frame, but the jury's out on this, and there are various methods/approaches. I used my preferred method as the frame acts as the perfect engine stand (in combination with a bike lift, of course).
- The front wheel needs to be a fair way off the ground to allow easy removal.
- There's no need to remove the fork top nuts in order to remove the forks.
- A special nut holds together the head races, but it can be undone with a shock absorber 'C' spanner.
- When removing the bottom yoke, watch out for all the loose ball bearings – or stand helpless as you listen to them skitter away across the workshop floor!
- Always take photos of the order of assembly of parts that have multiple washers and spacers, etc.
- To easily remove the Allen set screw from the bottom of the fork legs, use a cordless impact driver. Sooooo much easier than other methods.
- Removing the front fork oil seals is always a problem – use the correct tool and plenty of heat.
- Applying heat and using a short, sharp blow is probably the best way of encouraging parts to come undone that don't want to – especially when you'll be renewing oil seals, etc, anyway, and it doesn't matter if they are damaged.

16.20 Oil seal removal tool in place, with leg protected by cardboard.

16.21 Oil seal removed after heating the leg and applying a sharp blow to the removal tool with a lump hammer.

www.velocebooks.com
New book news • Special offers • Newsletter • Details of all Veloce books • Gift Vouchers

Chapter 17
Dismantling the front & rear wheels

My next job was to dismantle the front and rear wheels as I wanted to chrome the wheel spindles, so I could finally take everything to the chrome platers', which was an urgent job as there was such a long lead time.

Beginning with the front wheel I took the usual 'before' photos to help with reassembly later. See photos 17.1 and 17.2 of the left and right sides of the front hub and wheel spindle. I then removed the front disc and wheel spindle from the hub, having first loosened the locking tabs (see photo 17.3) and removed the dust cover from the other side of the hub.

Next, I removed the spokes. In order to undo these I needed to first remove the tyre, which came off easily enough together with the inner tube using a couple of tyre levers. Unfortunately, with the tyre off, I quickly realised that there was no way I could undo the spokes as they were very tight and rusted solid: I couldn't get a single one to loosen. I therefore took the pragmatic decision to simply cut them off with my Dremmel (see photo 17.4) as I intended to replace them anyway, and couldn't see another way round the problem. Just be aware that, with the tyre removed,

17.1 Right side of wheel hub.

17.2 Left side of wheel hub.

the highly-tensioned spokes will fly out of the rim at great speed when cut! It's very dramatic and a tad dangerous.

After much fun with the Dremmel, all of the spokes were finally removed. See photo 17.5 of the hub now looking like a creature from a sci-fi film. I removed the circlip and grease seal from the right-hand side of the hub to expose the bearing – see photo 17.6 – and was then able to drive out the bearing from the other side together with the spacer tube (see photo 17.7), followed by the left side bearing (see photo 17.8). My MO for bearing removal was simply to heat the hub with a blowtorch before raising it off the bench with blocks of wood to give clearance for the bearing to come out, and then tapping out the bearings with a drift. Note the manual on the bench. As factory workshop manuals go it's a really good one, so always read the procedure *BEFORE STARTING WORK*, and keep it handy for reference during the operation.

I cannot emphasise enough the importance of using heat to remove and install bearings in alloy casings. If you use heat the bearing will slide in or out easily without fuss. If you don't apply heat to the alloy then the bearing will refuse to come out, and you will score the surface of the alloy trying to remove it. This will mean that the hole is now enlarged, and the

DISMANTLING THE FRONT & REAR WHEELS

17.3 Disc and wheel spindle, etc, removed.

new bearing will be loose when fitted, and prone to spinning in the housing, so making it even looser and leading to major mechanical problems. Use heat, every time.

With the front hub now stripped it was time to look at the rear hub. I removed the tyre and rim together with the tyre grips. (I wasn't sure whether or not to refit the tyre grips to the rear wheel as I find them a bit ugly. Luckily, my mind was made up for me when the replacement rear rim arrived without holes for tyre grips. Remember that my original rear rim was dented and so was scrap – apparently they can never be fully straightened.) I then cut off the spokes as per the front wheel.

With rim and spokes out of the way, I removed the first bearing from the rear hub. See photo 17.9. I then inverted the hub and drove out the second bearing. See photo 17.10 of the bearings and spacer on the

17.4 Tyre removed and beginning to cut spokes off with a Dremmel.

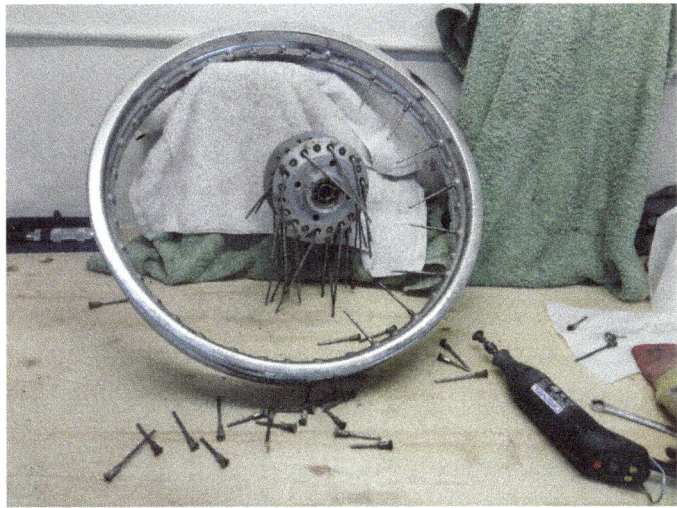

17.5 All spokes removed leaving the hub looking like an extra from *War of the Worlds*!

17.6 Removing the circlip and grease seal to expose the right side bearing.

17.7 Right side bearing knocked out together with the distance piece after applying heat.

17.8 Removing the left side bearing with a large drift – and more heat.

17.9 Drifting out the rear hub bearings with heat – note the manual on the bench!

17.12 Drifting out the large bearing from the sprocket carrier.

17.10 Rear hub bearings and spacer removed.

17.11 Rear sprocket removed from the carrier with the aid of my impact driver – any excuse!

17.13 Preparing to remove the rear brake shoes.

bench. There is also a large bearing in the rear sprocket carrier, so I removed the sprocket from the carrier using my cordless impact driver (any excuse!), and drifted out the large bearing in the same manner as for the hubs. See photos 17.11 and 17.12. The hubs were now stripped and ready for cleaning/polishing and rebuilding.

My last job was to remove the rear brake shoes from the back plate. To do this I removed the split pins from the retaining spigots (see photo 17.13) and, with the retaining plate removed, the shoes were ready to come away. The shoes then came off the back plate with the operating shaft. A few taps on the operating shaft eased the shaft out through the back plate and the shoes were off without fuss.

LESSONS LEARNT

- If you cut through spokes with the tyres off they shoot off at high velocity!
- Always, always, always use heat to remove/replace bearings in alloy castings. But be aware that the very localised heat from a blow torch can damage the metal. The more general the heating the better – so use an oven to provide universal heating wherever possible.
- A cordless impact driver – cost: £160; value: priceless!
- Brake shoes slide off the back plate with the operating shaft.
- Workshop manuals (the *Kawasaki Service Manual* amongst others) are great – but only if you read them! Ideally, read through the entire process before starting work, and keep them handy for reference as you undertake the operation. (But have I always followed my own advice on this? Of course not!)

Chapter 18
Vapour blasting, chroming & powder coating

The bike was now fully stripped, and all parts were ready for refurbishment prior to reassembly. As it was important to get the restoration finished relatively quickly (I had a publishing deadline to meet – so much for the leisurely life of retirement!), it was vital to get all parts refurbished as soon as possible.

Top priorities
• Get the wheel hubs polished so that they could be sent off for rebuilding ASAP (estimated wheel build completion time: six weeks).
• Get all alloy parts vapour blasted ready for polishing and reassembly. This included the crankcases, cylinder block, cylinder head, cam cover, alternator cover, oil breather cover, rear sprocket carrier, inner points cover, lower fork legs (replacement legs as others were damaged when the trailer went over – and the replacements were painted black), carburettor bodies, tops and float chambers, brake back plate, and clutch cover (estimated completion time: three weeks).
• Prepare parts for plating and take to a new chrome platers with a much shorter lead time than my usual company (estimated completion time: six weeks).
• Prepare tank and other panels and take to painter (estimated completion time: three months).
• Send speedo and tacho for reconditioning (estimated completion time: six weeks).

Medium priorities
• Check cylinder head on return from the vapour blaster, and have any necessary work done – in my case, all new exhaust valve guides and two sparkplug threads helicoiled (estimated completion time: two weeks).
• Check cylinder barrels on return from vapour blaster and for any other necessary work, eg, a rebore. In my case, all that was required was to hone the cylinders following the vapour blasting.
• Buy essential parts to reassemble engine: gasket set, oil seal set, new crankcase bolts and cover screws, engine assembly oil, gasket cement (Wellseal), Loctite bearing fix, Loctite Threadlock, plus any new parts required following inspection – luckily, that wasn't too much – new alternator cover and points cover – both damaged beyond reasonable repair so easier to buy new, plus a new cam chain, cam chain guide and camshaft bearings.
• Polish all engine casings to a varying degree of finish ready for assembly.
• Polish lower fork legs when returned from vapour blaster (the forks and front wheel are required early on in the restoration so that the frame can hold the engine).
• Buy and fit new tyres for same reason as above.
• Buy all parts to refurbish forks and front wheel, eg, front fork oil seals, front wheel bearings, etc (for same reason as above).
• Book in wheels for new tyres to be fitted as soon as they return from the wheel builders (for same reason as above).

Low priorities
(at start of rebuild)
• Replace and refurbish electrical items.
• Buy parts not required immediately eg: rear shock absorbers, rear chain and sprockets, handlebar switchgear, new exhaust system (at the time of writing I have no idea where I'm going to get the money for that!), front brake lever and master cylinder, and chain

guard (missing from my bike).
• Refurbish parts such as the brake callipers, which could be done later.

I prepared the wheel hubs for rebuilding by first cleaning them, giving them a machine polish (see separate chapter on this), and then sending them off to be rebuilt. I chose Black Cat Wheels in Wolverhampton this time as I'd heard good reports.

The front wheel rim was in amazingly good condition, so I just gave it a thorough clean and polish, and sent it off to be re-used as-was. Unfortunately, my original rear rim was dented and couldn't be repaired (once dented they can't be trued-up again), so I had to find a replacement.

All wheel rims for the Z900 range were made by Takasago and stamped as such (Takasago 303), together with the date of manufacture. If you want a completely original bike, Takasago rims are very desirable, and ideally ones with a similar date stamp to the rest of the bike. I wasn't too bothered about 100 per cent originality, and to keep the rims authentic I'd have had to buy an old rim for a small fortune, and then pay out again to have it rechromed.

In the end, I bought a new rim from Z Power which was unstamped. An unstamped rim is slightly better than a new rim with a different maker's stamp on it eg: Devon Rims, so I was happy (no stamp is better than the wrong stamp). The hubs and rims were then sent on their way to Black Cat.

After this I prepared the bodywork parts for painting as I knew this had quite a long completion time. I removed the badges, etc, and cleaned and sealed the inside of the petrol tank before taking the parts to Mark Hutchinson in Pontefract for painting. (See separate chapter on preparing and painting the tank.)

Next, I removed as much old gasket as I could from the crankcases and barrels before sending them to be vapour blasted. The problem with this is that blast cleaning won't remove old gasket as gasket is soft and pliable and the beads simply bounce off. To remove gasket residue I use my trusty scraper (see photo 18.1), but you have to be very careful not to damage the facing edges as the metal is so soft. In the past I have tried various chemicals to remove the gasket, but nothing has worked for me. I also had to remove the old gasket from the base of the cylinder block, but it was a real pain.

In the end I had a brainwave and used Nitromors paint stripper on it. See photo 18.2. The result was a toxic, sticky mess of green gunge that made no impact on the gasket whatsoever, though made the job twice as messy. Consign that 'brainwave' to the 'ideas that didn't quite work' cupboard. I had to persevere with my scraper, and eventually got it cleaned off.

The crankcases and the myriad of other parts were then taken to the blast cleaner for vapour blasting (I had already dismantled the carburettors – see separate chapter on this). Vapour blasting (or aqua blasting, as it is sometimes known)

18.1 Removing the crankcase gasket.

18.2 Removing the cylinder base gasket.

VAPOUR BLASTING, CHROMING & POWDER COATING

is good for cleaning alloy parts, as it gets the grime off without damaging the cases – ordinary blast cleaning is too aggressive. However, even though it is gentle it will still pit surfaces that are already smooth such as polished alloy covers. For this reason you should really take only non-polished parts, such as crankcases, for vapour blasting. I did take some polished cases for vapour blasting – the clutch cover, for example – as they were very dirty and had deep scratches in them, which meant that they would have to be prepared with a coarse abrasive to remove the scratches before repolishing (see separate chapter on polishing), and so it was easier to have them cleaned in all the nooks and crannies by blasting as they required refinishing, anyway. Hence, a lot of parts were destined for the blast cleaner.

I also sorted out all the parts that required blast cleaning and powder coating – the frame, main stand, side stand, swinging arm, engine mounting plates (although I stripped the two triangular ones and had them chromed), top and bottom yokes, etc, and took these to the blast cleaner as it does both jobs. Note that I was going to have my brake callipers blasted and powder coated, too, but the company wouldn't do them as it had had problems in the past with callipers warping with the heat and seizing the piston in the calliper. I'm not sure of the veracity of this claim, but blast cleaning was all that was on offer – I had to finish the callipers myself. See separate chapter on these.

Also note that Z900 frames were originally spray painted and not powder coated (although apparently the paint quality wasn't high), so, if you want to keep to 100 per cent originality, don't powder coat the frame. Personally, I wanted a well-painted frame that would last – so powder coating it was.

Finally, I sorted out all of the parts that required chroming or rechroming (a couple of parts weren't originally chromed, but I wanted these done, too: some of the engine mountings and carburettor parts and wheel spindles, etc.) Before taking the parts to the plater I took photos that I clearly labelled. See photos 18.3 and

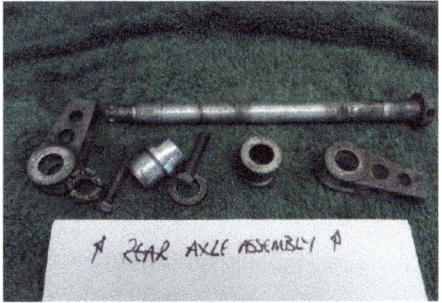

18.3 Parts labelled for identification, ready to go to the platers.

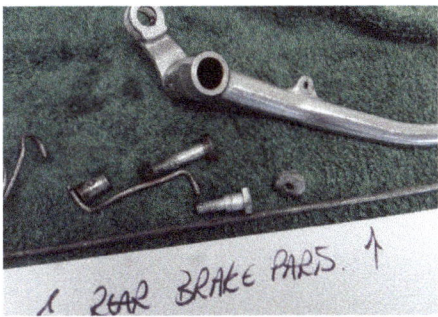

18.4 More labelled parts for the platers.

18.4. I did this because, when all of the parts come back from the plater in one big box, I can guarantee you will have no idea what these collections of nuts, bolts, washers, etc, are, let alone where they go. I therefore took photos of parts in their order of assembly so that I had some chance of identifying them and putting them back together in the right order.

Phew! After a fairly crazy week I had managed to get all of the requisite parts to the blaster, powder coater, chrome plater, painter and wheel builder. You may have noticed that I hadn't sent the speedo and tacho for reconditioning, and this was because I discovered that the cost of brand new ones was almost exactly the same as reconditioning my originals. Again, as I wasn't too bothered about originality I decided to buy new items (and, of course, kept my originals safe). End of story. Note that new originals may not be available for the earlier Z1s with their slightly different speedo markings (in 20mph increments), and no brake light failure warning bulb in the tacho.

The first things to come back were the parts that had been blasted and powder coated. They returned looking wonderful: clean and shiny. See photos 18.5, 18.6, 18.7 and 18.8

18.5 Crankcases and barrels back from vapour blasting.

18.6 Assorted parts returned from vapour blasting.

18.7 Cylinder head and cam cover vapour blasted.

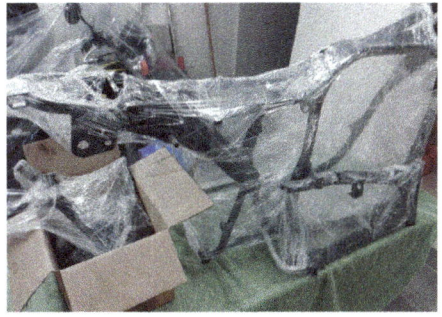

18.8 Frame, swinging arm, yokes, etc, back from the powder coater.

of the various parts. All looked good but closer inspection revealed the real Achilles heel of vapour blasting: minute glass blasting beads left over

HOW TO RESTORE KAWASAKI Z1, Z/KZ900 & Z/KZ1000

18.9 Beading left from vapour blasting – now imagine what the oilways were like!

from the cleaning process all over the inside of the alloy casings (and carburettors, etc). See photo 18.9 of some of the beads sitting in the crankcase.

Now, these beads are really, really bad news: they clog up and block small airways in the carburettors, and cause massive wear inside the engine if allowed to mix with engine oil and pumped round your brand new engine. Yes, coarse beads of hard-wearing glass being pumped round your engine and bearings, etc – doesn't bear thinking about.

This remains the major problem with vapour blasting, and it was so bad on this engine that I would honestly think twice before having it done again. I love bling, etc, but the residual beads were so bad it took forever to try and clean the cases, and led to major problems.

I rinsed the casings in the sink several times before giving them a good swill down with the hose in the back garden in an effort to remove all of the beads, after which I spent quite a bit of time polishing the casings (see next chapter on polishing), and used a tap to run through all the (many) thread holes to check they were clear. Using a tap to clear out the threads made me realise just how many beads there were lurking in the depths of blind holes, etc, even after thorough cleaning. (Use of a tap is shown later in photo 27.2).

I decided that the cases still weren't clean enough, and made the mistake of searching on YouTube for some ideas of how best to clean them. One video showed a chap cleaning his cases in the dishwasher, which seemed like an excellent idea. I therefore took both crankcases and managed to get them into our twin drawer dishwasher – they only just fitted (unfortunately). I added a dishwasher tab in each drawer, switched on the machine and left it to it. When the cycle was finished I excitedly opened the drawers to discover, to my horror, that the dishwasher had turned both of my shiny crankcases, which I'd spent a load of money on getting blast cleaned and then polished, a really horrible, dark grey. See photo 18.11 of one of the cases after washing (compare it with photo 18.10 of before I put it in the dishwasher). I subsequently read a comment from someone on the YouTube video warning not to use dishwasher tablets to clean the cases as the ammonia in the detergent would react with the alloy, turning it dark grey. Bugger.

I then, stupidly (I mean, really stupidly) looked at other videos on YouTube about the best way to remove the dark grey staining from the cases, and quickly found another clip of a chap who recommended using foaming oven cleaner on engine cases to clean them. I therefore went out and bought a couple of cans, set up the workmate in the driveway, and liberally sprayed one of the cases with the cleaner. After about ten minutes I used my jet washer to wash off the oven cleaner. The result? Cases that were even darker grey than before! Oh, no! After stopping to think for a minute (I should have done this before) I realised that oven cleaner is virtually pure ammonia, and I had actually been making things worse by using it to clean the cases! Damn, Damn, Damn! See photo 18.12.

I now had cases that I'd spent a lot of time and money on getting shiny that were a horrible dull grey. Not only that, but, as the grey was the result of a chemical process, it wasn't going to come off easily. I tried brake cleaner and carb cleaner but they did nothing. I finally came to the conclusion that the only way forward was to use mechanical cleaning methods to clean the cases.

I duly bought several different sizes and styles of fine abrasive wheels and cups (mainly from Frost Auto Restorations), and set about the very laborious task of trying to reclean the cases with the aid of the brushes and a cordless drill. See photo 18.13. However, I quickly realised that this was an almost impossible task, and no matter how many different sizes

18.10 Cleaning the crankcases for the umpteenth time.

VAPOUR BLASTING, CHROMING & POWDER COATING

18.11 Crankcases back out of the dishwasher – disaster!

18.12 Using oven cleaner and a jet washer to try and retrieve the situation – just making it worse!

18.13 Trying mechanical means of cleaning the cases back up again – without success.

18.14 Crankcases back from the vapour blast cleaners – again! Back to square one.

and types of brushes I had, it was impossible to get into all the crevices and corners. I finally took the decision I had been resisting, and took the crankcases back to the blast cleaner to be cleaned a second time!

In the end I'm glad I did this, as they told me that the black on the cases was really hard to get off as the surfaces of the cases were hardened by the chemical process that had turned them black (the cases were apparently even harder to clean the second time round than they had been when first done): without blast cleaning I would have been snookered.

The cases finally returned from their second stint at the blast cleaner nice and clean (again). See photo 18.14. However, I was now back to square one with regard to how to clean the cases effectively and remove all traces of glass beading without discolouring them.

To begin with, I thought I'd put them back in the dishwasher (!) but this time on the rinse cycle, without any soap tablets. I duly prepared the dishwasher by putting it on rinse a couple of times to remove any residual soap before washing the cases. I decided against it, however, as there was clearly still some soap in the dishwasher, and it just wasn't worth the risk. In the end, I cleaned the cases with the jet washer alone as I thought this would do the job without risk of the cases turning black.

The cases were finally cleaned and free from glass beading, and ready for final polishing before reassembly. I also spent a lot of time using a tap to clean every thread on the cases. I'm not sure if it was as a result of the vapour cleaning or the episode with the dishwasher, but the threads were in a really poor state, and took a lot of cleaning with the tap. I've not known it happen before but it was a real problem with this engine. If I'd not done this, most of the screws and bolts would never have screwed in properly, and casings would not have been properly tightened. They really were bad.

I also decided to clean up the old 8mm crankshaft bolts rather than buy new ones for reasons of economy, and, as they're under the engine, they're hardly visible at all. See photo 18.15.

LESSONS LEARNT
- Removing old gasket is never easy.
- Label and take photos of parts being sent away for chrome plating/ other work – at least that'll give you some idea of where they go!
- Frames weren't powder coated originally, but the finish is so good what's not to like?
- Vapour (or aqua) blast cleaning leaves behind hundreds of tiny glass beads that require thorough cleaning to remove.
- Don't put your freshly-cleaned cases in the dishwasher with a soap tablet – they'll react with the ammonia in the detergent and turn black.
- Don't try to remove the black from the cases you've just accidentally washed in the dishwasher by spraying them with oven cleaner – they'll just turn even darker! (For the same reason)
- Having finally cleaned your cases and washed away any glass bead residue, carefully run a tap down all of the threaded holes – there are over 100 on the crankcases alone!!

18.15 Cleaning up the crankshaft bolts.

73

Chapter 19
Polishing engine casings and other alloy parts

One very arduous, laborious, but yet particularly satisfying job, is polishing the various alloy parts on the bike. A big debate exists in the restoration world about how shiny and polished an engine, etc, should be. My feeling is that this is entirely up to you, and I'm just going to give guidance on how to achieve a highly polished finish if you want one. End of.

All-in-all I spent at least a solid week polishing various alloy parts. It's a real pain of a job, but if you want a nice shiny engine, then it has to be done. There's one simple basic rule: the more work you put in, the better finish you'll get.

If you want to achieve a really highly polished finish to your alloy parts then the only way to do this is to use some kind of buffing machine, as hand polishing alone simply won't do it. To achieve a polished finish on parts such as crankcases and cylinder heads (that you can't get on a buffer due to their convoluted shape), you'll need a variety of mildly abrasive brushes and some wet-and-dry emery cloth.

For a real mirror finish you'll need a polishing wheel with a variety of mops (see photo 19.1). I use a converted bench grinder that I hold

19.1 Polishing wheel, buffing mops and grit mops.

in the vice (I used to clamp it direct to the bench but the mountings weren't up to it). I then have five different polishing mops, although I usually use only four. The most abrasive I have are two grit mops of 150 and 240 grade (similar to emery cloth). The 150 grade is only used on really rough castings that have a very uneven surface from the casting process, and which have never been polished before. In my case I didn't use the 150 grit mop at all on this bike – it's just too coarse and you can easily do more harm than good.

The next grade down is the 240

POLISHING ENGINE CASINGS & OTHER ALLOY PARTS

19.2 One leg after being polished with a fine 240 grit.

19.3 One leg after polishing with a grey polish and then with a medium (green) polish.

19.4 Final polish with a soft blue mop.

grit mop (on the left in photo 19.1) which is still pretty coarse, and only used for parts that are too uneven for polishing alone. I used the 240 grit on any parts not previously polished, plus any that had been vapour blasted, and any with deep scratches or dents that were too deep to polish out.

Note that if you vapour blast any parts they will come out rough even if they were polished previously. In my case this included parts such as the clutch and gearbox outer casings, which I'd had vapour blasted. These were so dirty and damaged I thought it easier in the long run as the scratches and gouges had to be flattened out with a grit mop, anyway. However, if you can get away without vapour blasting parts already polished then the whole job is much easier.

After the 240 grit comes the first of the polishes: the grey polish and mop (the grey polish should leave you with a pretty shiny piece of metal). See photo 19.2. After this it's the medium green polish, which achieves a very good shine. See photo 19.3. Finally, comes the blue polish with the softest mop. See photo 19.4.

Polishing technique

- Screw the first mop onto the buffer, remembering that they are all left-hand threads.
- Apply grit sparingly to the grit mop if the part requires this to begin with because it's too rough just to polish (use a sisal mop that is closely stitched, and therefore very hard). Be aware that grit is very abrasive and you can easily do more harm than good if you're not careful. Apply grit frequently but sparingly to the mop.
- After finishing with the grit mop (if required), go on to the polish mops, beginning with the coarsest first. Harder sisal mops are stitched, and the more stitching the harder the mop. Apply polish frequently but very sparingly – if you start getting polish residue on your work the chances are you've got too much polish on the mop. Use harder mops to begin with, and work your way down to the softer mops.
- Don't push too hard – if the buffer slows right down you're pushing too hard.

- There will always be some polish residue left over, and this can be removed with either French chalk that comes with most polishing kits, white spirit, or when you give the piece a final hand polish with Solvol Autosol.

The good news is that every time you polish something you get a little better at it (like most things), and, as a general rule, if you don't get a decent shine after using the grey polish the work might need more work with a fine grit first.

Don't forget that what you're doing is gradually removing uneven/

19.5 Preparing to polish the head and other parts.

75

HOW TO RESTORE KAWASAKI Z1, Z/KZ900 & Z/KZ1000

cast finishes by slowly cutting down the roughness with successively finer polishes. Consider that the highly polished surfaces on your engine began life with a cast finish like on crankcases, and are only shiny due to careful polishing.

I'm certainly no expert but I can get a decent finish on most parts after a few engines' worth of practice. Even now I know that the professional polishers (at the chrome plater) can still produce a way better mirror finish than I can (it's a bit like trying to teach yourself plastering if you've ever tried that: you get better at it each time, but it's a long learning curve). Having said that, polishing alloy parts to a wonderful shine is one of the really rewarding jobs on the bike – but also one of the most time-consuming and dirty – note that I try to do my polishing outside whenever possible to prevent the workshop getting covered in thick, black dust. See photo 19.5.

The second type of polishing (for those who want it) is to try and polish parts that can't be buffed due to their odd shape and size, such as crankcases, cylinder barrels, and cylinder heads, and for these I use a cordless drill with a variety of fine bristled brushes (not steel brushes as these are too abrasive), combined with a selection of wet-and-dry emery cloth. I occasionally use brass brushes but I find these hard to source, and they can be a bit too aggressive as well). I have a wide selection of shapes and sizes for different jobs. See photo 19.6. With these I have a selection of wet-and-dry emery cloth from 240 down to 2500 grit which I always use wet. See photo 19.7.

To begin with I used the cordless

19.6 Various abrasive mops for cleaning and polishing parts that can't be buffed on the wheel.

19.7 Wet-and-dry emery paper graded 240 to 2500 grit.

drill and the flap wheels as far as possible, and then finished off the work with wet-and-dry to remove the scratches left by the flap wheels. The level of finish is dictated by how much graft is put into the work with the wet-and-dry cloth. The higher the grade of emery cloth, the higher the level of finish, but I needed to work my way slowly from 240 to 2500 grade – and this took a lot of graft. Luckily, I like a bit of a shine on my cylinder head, etc, but not too much so there wasn't a great deal of graft to be done with the emery cloth. Hurrah! See photos 19.8 and 19.9.

After all of this I finished off the job with Solvol Autosol to remove any light scratching left by the emery cloth, leaving the work with a lovely deep finish. See photo 19.10. Photos 19.11, 19.12 and 19.13 show some of the casings that have been polished using different methods.

19.8 Cylinder head before polishing.

19.9 Cylinder head polished with abrasive wheels and emery cloth.

19.10 Final finish with Autosol.

POLISHING ENGINE CASINGS & OTHER ALLOY PARTS

19.11 Crankcase polished with abrasive wheels and emery cloth.

19.12 Cam cover buff polished.

19.13 Buff polished clutch cover.

19.14 Dremmel with wire brush and flap wheel attachments.

19.15 Parts being washed in a jam jar of white spirit.

I also used a Dremmel multi-tool with a variety of bits for odd bits and pieces such as nuts and bolts, and hard-to-reach nooks and crannies on occasions. I used small sanding flap wheels, stainless steel brushes and brass brushes, but the flap wheels were pretty abrasive, the stainless brushes tended to leave the metal quite dark, and the brass brushes wore out quickly, so beware. See photo 19.14.

I also had a selection of jam jars for de-greasing nuts and bolts, etc, before detailed cleaning and polishing. I put the nuts and bolts in the jar, together with some white spirit, and gave it a good shake for a couple of minutes. See photo 19.15. It worked a treat – but heavy nuts and bolts being shaken in a glass jar? Yes, I did have some 'incidents' – I think I shall invest in a plastic container or similar!

LESSONS LEARNT
- How much alloy you polish is up to you – some people love it; some hate it (but, as I always say: it's your bike).
- The only way to achieve a mirror shine is by mechanical buffing.
- Use grit to begin with if the surface is poor – but be careful.
- Use polish frequently but sparingly on the mop.
- If it doesn't shine with the grey polish it isn't right.
- Polish left on the job? Too much polish!
- Mop stalling on the buffer? Too much pressure.
- The quality of finish is directly proportional to the amount of effort you put in.
- Use wet-and-dry to obtain a polish on parts that can't be buffed – but be prepared to graft!
- Practice makes perfect.
- Glass jars and nuts and bolts aren't the best combination!
- Polishing is at once one of the most frustrating yet rewarding jobs on the restoration.

www.velocebooks.com
New book news • Special offers • Newsletter • Details of all Veloce books • Gift Vouchers

Chapter 20
Crankshaft, transmission & oil pump

With the cleaning and polishing of various alloy parts finally done, it was time to check that all was well with the crankcase internals. First and foremost was the crankshaft; the heart of the engine, if that's not right then the engine will never be right. See photo 20.1. The problem here is that it's very hard to check the crankshaft without specialist equipment (which I didn't have), and without dismantling it. I had two choices: I could send the crankshaft to a local specialist engineering firm (which also works on Formula 1 cars!) for checking and balancing, or visually check it myself and leave as-was.

The case for the first course of action was strong as the crankshaft showed signs of slight damage where it may have been dropped at some point in its life (see photo 20.2). The letters R and L written on the flywheels also suggested that it had been taken apart before. If nothing else, having the crankshaft checked gives peace of mind. However, in the end, I decided to just check the crankshaft myself for one simple reason: money. The cost of restoring any bike is high, and a Z900 is no exception: I was already sliding into debt. If I could, I would have had the crankshaft checked and balanced without a shadow of a doubt, but it was a case of needs must. (At this point in the restoration, in order to fund the restoration of the Z900 I had already been forced to sell my spare set of carburettors for the Z1A, and then, very reluctantly, my cherished Hinckley Triumph Thunderbird 900.)

The other problem with checking the engine generally was that, as I'd never actually fired up the bike before disassembly, it was impossible to know what, if any, faults there might

20.1 Crankshaft being checked.

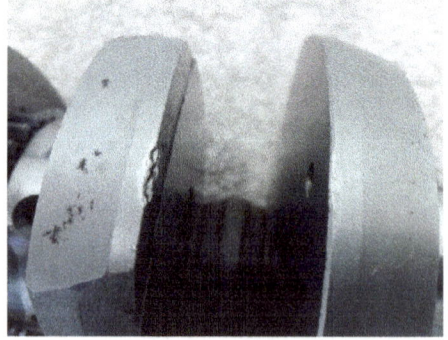
20.2 Unknown damage to crankshaft – possibly dropped.

CRANKSHAFT, TRANSMISSION & OIL PUMP

be, from a rumbling big end through to burning oil, or a faulty gear change, so checking all parts regardless was essential.

As it was I checked the crankshaft roller main bearings as far as I could, and pulled and pushed the roller big end bearings (on the bottom of the con rods), and checked the con rods visually for cracks and signs they weren't straight, or had any other damage (a chip on a con-rod can be fatal as this becomes a focus for stress and can lead to catastrophic failure), and all seemed well. This was a poor substitute for a professional check, however. It was fingers crossed – which really isn't the best engineering practice, but that was my problem. Do as I say, not as I do ...

Next up I checked the mainshaft, layshaft, and kick-start shaft. Once again, my inspection revealed that all appeared well with these. If I've not said it before, I'll say it now: as a British biker through-and-through who has only really ever worked on British bikes, and was once one of the loudest to be heard deriding 'Jap crap' and 'Rice burners,' I have been really impressed with the engineering of the Z1. It is so simple and yet so damned good! Problems that the British motorcycle industry struggled with for years, if not decades, are addressed and resolved at a stroke: having the transmission close enough to the crankshaft to enable the primary drive to be gear-driven rather than chain-driven, or having a clutch that works, or crankshafts with roller main and big end bearings, or horizontally split crankcases, or twin overhead camshafts, or an engine that is oil tight and has no fewer than four cylinders, or carbs that don't need tickling, etc, etc. Whatever your viewpoint on different marques, you have to acknowledge the engineering excellence of the Z1 (not to mention the fact that it looks incredible, was the fastest production bike in the world at the time, and cost less than many of its rivals!).

At this point I also checked the condition of the clutch basket. This has to be fitted before the crankcases are joined so requires checking prior to this. The clutch basket comprises two plates, riveted together with springs between them to act as shock absorbers. Check the plates and springs for wear, and have them repaired if necessary (I don't think they're available new): under heavy usage, such as drag racing, they can wear and become loose. I also checked the teeth on the inside rim of the basket for damage caused by the tabs on the clutch plates – again, all okay. See photo 20.3 of the clutch basket and gears being checked.

I then checked the actual gears and gear selectors for signs of chipped or broken teeth, discolouration that might be the result of overheating (or warping, in the case of the selectors) or signs of excessive wear in the bearings. I also laid the gearshafts back in the crankcase to check for excessive backlash (wear between teeth on the two shafts), which I did by eye and without the aid of a dial gauge, but they felt okay to me. I decided to partially strip the shafts anyway, in order to give them a

20.3 Transmission shafts, clutch basket and kickstart shaft laid out for inspection.

closer inspection and gain insight into their workings.

I began to strip the gearbox mainshaft by removing the circlip on the end, which freed up the outer bearing and first two gears. See photo 20.4. It was at this point that I discovered the three ball bearings hidden under the 4th gear cog that helps when selecting neutral when the bike is stationary. The clever idea behind this is that, when the mainshaft isn't turning, at least one of the three ball bearings falls into the hole in the mainshaft (by gravity), and prevents 4th gear from sliding along the shaft. This, in turn, means that only neutral can be selected, so there's no danger of going straight into 2nd gear when trying to find neutral at standstill. As the mainshaft begins to rotate when the bike begins to move, the three ball bearings are thrown out of the holes in the mainshaft into holes in the 4th gear cog, now allowing it to slide along the shaft and for all gears to be selected. Oh, so simple and yet so clever! See photo 20.5 for a close-up of the ball bearings, and respective holes in the mainshaft and 4th gear cog. -

Note that I always laid out components in the order they were removed and took photos, which at least gave me a fighting chance of putting them back together in the right order! Having found no evidence of any problems, I decided to leave things, as there seemed little point in

20.4 Mainshaft semi-dismantled – with the three ball bearings that lock the gearchange.

stripping the shaft further for no real reason.

I duly reassembled the components, ensuring that the three ball bearings were correctly located, and that I didn't use grease to hold them in place, as this can cause them to stick and not function correctly.

Similarly to the mainshaft I partially stripped the layshaft; the only problem discovered being a slightly loose bearing which might begin to spin on the shaft. I therefore Loctited it in position. See photo 20.6. The two shafts I now deemed ready to be remounted in the crankcases. See photo 20.7.

I double-checked the state of the gearbox selector forks for straightness, any signs of damage or discolouration (overheating), etc, as any faults here could lead to poor gear selection. All seemed fine.

I then stripped the final component: the kick-start shaft. See photo 20.8. Having removed the outer circlip, I dismantled the various parts of the assembly to discover that there far more components to it than I would have expected! See photo 20.9. I checked the condition of the teeth on the two mating pawls, and these seemed fine, so I reassembled the shaft. The main item to note here is that there are marks on the shaft and the outer pawl which need to be aligned if the tension on the kick-start spring is to be correct when fitted. See photo 20.10.

Next up was the oil pump. See photo 20.11. Disassembly was quite straightforward (the gauze filter simply prises out) and the unit was soon apart. See photo 20.12. Note that the drive vanes and spindles do come out of the housing, but that I left them in situ as they should be replaced in their original position to avoid excess wear. I therefore took these out one at a time to inspect and then refit them. The vanes looked to be in good condition with no gouges or scratches, and so I checked them for excess play/clearances. See photo 20.13. I then thoroughly cleaned all parts ready for assembly. See photos 20.14 and 20.15. Note the various sealants and cleaners used –

• I always used a proprietary engine assembly lubricant when rebuilding an engine. Wear on a newly rebuilt engine on initial start-up can be very high, so using a proper lubricant is essential. Normal engine oil isn't really suitable as it's too thin, and tends to run off before the engine is ready to start. Always use engine assembly lubricant.

• Threadlock. Where threads are required to be locked (as with the

20.5 A close-up of the shaft with the groove for the ball bearings which are seen below the gears.

20.6 Preparing to lock a slightly loose bearing on the layshaft.

20.7 The gear shafts ready to be re-installed.

20.8 The kickstart assembly.

20.9 The kickstart shaft dismantled and checked.

CRANKSHAFT, TRANSMISSION & OIL PUMP

20.10 Aligning the punch marks on the shaft and the ratchet.

20.12 The pump dismantled.

20.11 The oil pump assembly ready to be stripped.

20.13 Checking the play in the oil pump.

oil pump mounting bolts), I use a medium-strength threadlock on the threads. (I also use a lower strength threadlock on any studs that don't require locking, but which may be prone to oil leakage down the threads, so the threadlock acts as a sealant in this case).

• Wellseal. As a British biker you are brought up on this rather than mother's milk. The only engine gasket sealant I would ever use (other gasket sealants are available, however).
• Cellulose thinners – the only thinners that are effective on Wellseal,

20.14 Cleaning and preparing the oil pump for reassembly.

20.15 Assembly progressing.

20.16 Oil pump assembled – incorrectly!

20.17 Drive wheel reassembled in the correct order with the washer underneath the gear wheel *not* outside.

and used to wipe away any excess sealant.

The last element of the oil pump assembly was the large drive gear which I mounted and held in place with its circlip. See photo 20.16. I thought I had covered all bases by marking which way round the large drive gear was fitted before dismantling (note the word 'OUT' written on the drive gear so I knew which way round it went), but, when I checked that all was well with the pump by spinning the drive gear, I immediately discovered that something was catching somewhere. On closer inspection I realised that I had incorrectly fitted the washer next to the drive gear on the outside of the drive gear, which meant that the drive gear was now too close to the pump body, and was fouling on the mounting screws. I moved the washer to inside the drive gear and all was well. See photos 20.16 and 20.17. Such a simple little error that could have had catastrophic consequences if it hadn't been discovered. Always check that everything is turning/running freely at every step to avoid major problems.

As it was, all was okay and the crankcases were ready to be reassembled.

LESSONS LEARNT
• The crankshaft should be professionally checked wherever possible.
• Kawasaki (Japanese?) engineering is superb.
• You can't select gears when the mainshaft is still – so don't try going through the gears with the engine on the bench.
• If dismantling the kick-start assembly, align the punch marks on reassembly.
• Always use a proper engine assembly lubricant.
• Wellseal: the answer.
• Check that parts are turning or running freely at every stage of reassembly. This helps identify what is jammed and prevents having to dismantle too much (don't just check things at the end of assembly as you won't know which part is the problem).
• Note that I renewed the cam chain as a matter of course. This can only be replaced with the crankshaft removed, so it would be a false economy not to replace it with the engine stripped, regardless of condition.

Chapter 21
Assembling the crankcases

At last – time to begin reassembling the engine! It's worth noting that, by this time, all the hard work had been done: de-greasing, vapour blasting, removing gasket gunge, tapping the threads, cleaning and polishing the cases. With all of this finally behind me, it was time for the fun part: reassembly!

The first components I fitted to the bottom half of the crankcases were the gear selector drum and the gear change selector fork that runs on it. See photo 21.1. (Note that all parts were given a generous coating of engine rebuild lube before being assembled.) Having inserted the drum into the crankcase I slid the selector fork over it before tightening and locking its locating bolt (note that the short side of the selector goes towards the drum, and that the fork locating bolt engages with the central groove on the drum). Also locate the tip of the locating bolt in a little dimple in the drum, which sets the drum in neutral. See photo 21.2 with the fork not yet correctly located.

Next up was the drum positioning bolt which was inserted, torqued, and locked with its locking washer. See photos 21.3 and 21.8. After this it was time to mount the

21.1 Preparing to fit the gear change drum with engine assembly lubricant.

crankshaft in the upper half of the crankcase. The most important thing to remember is to fit the cam chain over the crankshaft before mounting: if you forget to do this then you've an awful lot of disassembly and reassembly to do later! After this, when it comes to actually mounting the crankshaft, it's very important that the dowels in the bearing faces of the crankcases locate and engage with the drilled holes in the crankshaft bearings. These dowels ensure that the holes for the oilways to the bearings line up. I had difficulty getting mine to line up because you can't see the holes as they're at the bottom of the crankshaft. In the end, I

HOW TO RESTORE KAWASAKI Z1, Z/KZ900 & Z/KZ1000

21.2 Mounting the selector fork – short side towards drum, in the middle slot, using a locking tab.

21.4 Marking the main bearings to ease correct fitting. Don't forget the cam chain! Also note the 'L' on the crankshaft.

21.7 Layshaft fitted together with the clutch basket.

21.3 Torquing up the drum positioning bolt.

21.5 Main bearing cap fitted and torqued down.

21.6 Main shaft in position. Don't forget to fit the semi-circular fitting ring.

marked a line on the bearings roughly opposite where the holes were, so that at least I had some chance of aligning them. Eventually, this worked (my marks weren't that accurate!) See photo 21.4.

With the crankshaft correctly located, the next job was to fit the central bearing cap and torque it (you can't do this later when the crankcases are joined as the lower crankcase is in the way). See photo 21.5. Note that the tightening sequence for these bolts is very usefully cast into the bearing cap.

I turned back to the gearbox and began assembling the various shafts, again, in the top half of the crankcase. First up was the mainshaft (output shaft) that sat nicely in its mountings. The main thing to note are the two semi-circular locating rings that go in grooves in the bearings on the ends of the mainshaft and layshaft (driven shaft), and hold them in position by engaging with two similar grooves in the upper crankcase. See photo 21.6. At this point I have to admit that somewhere along the line I had lost these two rings. I've no idea where or how, but they were gone, even with my very careful procedure for bagging and tagging all parts – you can never be too careful. At first I was devastated to learn that these were no longer available – such simple components but such an essential part of the engine. However, having checked, it was found that, in fact, they are available, so I immediately bought a pair. Lucky escape. Without these the entire rebuild would have ground to a halt.

The mainshaft was followed by the layshaft, with the clutch basket slid onto the end of it. See photo 21.7.

Turning back to the lower crankcase, I slid the gear selector shaft into place together with the remaining two selector forks; this time the forks have the long side facing the drum. See photo 21.8. The selector shaft is then held in place with a circlip. See photo 21.9. I also fitted the oil pressure relief valve, and locked it with its tab washer. See photo 21.10.

Turning back to the upper crankcase, I slotted the kick-start shaft in place and mounted its stop plate in the edge of the casing with its two small bolts, which were then locked with a tab washer. I also fitted the small 'O' ring seal in the centre of the crankcase which seals the oil supply pipe. See photo 21.11. Note that the 'O' ring seal goes into the crankcase flat side down, so the ridged top can be seen – the same goes for the oil pump 'O' ring seal.

The cases were now ready for reassembly, so I coated both mating surfaces with Wellseal and waited a few minutes for it to go off before mating the cases. See photo 21.12.

I used this time to triple-check that everything was okay and in the right place, and then carefully lowered the bottom casing onto the top casing, ensuring as I did so that the selector forks engaged correctly with their respective gears and didn't come unseated. See photo 21.13. I gently tapped down the casing, only to discover that it wouldn't seat properly. A quick check revealed

ASSEMBLING THE CRANKCASES

21.8 Selector shaft and remaining two selector forks in place, with long ends towards the drum.

21.10 Oil pressure relief valve fitted and locked with a tab washer.

21.13 Ensuring the gear selector forks locate correctly as the crankcases are joined.

21.9 The selector shaft held in place with a circlip on the outside.

21.11 Kickstart shaft and stop plate fitted, and centre oil seal in place.

21.14 The two halves don't seem to want to fit together – the layshaft bearing has not located with its dowel mounting.

that the bearing on the layshaft had come unseated from the dowel in the crankcase, and was preventing the cases from closing. See photo 21.14.

Having properly located the dowel the two halves came together and I began bolting them together with the remaining 8mm crankshaft mounting bolts. See photo 21.15. Note that, as with the bearing cap, the tightening sequence for these bolts is cast into the casing. The last two bolts need to be threadlocked and then sealed under the head to prevent oil leaks. See photo 21.16 and 21.17.

After this, I loosely inserted and then torqued the many 6mm

21.12 The two crankcase mating faces prepared with Wellseal gasket sealant – curing prior to assembly.

21.15 The crankcases now correctly fitted.

21.16 Using blue hermetite and threadlock to seal the two outer rear crankshaft bolts.

21.17 All the crankshaft bolts fitted and torqued down – the two outer rear ones sealed and threadlocked.

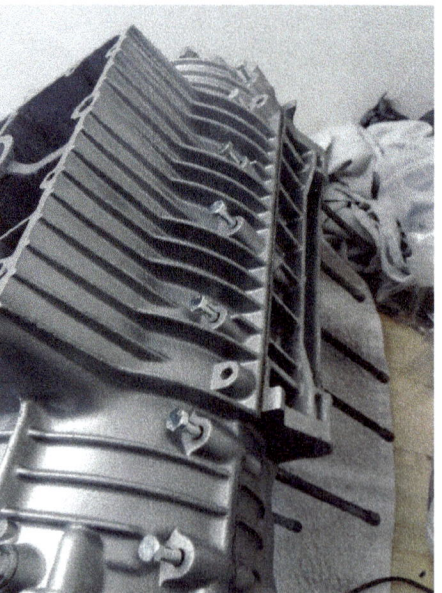

21.18 Inserting the crankcase bolts before torquing them down.

crankcase mounting bolts. See photo 21.18. Note that there is another bolt that requires locking and sealing: the long bolt to the rear of the clutch housing. See photo 21.19. Note also in this picture the location of two of the four wiring clips that go on some crankcase bolts.

With all of the underside bolts fitted I turned over the cases and fitted the remaining five bolts to the top of the casing. See photo 21.20. Note the location of the remaining two wiring clips.

With the crankcases now successfully united, I turned my attention to the oil pump and the sump. The first job was to fit the 'O' ring oil seal in place in the bottom of the crankcase ready to take the oil pump. See photo 21.21. After this I fitted the oil pump assembly using threadlock, and torqued the bolts to the required setting. See photo 21.22. Note that there are two locating dowels on the bottom of the oil pump body that locate into recesses in the crankcase to ensure perfect alignment

It was then time to fit the sump, so I duly coated the two mating halves with Wellseal before fitting

ASSEMBLING THE CRANKCASES

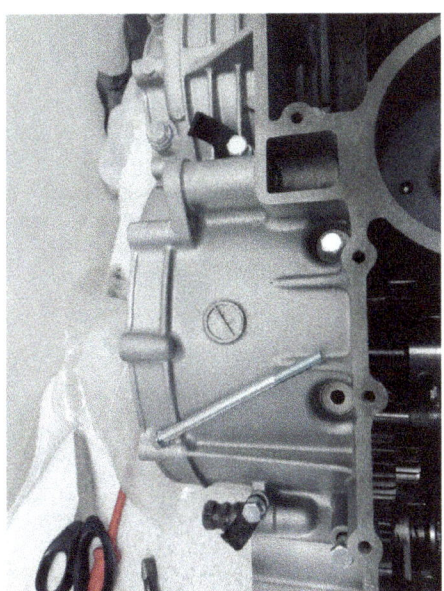

21.19 This long crankcase bolt also requires threadlocking and sealing. Also note the position of the two cable clips.

21.20 Inserting the five crankcase bolts on the top of the casings – note the position of the two cable clips.

21.21 Oil pump 'O' ring in position, ridged edge uppermost.

21.22 Oil pump fitted with mounting bolts, threadlocked and about to be torqued down.

21.23 Sump waiting to be fitted. Note the sump gasket and large 'O' ring for the oil filter aperture ready to go on first.

21.24 Sump being fitted.

21.25 Shaving off excess gasket and wiping off excess gasket goo with cellulose thinners.

21.26 The oil filter and various drain plugs etc, ready to be installed.

21.27 Fitting the oil filter.

the gasket and large 'O' ring seal round the oil filter aperture. See photo 21.23. Next, I fitted the sump and tightened the bolts. See photo 21.24. Note that, as usual, I loosely screwed in all of the bolts first to ensure I had the right bolt in the right hole by checking that they all sat proud of the casing by the same amount when loose. I then shaved off any excess gasket that protruded beyond the cases to give a really nice finish, and cleaned off any excess Wellseal with cellulose thinners. See photo 21.25.

The next job was to fit the oil filter assembly and various drain plugs to the bottom of the sump. I duly gathered together the parts and fitted another large 'O' ring seal to the bottom of the filter housing. See photo 21.26. I then mounted the filter assembly to the sump (see photo 21.27) with the small spring on the mounting shaft between the filter and the circular filter housing – which can't be seen in the photo. With the filter in place, I refitted the two oil drain plugs – the main one to the front of the sump and the one for the oil filter in the filter housing. They both received new 'O' ring seals, see photo 21.28.

The next job was to fit the kickstart mechanism. The kickstart return spring has a straight tang at one end and a right-angled tang at the other. See photo 21.29. There is a hole in the crankcases for the tang on the spring. See photo 21.30. Insert the tang into the hole and use small mole grips or similar to rotate the spring anti-clockwise, then insert the other, right-angled tang into the hole in the shaft. See photo 21.31.

87

HOW TO RESTORE KAWASAKI Z1, Z/KZ900 & Z/KZ1000

21.28 Oil filter and drain plugs all fitted.

21.29 Kickstart spring with straight tang on one end and right-angled tang on the other

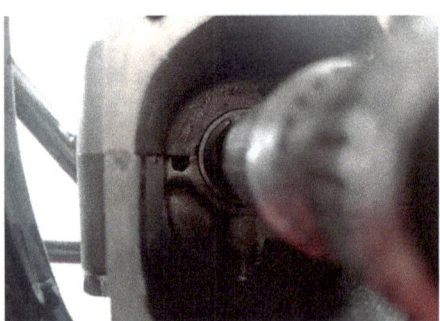

21.30 Hole in crankcase for the tang on the kickstart.

21.31 Kickstart spring fitted, with straight tang in the hole in the crankcases and bent tang in the hole in the kickstart shaft.

Slide the alloy spacer over the shaft, under the spring. See photo 21.32. The outer case (with a new oil seal fitted) is now ready to be fitted. See photo 21.33. Fit a new gasket, lubricate the oil seal and feed it carefully over the kickstart shaft to avoid damaging the lip, and finally fit the four mounting screws. See photo 21.34.

I then turned the engine so that it was the right way up: assembly was now complete and the engine ready to fit into the frame! See photo 21.35.

I had already decided that the easiest method of full engine assembly was to return the half-built engine to the frame whilst it was still light and small enough to move, and then finish assembly in the frame, using the frame as a glorified engine stand. This had worked

21.32 Alloy spacer slid on the shaft, underneath the spring

21.33 Outer cover polished and a new oil seal fitted.

21.34 Outer cover in place with a new gasket and a smear of Wellseal. Take care not to damage the new oil seal when sliding the cover over the shaft.

well on disassembly so it seemed logical to use the same method for reassembly. I've seen various methods used when rebuilding the engine, most notably heaving the fully rebuilt engine into the frame, or laying the engine sideways on the ground and then lowering the frame over it, but I decided that, in my case, it made sense to replace the half-built engine in the frame.

LESSONS LEARNT

• If possible, do all of the cleaning, painting, machining, etc, first so that you can relax a bit and get into reassembly mode.
• Check and check the order that everything goes back in before final assembly/tightening up – just one small part inserted the wrong way round will cause a lot of heartache (and necessitate dismantling/rebuilding).
• I think I'm pretty damn meticulous about bagging and tagging all parts – but even so I lost the locating rings for the gearshafts – and this was almost a disaster. Only goes to show that you can't be too careful. (To date, I still haven't found the rings; I think I must have thrown them out by accident, probably with some old workshop tissue/rag.)
• I use Wellseal to join the crankcase halves, and on all other gaskets. Others may well recommend different gasket cement.
• I always loosely insert all bolts in a casing before tightening them to ensure I have the right bolt in the right hole – they should all protrude above the casing by the same amount.
• There is no better feeling than assembling clean and beautiful parts on an engine.

21.35 Crankcases together and ready to be slotted into the frame! Oh, yes.

Chapter 22
Reassembling the front forks

With the crankcases now reassembled and ready to fit back into the frame, the obvious next step in the process was to ... rebuild the front forks! To explain: as I had decided to complete the engine rebuild with the engine in the frame, I first needed a standing frame in which to put it – and at this point in time I didn't have one, so it was on with the front forks.

I had bought a set of second-hand replacement forks to replace those damaged in the trailer 'incident,' and disassembled them to check they were okay, and to take the best parts from each set to make one good one. The first thing I realised was that the stanchions on my replacement forks were in a fairly poor state compared to my originals with slightly pitted chrome, so I kept my originals.

I readied the stanchion internals for reassembly – in the correct order. See photo 22.1. Note that the spacer tube has a slight chamfer at one end, and this goes towards the bottom of the fork leg. See photo 22.2. The various spacers and springs are held in place by a circlip at the bottom.

With the stanchion internals in place, it was time to fit new oil seals, and these can prove tricky. Various bespoke tools exist for fitting front fork oil seals, but I don't own one, and if fork seals aren't properly fitted they can easily leak. So I very carefully fitted the new seals by heating the lower fork legs and lubricating the seal with WD40, driving home the seals with a drift that just fitted the perimeter – in this case, an old, large diameter socket. See photo 22.3. I usually find that this method works well, though it's a lot trickier than the above description suggests! I then liberally greased the lips of the seals. There is a special (red) grease just for this purpose, but I didn't have any, even though seals are often supplied with a little sachet of red grease (not in this case) so I used ordinary grease – I hope I don't live to regret it!

22.1 Stanchion internals.

22.2 Note that the chamfer on the distance piece goes towards the bottom.

22.3 Inserting new oil seals using heat, WD40 and a suitably sized socket.

Next up were the internal damper rods. As I inspected them for excess wear, etc, I suddenly realised that the damper rods weren't a matched pair, and probably from slightly different model years. See photo 22.4. I therefore took one of my original damper units to create a matched pair. See photo 22.5. I then fully inspected the replacement lower fork legs only to discover that the studs on the bottom of one of the legs were bent. See photo 22.6. I used the time-honoured method of locking two nuts together to remove the studs – with the aid of a lot of heat in the case of one of them that didn't want to budge. See photo 22.7. I replaced the old studs with new ones using the same method.

With the studs successfully replaced I assembled the fork innards and slid them home, ready to be bolted together. See photo 22.8. However, I realised that the little alloy end cap doesn't go down into the stanchion with the damper rod, but is inserted in the bottom of the stanchion and the damper rod then lowered into it. See photo 22.9. With everything successfully located, I applied threadlock to the bottom Allen screw and fitted a new sealing washer. I used threadlock not as a lock but as an extra oil seal – you don't want these screws leaking as they're such a pain to replace. See photo 22.10.

22.6 Bent fork leg studs.

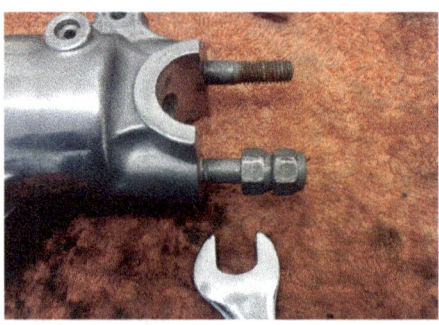

22.7 Using two nuts locked together to remove old studs.

I then refitted the Allen screw. I had used my fantastic new cordless impact driver to remove the screw, but didn't want to use it to replace it, as I might inadvertently do it up too tightly, or even tighten it so much that the thread stripped in the fork leg – impact drivers are very powerful. I therefore took my very long, flat-bladed screwdriver (bought for this very purpose a few years ago), inserted it into the stanchion, and twisted it until it jammed the damper unit and held it still enough for me to tighten the Allen key by hand. See photo 22.11. On reflection, I think I could have used my impact driver on its lowest setting actually, and tested how tight that was, but better safe than sorry.

With the stanchion screwed into the lower leg I slid the metal washer over the fork oil seal before holding it in place with the large circlip. See photo 22.12. I then slid down the dust covers over the seals. I fitted new seals to the drain screws and refitted them to the bottom of the legs. See photo 22.13.

After this, I assembled the main springs with their associated collets and spacers, and prepared to slide them into the stanchions. I think that, on some models, the main springs are graded in that there are tighter coils at one end than the other, in which case the tighter coils go to the top. In the case of the Z900, the coils are evenly tight throughout the coil so could be fitted either way up. See photo 22.14.

The last job was to fill the forks with oil. The manual advises 192cc

22.4 Mismatched internal damper units.

22.5 That's better.

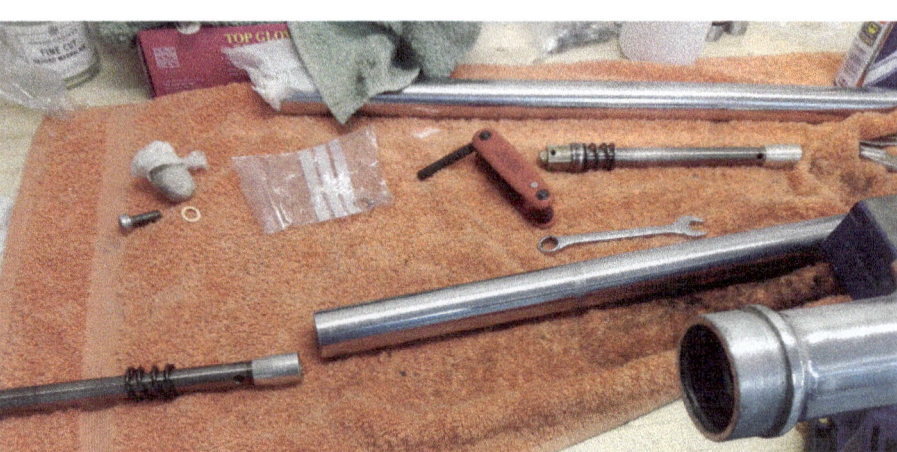

22.8 Preparing to assemble the forks.

REASSEMBLING THE FRONT FORKS

22.9 Inserting the alloy cap into the bottom of the stanchion.

22.10 Threadlocking the Allen screws to help them seal.

of 10 SAE oil. I had a spare bottle of 15 SAE and was tempted to use this instead as there surely wasn't much of a difference ... was there? Thankfully, it dawned on me that 15 SAE was, in fact, 50 per cent thicker than the required viscosity, and ordered some correct fluid on the net. When this arrived (some time later when the forks were fitted to the bike) I carefully filled each leg with the required amount, using a cheap cookery measuring jug, screwed down the stanchion caps and it was job done. See photo 22.15.

LESSONS LEARNT

- As with parts already on the bike, check all second-hand components to ensure they are correct and of serviceable quality before fitting.
- Fitting front fork oil seals – a seemingly straightforward job that can be a real nightmare.
- Don't use your wonderful new cordless impact driver for reassembly – it'll only end in tears.
- Hold the damper rods with a long screwdriver or similar to tighten the Allen screw at the bottom of the fork legs.
- If the springs are asymmetric the tighter coils go to the top.
- Use the correct grade of suspension oil in the fork legs – it's not rocket science.

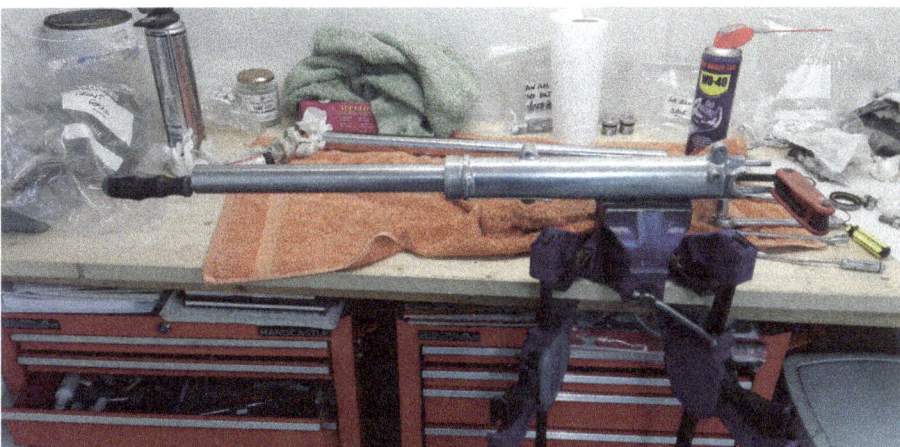

22.11 Locking the damper unit with a very long screwdriver to enable the Allen screw to be fully tightened.

22.12 Refitting the circlip on top of the fork oil seal washer.

22.13 Replacing the fork leg drain screws with new washers.

22.14 Preparing to insert the main springs.

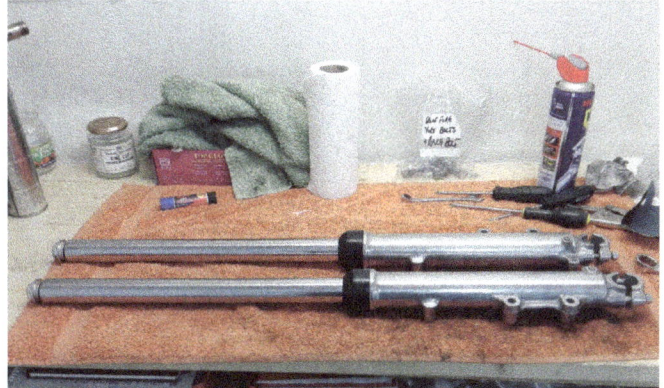

22.15 Fork legs assembled, ready to go back on the bike when refilled with oil.

Chapter 23
Rebuilding the wheels, brake discs & shoes

Next up were the wheels. The hubs had been blast cleaned and then polished, after which they'd been sent away for rebuilding with stainless spokes at Black Cat wheel builders. I'd had to buy a new rear wheel rim as the original was dented beyond repair, but, amazingly, the original front rim was in such good condition that not only was it usable, it didn't even require rechroming! Never had that before! The rear was a chrome rim without any maker's stamps on it. I really wanted to keep the original Takasago rim, but as this wasn't possible, second choice was to have a rim with no stamps from modern makers. I could also have bought a second-hand rim from Ebay or similar, but at the time there were none for sale so I decided to leave it. It's only a little thing, and I'm not really bothered about originality, but for some reason I'd have liked to have original rims. C'est la vie.

Whilst the wheels were away being built I had the wheel spindles and nuts chrome plated.

Now, I know many people who rebuild their own wheels, and I think it's something I'd like to have a go at myself sometime. You need a jig to be able to spin the wheels, with a pointer

23.1 Wheels back from the builders.

next to the rim to ensure trueness, and some good instructions. Bear in mind that some wheels are offset, with the hubs slightly to one side, so it's not always quite as easy as it seems. Anyway, for the sake of expediency I had them built for me this time. Doing it for the first time is bound to take ages, but also very satisfying, I'm guessing.

Just in time the wheels came and I fitted new bearings throughout so that new tyres could be fitted and balanced. See photo 23.1. Beginning with the front wheel I heated the hub on the left side with my blowtorch (see photo 23.2), and then inserted the cooled bearing, with a little oil round the edge, using a drift (a suitably-sized socket that sat nicely in the middle of the bearing) See photo 23.3. Note that I knocked in this bearing using a drift (socket) on the inner bearing race. This is not best practice, as new bearings should be driven home on the outer race to avoid damaging them. In this case the bearing wasn't that tight a fit, and I didn't have a drift to fit on the outer race – but still not ideal.

REBUILDING THE WHEELS, BRAKE DISCS & SHOES

Turning over the wheel I inserted the spacer tube (see photo 23.4), realising that although I'd marked it on removal, it didn't matter which way round it fitted in the hub as long as the large collet was roughly in the middle. With that dropped in, I once again heated the hub and inserted the second bearing in a similar fashion to the first, then inserted its large retaining circlip. See photo 23.5.

At this point I rang my local motorcycle shop to order new tyres so they would be ready when the wheels were finished. After much deliberation I chose Avon Roadriders, for several reasons: They were already fitted to my Z1A when I bought it and seemed to be fine; they weren't wildly expensive, and the tread pattern wasn't too futuristic: more in keeping with the age of the bike – although still slightly anachronistic. But tyre choice is always very personal and depends on a whole host of criteria (cost, originality, type of use (track days or weekend use or touring), looks, rate of wear, available tyres for rim size, etc). For me and what I wanted the Avons seemed the right choice.

Turning back to the left side I fitted the speedo drive collet, disc, and speedo drive retaining plate. See photo 23.6A. Just prior to this I'd made an unwelcome discovery: the pair of solid discs I'd got to fit the bike turned out to be an unmatched pair – one was 6mm thick and the other 8mm thick. See photo 23.6B of what appear to be a pair of discs, but on closer inspection were different thicknesses. Two different thickness discs for the same bike? Now, I do know that often discs were made thinner to reduce weight, or unsprung weight to be precise, especially when fitting twin discs, as the weight of two discs is obviously greater.* I think that, on most models, Kawasaki fitted a thicker disc (8mm) for single disc models and two thinner ones (6mm) for twin disc models. As my bike had started life as a single disc model, the original disc was therefore a thick one.

I had bought a second-hand right brake calliper, calliper bracket, and brake disc which, being part of a twin disc setup, meant it was a thinner disc. I now had one 6mm and one 8mm disc, which, I guess, I could have actually used, but it would have looked odd at the very least. The problem was that discs for the Z900 A4 model of either size (6mm or 8mm) are currently unavailable, so what to do? See photo 23.6C.

Whilst I was mulling over the best way forward I did my customary search of parts on eBay, and found a pair of discs – and not only that, but they were drilled discs which look so much better in my opinion. I immediately bought them and they duly arrived looking fine. I took them down to the engineer shop and had them skimmed; they came back looking superb! I gave the centres a coat of paint and they were ready to fit. Excellent. See photo 23.6A again.

Next up was the speedo drive which required dismantling, checking, and reassembling with a new grease seal. I secured the drive unit in the vice and removed the old grease seal with my seal remover. See photo 23.6D. With this removed, I dismantled the assembly and cleaned out all of the old grease with white spirit (see photo 23.6E), before reassembling the unit with new grease and a new grease seal. See photo 23.6F. I then loosely assembled the drive unit and wheel spindle (now that my parts had returned from the chrome plater) to check all was okay. See photo 23.7.

Turning to the other side of the hub, I greased the new bearing (which, I was surprised to discover, wasn't a sealed bearing – neither of the front ones were, but the rear ones were – although the rear sprocket one wasn't: strange). See photo 23.8 before fitting a new grease seal. See photo 23.9. I then refitted the second disc and slotted the wheel spindle spacer and nut onto the spindle. See photo 23.10. The front wheel was finished.

I then put the rear wheel bearings

---

* Basically, unsprung weight is any weight that is on a vehicle between the road and the suspension, (so the lower fork legs, callipers and discs, and the wheel itself on a motorcycle front wheel). Now, I'm not sure why, but unsprung weight has a considerable impact on the roadholding and handling of any vehicle, and the lower this is, the better the roadholding. This is why the legendary IRS (Independent Rear Suspension) on such Jaguars as the E-Type had inboard brakes (discs and callipers) which are therefore not in-between the road and the suspension, but after the suspension, and so help to reduce unsprung weight.

23.2 Heating the front hub ready for the first bearing.

23.3 Inserting the bearing with the aid of an appropriately sized socket.

23.4 The bearing spacer – whichever way round is fine.

23.5 Second bearing and retaining circlip fitted.

HOW TO RESTORE KAWASAKI Z1, Z/KZ900 & Z/KZ1000

23.6 (A) Speedo drive collet, securing plate and disc fitted to left side ... of what appears to be a pair of discs (B) – but one is 6mm and the other 8mm thick (C).

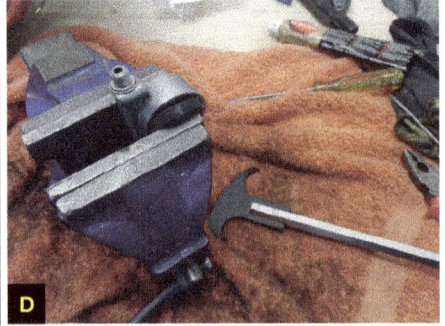  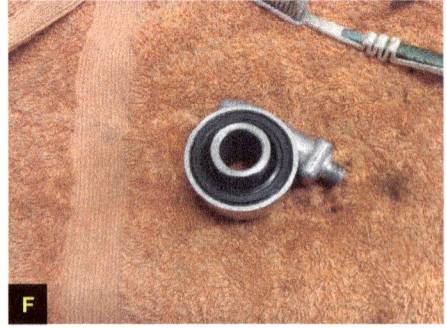

(D) Removing the old grease seal. (E) Cleaning and checking the speedo drive. (F) Speedo drive reassembled with new grease seal.

in the freezer to shrink them as much as possible (see photo 23.11), and heated the hub with my blowtorch for quite a time as there is a lot of metal to heat, and the bearing sits quite deep in the hub. When it was nice and hot I removed the bearings from the freezer and drove them home with the aid of another socket. See photo 23.12. I then inserted the wheel bearing spacer (see photo 23.13), realising that the collet on the spacer needed to be at

23.7 Speedo drive and wheel spindle in place.

23.8 Right side bearing greased.

23.9 New grease seal in place.

 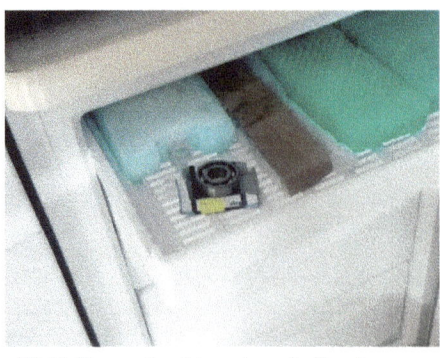 

23.10 Right side wheel spindle and spacer in place.

23.11 Rear wheel bearings in the freezer.

23.12 First rear wheel bearing in place.

REBUILDING THE WHEELS, BRAKE DISCS & SHOES

23.13 Rear wheel bearing spacer, only goes in one way round.

23.14 Inserting the rear sprocket carrier wheel bearing.

the end as the inside of the hub is cone-shaped so the collet can only go in one way in order to fit snugly against the sides of the thin end of the cone. With that inserted, I heated the other side of the hub and drifted in the second bearing. The wheels were now ready to have new tyres fitted, and were duly taken to the motorcycle shop for this to be done (I HATE fitting tyres, and will do anything to avoid it!).

While the wheels were away having their tyres fitted, I fitted the third rear wheel bearing to the rear sprocket carrier. See photo 23.14. Fitting was much as before, but be aware that, as this is a big bearing and there is a lot of metal on the hub carrier, it takes longer to heat the hub and cool the bearing. There's nothing worse than trying to fit a bearing, only for it to jam halfway because the housing isn't sufficiently hot. Your options then are to use brute force to try and fit it, or extricate it and start again. Anyway, the bearing was finally fitted.

At this point I decided to fit my new brake shoes to the back plate. As ever, this was difficult, but the method that worked for me was as follows.

First of all, apply a light coating of grease to the ends of the brake shoes, the two spigots at the bottom of the brake plate, and the sides of the brake operating shaft (not too much as you don't want to contaminate the shoes with grease – but neither do you want the brake to seize). Attach the springs to the brake shoes and then fit the operating shaft between the jaws of the brake shoes at the top; then lower the brake shoes onto the back plate, inserting the operating shaft into its tunnel. When the brake shoes are low enough, pull apart the bottoms and ease them onto the two spigots at the bottom of the back plate. See photo 23.15 of

23.15 Fitting the new brake shoes, number 1 on the left, number 2 on the right.

23.16 Washers and split pins in situ, holding the shoes in place.

23.17 Operating shaft pushed fully home and felt washer fitted.

the shoes finally in position (it's a bit of a struggle).

The main thing to note is that the brake shoes are handed and numbered 1 and 2: number 1 shoe goes on the left and number 2 on the right. If you look at photo 23.15 again, you should be able to see those numbers cast in the side of the shoes near the top. With the shoes tapped fully home I fitted the washers and split pins to the lower spigots to hold the shoes in place. See photo 23.16. I made sure that the operating shaft was pushed fully home, and then fitted the small felt

HOW TO RESTORE KAWASAKI Z1, Z/KZ900 & Z/KZ1000

23.18 Wheels and tyres completed.

dirt/grease washer round it. See photo 23.17.

The wheels were now finished! See photo 23.18 – wheel porn! (Note that I still needed to fit the rear sprocket and oil/grease seal to the rear wheel before that could be fitted.)

LESSONS LEARNT
• Purists always like to see original, stamped wheel rims, so watch for these if wanting to build an original bike.
• Stainless steel spokes, nickel-plated nipples and stainless rims – what's not to like? (I've always had a thing for nickel-plated nipples ...).
• Rebuilding the wheels yourself is an option.
• Inserting new bearings isn't easy but use as much heat as possible,** cool the bearings, coat the outsides with light oil, and find something suitable to use as a drift – or buy a bearing fitting tool (not sure why I never have).
• Twin disc models have thinner discs than single disc models.
• New discs for a Z900A4 are unavailable, currently.
• My rear wheel bearings were ready greased, sealed-for-life items (as is now normal), but my front bearings weren't: weird.
• Tyres: it's very much a matter of personal choice – ask on one of the forums on the internet or Facebook pages and you'll get 25 different answers.
• Fitting new tyres yourself – life's too short.
• There are three bearings in the rear wheel.
• Never be tempted to re-use old brake shoes, even if they look okay. They glaze over and deteriorate with age. New brake shoes will work so much better.

** Be aware that heating any metal, alloy included, can chemically change its composition, especially if heated unevenly (eg: with a blowtorch rather than in the oven) and weaknesses can occur. So be careful. I've never had any problems with heating parts with a blowtorch, but the metal can change molecular structure if over-heated.

Chapter 24
Fitting the head races, forks & front wheel

Time to sort out the frame ready to accept the rebuilt crankcases. I had already checked the frame for straightness by eye before having it powder coated, and it all looked fine. The very first job was to fit the newly powder coated main stand to the newly powder coated frame, which was quite straightforward if a little fiddly. The method I used was to put the stand roughly in position with the spring attached at both ends, and then use a bar inserted in the mounting holes to lever the stand into the correct position so that the (lightly greased) mounting bolts could be inserted. See photo 24.1.

After this I refitted the steering lock in the bottom yokes by holding it in place with its small grub screw. See photo 24.2. All I did to the steering lock was clean and oil it, and check that it turned with the ignition key before refitting it.

I then checked the state of the old steering head races and bearings. I inspected the ball bearings to discover that many of them were tarnished and had lost their chrome. If you look at photo 24.3, you may see this. I also checked the races to discover that there were dents in them where the bearings had sat in the same position for some time. See photo 24.4. I therefore decided to change the head races and upgrade them to taper roller bearings at the same time. If the original bearings had been okay I would probably have left everything as-was, but they needed changing so I decided to upgrade, as taper roller bearings are definitely better – although not enough to

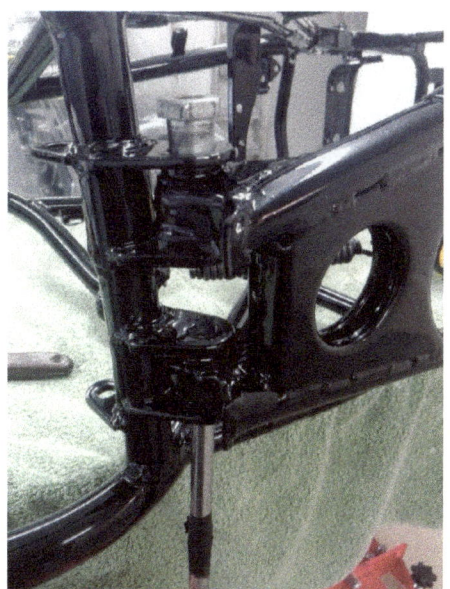

24.1 Fitting the main stand to the frame.

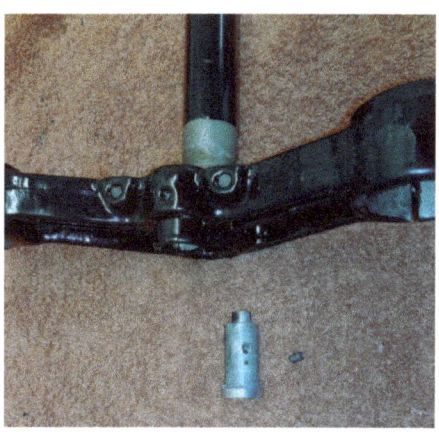

24.2 Steering lock ready to be fitted.

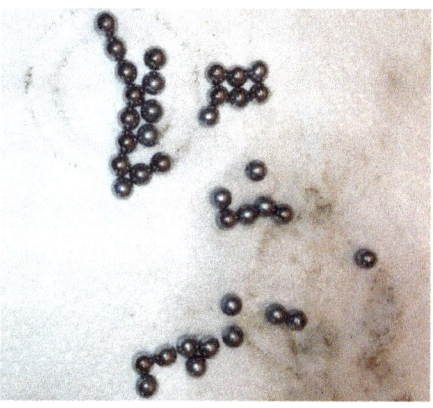

24.3 Old ball bearings have seen better days.

97

24.4 Worn bearing race.

24.5 Removing the old race from the bottom yoke.

24.8 New tapered roller bearing (finally) in place.

warrant changing bearings that are good. (I have two Triumph Tridents, one with roller head races and one without, and you'd never be able to tell which was which, especially in everyday riding conditions – and even on the track.)

Having made the decision to change the races I had to remove the old races from the frame and bottom yoke. Removing them from the frame was straightforward – I heated the head stock and then drifted out the races from the opposite ends with a long drift. Removing the lower race from the lower yokes was harder, however, and required a proper puller. Needless to say, I didn't have one, but eventually managed to remove the old one by using a combination of heat and drifts, and cold chisels/old screwdrivers put to use as drifts. See photo 24.5. It was a pain of a job.

In readiness for fitting the new races I put the bottom yoke and the new inner races in the fridge to shrink them as much as possible. See photo 24.6.

Having heated the head stock quite a bit with a blowtorch I inserted the inner races in the frame. See photo 24.7. Note that the top race sits quite a way down in the head stock, and needs to be carefully driven home to ensure that it's fully seated and sitting square in the frame. With both inner races in situ I heated the new inner bottom tapered race, and inserted it over the yoke stem, tapping it down until it was fully home. See photo 24.8.

Despite cooling the yoke and heating the bearing, the bearing was a real pain to fit. It didn't want to slide down the stem and, without the aid of the proper fitting tool, it wasn't easy to drive home, especially as the new bearings are in an alloy cage sitting on top of the bearing just waiting to

24.6 Cooling the upper bearing race and bottom yoke in the fridge.

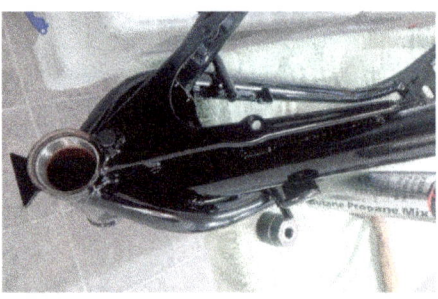

24.7 New tapered top bearing race fitted.

be damaged! Note that I used some waterproof grease to liberally lubricate the bearings before fitting them, as there's no way to add grease after they're assembled. As grease is slightly hygroscopic and thus attracts moisture, it made sense to use a waterproof grease, bearing in mind that this probably won't be changed again for another 40 years!

With the bearings finally located it was time to fit the lower yoke to the frame. Note that the top yoke is fitted separately, and the lower yoke can be attached to the frame without the top yoke. Be advised that there is a special castellated stem nut that goes under the top yoke, and is used to tighten the bottom yoke and head races. There is also a stem bolt that goes on top of the top yoke and holds the top yoke in

position (but doesn't affect how tight the head races are) – the stem bolt is the chrome bolt that is very visible on the bike. See photo 24.15.

The order of assembly of the various nuts and washers is shown in photo 24.9. Note that only the two on the left of the photo go on to the stem underneath the top yoke (the bearing cap and the stem nut), and the three on the right go on top of the top yoke (two washers and the stem bolt).

With the bottom yoke held in position, I fitted the bearing cap and then the stem nut. As with dismantling, I used the 'C' spanner made for adjusting forks to tighten the stem nut. The stem nut should be tightened just enough to ensure there is no play in the bearings, whilst still allowing the forks to turn freely and easily. Note that when I dismantled the yokes the stem nut had clearly been way over-tightened, damaging the bearings – and doing God knows what to the handling – it must have been a frightening ride! See photo 24.10 of the bottom yoke in position, with the top yoke loosely fitted just for checking before being removed again to fit the fork shrouds.

With the bottom yoke in position I prepared to fit the chrome fork shrouds. See photo 24.11 for the order of fitting of the various components. The shrouds and associated spacers and covers were stacked on the top of the bottom yoke, with the top yoke then added and held on to the shrouds with the stem bolt in place. See photo 24.12. It was then time to push the rebuilt forks into the yokes. I soon realised that the easiest way to do this was by removing the top yoke and inserting the forks up through the bottom yokes and shrouds, and then

FITTING THE HEAD RACES, FORKS & FRONT WHEEL

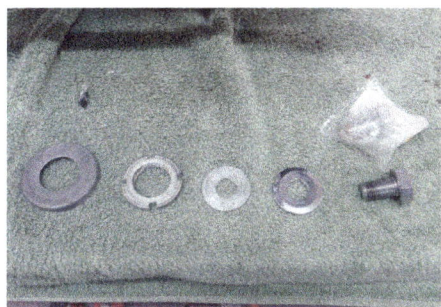

24.9 Order of assembly of top yoke with stem nut second from left and stem bolt on the right (new stem bolt in the little bag above it).

24.10 Bottom yoke in situ and top yoke loosely fitted.

mounting the top yoke. See photo 24.13 of the forks being inserted. Note that when I then added the top yoke, I ensured that the top of both fork stanchions was exactly in line with the top of the yoke to ensure both were exactly the same height.

With the top yoke in position I tightened the stem bolt, added the two chrome cable guides to the top of the forks, and inserted and tightened the four yoke pinch bolts and steering stem pinch bolt. I then bolted the handlebars to the top yoke to complete this section. See photo 24.14. Photo 24.15 shows the stem nut, top yoke, and stem bolt in position.

After this I bolted the rechromed front mudguard into position, together with the cable guides (two in my case as I'm fitting twin discs, so one each side). The cable guides go inside the mudguard – it's hard to fit them incorrectly due to their design. With the handlebars bolted to the top yoke, the frame was ready to accept the front wheel. See photo 24.16.

I then raised the bike onto its centre stand and strapped down the rear of the frame to lift the front forks well clear of the bike lift. This enabled me to then fit the front wheel and bolt it on with the bottom fork leg clamps. The clamps have arrows underneath to show which way round they go. See photo 24.17. I then tightened

and torqued the nuts on the clamp. It's important to tighten the front nuts first and then the rear so that, when completed, there is no gap at the front and a parallel gap at the rear. If the gap to the rear is uneven the clamps are on backwards. See photo 24.18. This clamping method feels strange to

24.12 Fork shrouds loosely fitted.

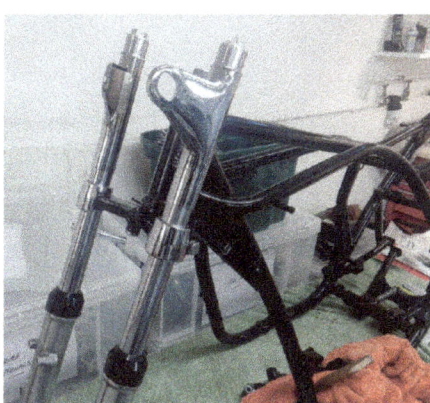

24.13 Fork shrouds fitted with forks inserted and top yoke removed.

24.11 Order of assembly of fork shrouds.

24.14 Yokes, clamps, stem bolt, cable guides and handlebars fitted.

HOW TO RESTORE KAWASAKI Z1, Z/KZ900 & Z/KZ1000

24.15 The stem nut and stem bolt fitted.

me as I have always tightened bottom clamps with an even gap both sides, but not on this occasion. I'm unsure of the engineering principles behind this (it makes for a stronger clamp, or it gives more even pressure on the spindle?) but that's the way it's meant to be.

LESSONS LEARNT
- Over-tightening head bearings will result in bad handling, and irreparable damage to the races in the long term.
- If the head races need changing it may be worth upgrading to taper roller bearings – but for normal road use you probably won't notice the difference.
- Fitting new head races – a real pain (unless you've got the requisite special tool).
- It's impossible to regrease the head bearings without dismantling the yokes after they're fitted, so make sure they're well greased – and possibly use waterproof grease. Also note, this means that the head bearings on most restorations will need replacing as they've probably never been greased.
- Grease is hygroscopic and attracts moisture.
- Fit everything (bottom yoke, forks and fork shrouds) before adding the top yoke.
- Learn the difference between the stem nut and the stem bolt!
- Don't forget to add the cable guides at the top of the yokes, and next to the front mudguard.
- Fit the front mudguard before fitting the front wheel: doing it the other way round is almost impossible.
- Check you've fitted the mudguard round the correct way – it's easy to to get it wrong! The slightly curved end to the front, and the flatter, squarer end to the rear.
- Fit the bottom fork clamps the right way round and tighten the front end first so there's no gap at the front and an even one at the back – strange, but true.

24.16 Forks all fitted, ready for the front wheel.

24.17 Wheel spindle clamps with the arrow pointing forwards.

24.18 Wheel spindle clamps with no gap at the front and an even gap to the rear.

Chapter 25
Replacing the engine in the frame

Time to refit the partially built engine in the frame – exciting! The first thing I did was enlist the help of my friend and neighbour, Rob; I really didn't want to drop the engine or knock over the frame over – or be left holding something that I couldn't put down until someone chanced by (yes, been there, done that!).

To begin with we carefully adjusted the strapping on the frame so that the front wheel was securely on the ground (after it had been raised to enable it to be fitted). See photo 25.1 of us beginning this process. My next job was to ensure that the cam chain was hanging out of the crankcase, and wasn't going to slip down into it. I also laid out all the various engine bolts, plates, spacers, etc, in exactly the right order on the bench, so I could insert them in the correct positions as soon as the engine was in place without having to try and work out what went where.

With towels I covered the bottom section of the frame to avoid it being damaged (and towels are relatively easy to remove later). Having done this, Rob held the frame whilst I simply lifted the half-completed engine into position.

25.1 A smiling Rob helping to adjust and strap down the frame.

This went surprisingly smoothly, the only slight problem being that I briefly trapped my arm between the engine and the frame as I lifted it in, but this saved the engine and frame from damage so was well worth it!

We removed the towels and the engine slotted into position without fuss, and was soon bolted in place, with the cam chain cable-tied to the top frame tube. See photo 25.2 of a still-smiling Rob with the engine in situ.

I then took some time to fully strap down the bike so that I was 100 per cent sure it was safe and secure, and able to withstand the rigours of reconstruction. See photo 25.3.

The only real item of note in this process was that the two bolts on the left rear upper engine mounting are of differing lengths, with the longer bolt going to the top. See photo 25.4. Although on my Z1A they are of equal length.

LESSONS LEARNT
- This is one way of refitting the engine – there are others.
- It's always a good idea to ask a friend for help rather than risk major damage or becoming stuck.
- Note that I had deliberately only partially built the engine, for two reasons: firstly so that it was still light enough to carry easily, and secondly so I could use the frame as a glorified engine stand to rebuild the rest of the engine.
- Putting the engine back in the frame was a major milestone!

25.4 Note that these two mounting bolts are of different lengths.

25.2 The engine back in the frame – and Rob's still smiling!

25.3 The bike now fully strapped down.

Chapter 26
Refitting the pistons & cylinder barrels

With the engine back in the frame the next job was to check and fit the pistons and the cylinder barrels. First of all I checked the pistons and piston rings as thoroughly as I could. Both the pistons and bores looked to be in good condition, thankfully, as replacing the pistons and having a re-bore was an expense I could do without – even replacing the rings wasn't something I wanted to have to do.

Various checks are specified in the *Kawasaki Workshop Manual*, with working tolerances given, so I followed these. First of all, I checked the wear on the pistons themselves. See photo 26.1. Next up, was thickness of the piston rings (see photo 26.2), followed by piston ring gaps. See photo 26.3 of the rings inserted in the bottom third of the bores, and the gap being checked with feeler gauges. After this, I checked that the grooves in the pistons for the rings weren't excessively worn: see photo 26.4. Finally, I checked the open gap on the rings to ensure these had not lost their springiness over the years. See photo 26.5. I'm pleased to say that all measurements were within the tolerances given in the *Kawasaki Workshop Manual*, so the pistons and rings were re-used. I hoped that this proved to be a prudent rather than a poor decision (I'm very glad to report that now the bike's finished it runs very well with no hint of smoke or piston slap).

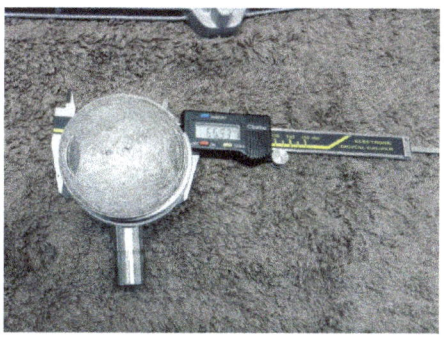

26.1 Checking for piston wear.

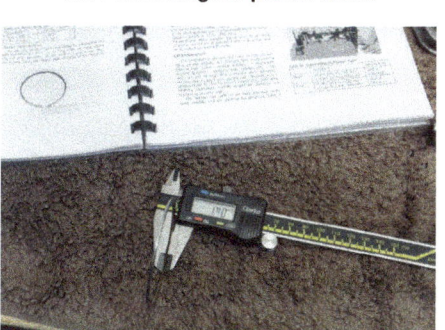

26.2 Checking ring thickness.

26.3 Checking ring end gaps.

26.4 Checking ring groove wear.

It's also worth noting that Kawasaki numbers its cylinders left-to-right 1-2-3-4. I am used to British bikes where they are numbered right-to-left, with No 1 cylinder being on the right. I stuck with Kawasaki's

HOW TO RESTORE KAWASAKI Z1, Z/KZ900 & Z/KZ1000

26.5 Checking springiness of rings.

26.6 Fitting new gudgeon pin circlips to the pistons.

method of numbering the cylinders, with No 1 cylinder being on the left (as you sit on the bike).

Having decided to re-use the pistons and rings, I gently heated the pistons and con rods before fitting the former by sliding home the gudgeon pins. Note that it is very easy to damage the con rods by applying heat to them, so they should be only lightly warmed to avoid this. Also note that each piston has an arrow on the crown showing which way it should be fitted. I also ensured that each piston went back in its original position. Although I was going to hone the cylinders, I thought it best to return everything to the same place wherever possible.

With the pistons in place I fitted new gudgeon pin circlips, and, in order to do this, I covered the crankcase opening with towels to ensure no errant circlip pinged off and ended up in the crankcase. See photo 26.6. When the circlips were fitted, I rotated them to ensure that the opening in them didn't align with the little opening in the piston side. I had previously cleaned the piston crowns, and removed all the carbon deposit which can cause overheating and pre-ignition.

I then turned to the cylinder barrels. A quick inspection showed that, despite having been blast cleaned, there were still small stones and dirt in between the cylinders, which needed cleaning out to maximise airflow and thus cooling, especially of the two middle cylinders. See photo 26.7. Having cleaned the fins, I measured the tops and bottoms

26.7 Cleaning detritus from between the cylinders on the barrels.

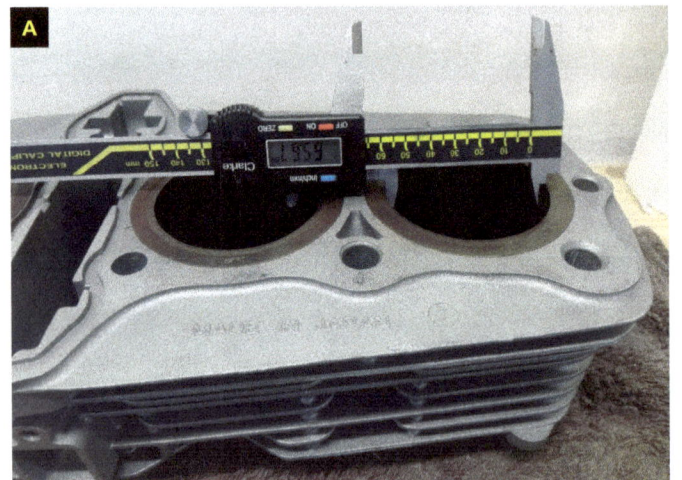

26.8 A. Measuring the top of the bores; B. Measuring the bottom of the bores.

REFITTING THE PISTONS & CYLINDER BARRELS

of the cylinder bores to check that they were all still in tolerance, which they were. See photos 26.8 A and B. Note that the measurements should, ideally, be taken a little further down the bores, for which a proper internal micrometer/bore gauge is required, which I didn't have, so I went with the measurements from either end of the bores as they were well within the tolerances given in the workshop manual. With the bores within tolerance but showing signs of slight rusting, I prepared to hone them using a three-legged honing tool in my cordless drill. See photo 26.9.

Having applied a little light oil, I honed each cylinder, trying to create a cross-hatched pattern by running the honing tool up and down the barrels quite quickly. See photo 26.10. As I honed one of the cylinders, I noticed a vertical score at the top of the bore which wasn't great news. See photo 26.11. However, after a little more honing I managed to remove the mark altogether. See photo 26.12. I hoped that my faith in the pistons, rings and bores (and Kawasaki engineering) would not be in vain.

I replaced the old, broken cam chain guide with a new one. See photo 26.13 of the old and new one. I then screwed it back into the tunnel on the cylinder block. See photo 26.14. I also refitted the central cam chain guide in the top of the crankcases using new rubbers – conveniently marked as to which way up they went – as with all parts that required fitting a certain way round. See photo 26.15.

I had already refitted the piston rings to the pistons, but double-checked that I had them in the right order and the right way up, as per the diagrams in the workshop manual. I then turned the top and bottom piston rings on each piston so that the gaps faced forward, and the middle ring so that the gap faced backward. See photos 26.16 and 26.17.

As with the bottom fork clamps I was confused by this. I was always taught to space the ring gaps evenly round the piston, and ensure that none of the gaps was directly in line with either the front or rear of the piston, where most wear occurs. Here, I was being told to actually line up two gaps (top and bottom rings) and align all three ring gaps directly with the front and rear of the bores! What the engineering thinking is behind this one is totally beyond me – but you know what they say: every day in the workshop is a school day.

It's also important to ensure that the large spigots at the bottoms of two of the cylinder head studs are at the front two corners, not the rear, where they will also fit. In my case, of course, this wasn't a problem as I'd not removed either the cylinder head studs or the two spigots in the first place. See photo 26.18.

I next fitted round the base of each cylinder the four new red 'O' ring seals (see photo 26.19) before placing a new cylinder base gasket in position, fitted dry. I used towels to hold the pistons relatively securely but gently in an upright position, and

26.9 Preparing to hone the cylinder bores.

26.10 Honing the bores.

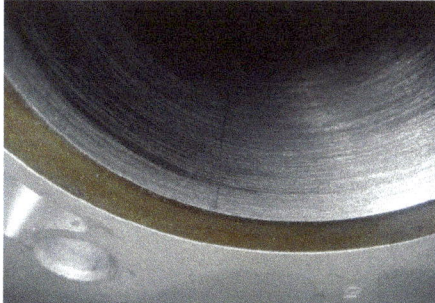
26.11 A vertical score in one of the bores – bad news.

26.12 The score has been honed out.

26.13 The new and the remains of the old cam chain guide.

HOW TO RESTORE KAWASAKI Z1, Z/KZ900 & Z/KZ1000

26.14 The new guide in situ.

26.16 The top and bottom piston ring gaps to the front.

26.18 The two spacers on the cylinder head bolts on the front corners – not the rear.

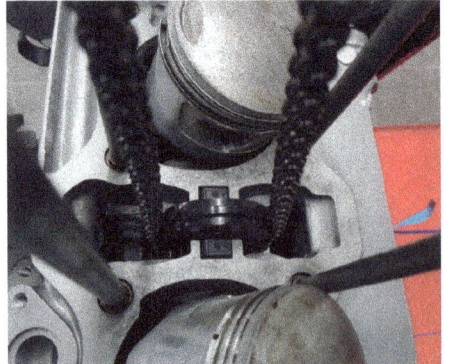

26.15 The central cam chain roller in situ with new rubbers.

26.17 The central piston ring gap to the rear.

26.19 New O rings fitted to the bottom of each cylinder.

all was ready to replace the barrels. See photo 26.20.

Now, I didn't have the special tool for holding the pistons still, referred to in the manual, so I fitted the cylinder barrels by hand. The bottoms of each cylinder are nicely chamfered, so if you're careful enough, you can lower the block onto the pistons and gently ease the piston rings into the bores using the chamfer to compress them. The first thing I did was to once again call upon my neighbour, Rob, to take the weight of the barrels whilst I concentrated on feeding the rings into the bores. In retrospect, I think you could probably do this entire exercise on your own, but only with a lot of practice, and even then it'd be difficult, so better to have a friend to help.

I double-checked that the cylinder barrels were the right way round: this may sound silly but I'll bet there's been a fair degree of heartache in the past where people have accidentally put the barrels on backwards! Having established that the barrels were indeed the correct way round, we fed the dear old cam chain through the tunnel, and once

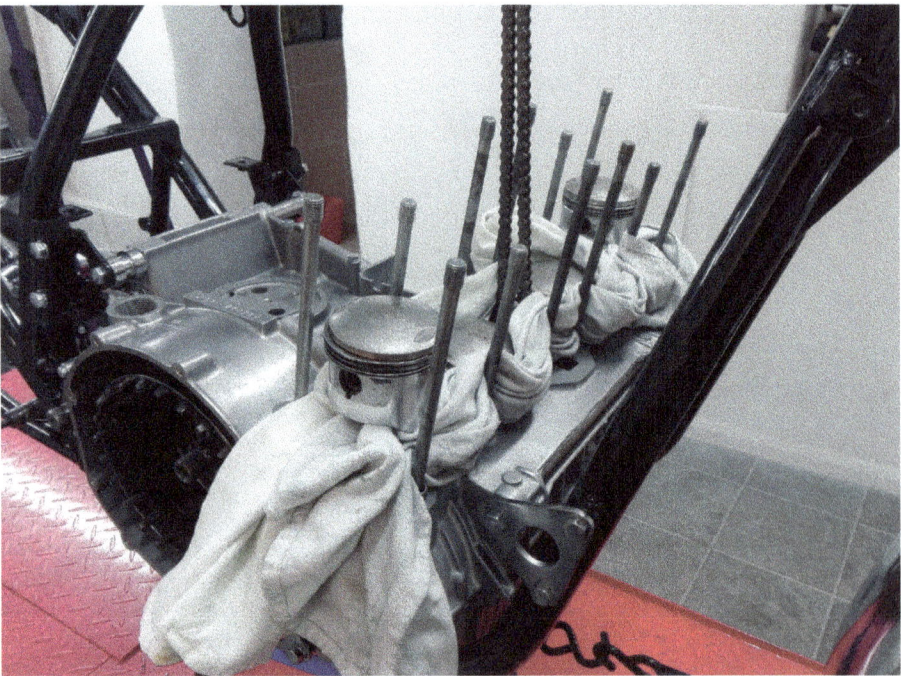

26.20 New cylinder base gasket fitted dry and pistons held in position with towels.

again secured it to the top frame tube with a cable tie to keep it out of the way and safe. We then slowly lowered the barrels onto the pistons, removing the supporting towels as we went, and gently squeezing and feeding piston rings into cylinder bores. See photo 26.21 of the barrels with the piston rings of the two outer cylinders safely inside their cylinders.

REFITTING THE PISTONS & CYLINDER BARRELS

26.21 Cylinder block half way on with the two outer pistons in their bores. Cam chain secured to frame.

26.22 The cylinder block in position – all looking good.

A little while later – and with great relief – we finally had all four pistons fitted without hearing the sound of snapping rings, and the barrels were fully tapped home. See photo 26.22.

The first thing I did after this was gingerly turn over the engine to check for any scoring on the cylinder walls, which would indicate a broken or unseated piston ring or circlip. Thankfully, all seemed well. I once had a ring that wasn't seated properly (a nasty 3-piece oil ring), and it made a horrible mess of the cylinder wall after only a couple of turns of the crankshaft.

LESSONS LEARNT
• To re-bore or not to re-bore: that is the question. If the engine's quite low mileage and hasn't been smoking or making strange rattling sounds (piston slap), I'd say 'not.' The problem in this case was that, whilst I was pretty sure the mileage was correct, I'd not seen or heard the engine running, so had no idea if there were any problems with the engine smoking or rattling, etc. I decided that bore, piston and ring condition was such that a re-bore wasn't necessary – but each case must be examined on its merits. One of the jobs most frequently carried out unnecessarily is a re-bore. Don't simply assume it needs one.
• A whole host of checks can be made on the pistons and rings, etc, and these are all outlined in the *Kawasaki Service Manual* – an essential publication.
• Most parts on the engine that require fitting a certain way round on the engine are marked as such – and this includes the pistons.
• The piston rings should be fitted with the gaps to the front and rear as detailed above.
• With care, the cylinder barrels can be fitted by hand without piston ring compressors or the special tool to support the pistons.
• Fit the cylinder base gasket dry, and slide the four 'O' rings onto the bottom of the cylinders.
• Don't forget to fit the intermediate cam chain guide in the top of the crankcases, or the guide in the tunnel in the barrels.
• Check the barrels are the right way round!
• Don't let that flipping cam chain drop!

www.velocebooks.com
New book news • Special offers • Newsletter • Details of all Veloce books • Gift Vouchers

Chapter 27
Reassembling & refitting the cylinder head

Time to sort out the cylinder head. Before taking it to be vapour blasted I removed the valves with the aid of a valve spring compressor. If you wish to see detailed guidance on this, I would recommend watching this video on my YouTube channel: www.youtube.com/watch?v=yjIbVtzFJUE. I gave it a more comprehensive examination on its return, from which I established that the head was flat and true and didn't require skimming (which would have been unusual), and no fins were broken or damaged. However, I realised that the exhaust valve guides were quite badly worn, especially on No 4 cylinder, and so decided to have a full set of exhaust guides fitted. I determined the wear in the guides by inserting the valves in their respective guides, and then seeing how much sideways play there was; there was clearly quite a bit in the exhaust guides. Note that in order to ascertain the amount of wear in the guides, you have to insert the valves nearly all the way in before rocking them to determine the amount of play – there will be quite considerable play if the valve is inserted only a short way into its guide.

I also noted that two of the four sparkplug threads were badly

27.1 Cleaning out the oilways.

damaged and needed helicoiling. As I have no inclination to try and remove and replace valve guides, and not much more enthusiasm for inserting new threads (although this job is a lot better than replacing valve guides), I took the head to my local engineering shop to have this done. I'm glad I did, too, as, when I went to collect it, they told me what a horrible job it had been trying to remove the old valve guides, which didn't want to come out – and that was with all their special tools and presses, etc. Sometimes, discretion is the better part of valour.

With the head back from the engineer's, I gave it a thorough clean with water, compressed air, and a set of brushes – especially the oilways.

REASSEMBLING & REFITTING THE CYLINDER HEAD

Even then, I wasn't too sure I'd got out all of the blast cleaning beads. See photo 27.1. I then ran a tap down all the stud holes in the head. For whatever reason, all of the threads in the head were in really poor condition, and required quite a bit of effort to clear. I'm not sure why this is, but it would appear to be something to do with the vapour blasting, which somehow reacted with the metal in the threads to corrode them in some way and make them very tight. See photo 27.2 of tapping the inlet threads – note the large amount of crud lying on the bench that's been cut out of various threads.

I then checked the valve stems for excessive wear, but they seemed okay (see photo 27.3), so I gave them a thorough clean, finishing off with Scotch-Brite (a wonderful cleaning material that is quite abrasive without scratching) for a nice, shiny finish. I then loosely inserted the valves into their guides and checked the amount they protruded above the head (they were all still within tolerance: see photo 27.4). I especially checked this because, as I'd had new guides fitted, the engineer had re-cut all the valve seats (including the inlets), meaning that the valves sat deeper in the combustion chambers. Even though the valve stem protrusions were still within tolerance, I knew that much smaller shims would now be required on the tappets.

With the guides and valves deemed serviceable, I ground in the valves, using two methods – by hand and by machine. I began lapping the valves by hand using my old wooden shaft and lapping paste. See photo 27.5. I attached the sucker to the valve head, applied some coarse grinding paste, and began lapping

27.2 Running a tap down all the threads.

27.3 Checking valve stems.

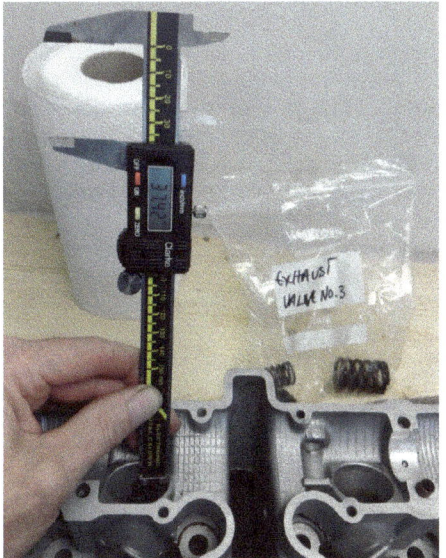

27.4 Measuring how far the valve stem protrudes above the cylinder head.

27.5 Preparing to lap in the valves.

HOW TO RESTORE KAWASAKI Z1, Z/KZ900 & Z/KZ1000

27.6 Lapping the valves manually.

27.7 Lapping the valves with a special powered tool.

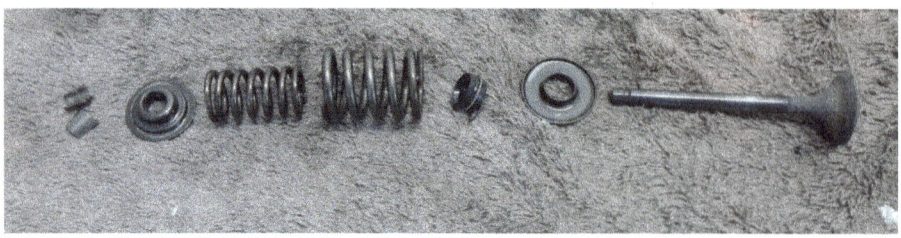

27.8 The valve assembly.

in the valves by rolling the shaft between my hands, like trying to light a fire with a wooden stick. See photo 27.6. Needless to say, after a while I'd had enough of this and attached the special lapping tool to my cordless drill (which rotates the valve backwards and forwards), and used that instead. See photo 27.7. I started each valve with coarse paste and finished with fine paste, ensuring that all of the paste was fully removed each time. You know that the valves are properly ground in when the mating surface turns a uniform grey around its circumference.

With the valves lapped in it was time to begin reassembling the head. The component parts of each valve assembly can be seen in photo 27.8, from when I removed the valves from the head. I began by fitting new oil seals to the tops of the valve guides. Luckily, I had only fitted two when I realised my mistake – see photo 27.9. Can you spot it? – I hadn't fitted the valve spring seats before the seals, and the seats won't go over the seals. I therefore had to prise off the seals (terminally damaging them in the process) before fitting the spring seats, and then fitting the new, new stem seals. You live and learn. See photo 27.10.

I then checked the valve springs for length as they are known to compress with age. The larger, outer springs were fine, but the smaller, inner springs were a bit on the short side, so I replaced them with new. See photo 27.11. As with many parts of the engine I could have replaced them with uprated items but decided not to for the usual reasons –
• Uprated parts are more expensive.
• I wasn't planning on racing the bike so didn't need to try and wring every ounce of power from the engine.
• Less stress on the engine and mechanical parts should mean greater reliability.
• Unlike most bikes I've worked on (mostly British, it has to be said), the Kawasaki Z900 engine is incredibly well sorted, and doesn't really have any weak points that require upgrading/modernising (apart from the front cam chain guide for which there is no upgrade available).

With new springs in hand I refitted the valves and valve springs

REASSEMBLING & REFITTING THE CYLINDER HEAD

27.9 New valve stem seals fitted – but what's been forgotten?

27.10 New, new valve stem seals fitted – *after* the valve spring seats!

27.11 Checking valve springs – too short.

27.12 Fitting the valve springs.

with my valve spring compressor. See photo 27.12 of the collets being inserted on a valve stem. The main item of note here is that I needed to keep the frame of the compressor in line with the camshafts, so that it didn't foul on and possibly damage the top edges of the cylinder head. Before too long, all of the valves were refitted in the head. See photos 27.13 and 27.14. If you wish to see detailed guidance on refitting valves, then I would recommend watching this video on my YouTube channel: www.youtube.com/watch?v=CPjQ5i5nWBQ .

I then gave each valve stem a good wallop with the soft end of a lump hammer to ensure they were seated properly (although I later discovered that, even then, one of the exhaust valves wasn't fully settled).

The head was now ready to fit on the barrels so I fitted the two cam chain idler gears in the top of the barrels. The one to the rear has the mechanism that the cam chain tensioner acts on to tension the chain. See photo 27.15. Note the idler gear mounting rubbers have 'up' written on them, the same as those for the roller guide on the top of the crankcases – these go to the top! I also fitted a new rubber seal to the cam chain aperture. Note that the seal didn't quite sit properly in its groove, so I held it in place with some Wellseal. I then fitted two new cylinder head gaskets over the cylinder head studs, with the larger elliptical metal surfaces around the cylinders facing upwards. I fitted this gasket dry. See photo 27.16.

I re-annealed the copper washers that go under the cylinder head nuts by heating them until they were cherry red, and then quenching them in water. See photo 27.17.

27.13 Valves fitted 1.

27.14 Valves fitted 2.

HOW TO RESTORE KAWASAKI Z1, Z/KZ900 & Z/KZ1000

27.15 Fitting the cam chain guides and rubber seal.

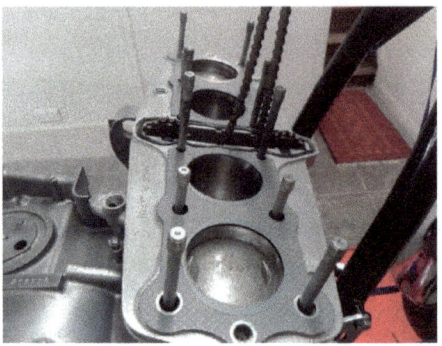

27.16 Cylinder head gasket fitted dry and with the larger metal flanges round the cylinders facing upwards.

27.17 Annealing the copper washers for the cylinder head nuts.

27.18 Cylinder head fitted in position and cylinder head nuts loosely tightened.

27.19 Torqueing up the cylinder head nuts.

Annealing them makes them soft and malleable again so they would flatten slightly when the nuts were torqued, and provide a leak-free seal on the studs that have oil flowing over them to lubricate the camshafts.

Actually fitting the head was quite straightforward. First of all I checked I had the head the right way round (yes, this can go on backwards too!) before resting it on the rear of the engine and feeding through the cam chain. I then sat the head on top of the studs whilst I cable-tied the cam chain to the top rail of the frame (again!). I then slid the head down over the studs and loosely fitted the 12 cylinder head nuts and two small outer bolts. See photo 27.18. The main item of note was to ensure that the central rubber oil seal remained in its groove and didn't come unseated before the head was home. After this, all that remained was to torque the cylinder head nuts in the weird order prescribed in the manual (another counter-intuitive sequence like that of tightening the crankshaft bolts, and of piston ring orientation) and the head was back on. See photo 27.19.

LESSONS LEARNT
- To get an engine to run well one of the most important components is the cylinder head, so it's important to get this right,
- If you want more power, quite a few upgraded parts are available to improve performance.
- If in doubt, farm out the work. I know my limitations, so get specialists to complete work for me that I either can't do or really don't like doing,
- On the other hand it's always good to learn new skills – you just have to get the balance right.
- Scotch-Brite is a great cleaning and polishing tool – just make sure to buy the heavy-duty pads and not the ones for washing-up!
- Annealing copper (as with washers and some cylinder head gaskets) makes it soft again. The jury's out as to whether you heat it and then leave it to cool or heat it and then quench it. I'm no metallurgist so can't comment on this. I quench the copper as it's more fun!
- Both the cylinder base and cylinder head gaskets are fitted dry.
- Fit the head gasket with the large metal rings uppermost.
- Fit the valve spring seats before the valve stem seals.
- Tighten the cylinder head nuts in the strange order specified in the manual.
- Do you torque nuts up or down? Just realised I'm not sure, so interchange both words at random!
- Every day in the workshop is a school day – if you think you already know it all then you're a poor mechanic.
- Note that there is a locating dowel at each end of the cylinder head that may have been removed by the engineers whilst machining etc – check they are still there!

Chapter 28
Camshafts, tappets & oil pressure switch

With the cylinder head in position it was time to fit the camshafts and adjust the tappets. First off, I refitted the tappet buckets with the shims on top. See photo 28.1. Unfortunately, I couldn't put the buckets in the same places they had come out of due to my idiocy when taking apart the head. In this case, I just checked that they all fitted well with no looseness or tightness, and hoped for the best. Likewise, I had no idea which shim went where, so fitted them at random (although I knew this would make little difference due to having had the valve seats recut).

I then tapped the new camshaft bearing shells into place on the head and in the bearing caps. See photo 28.2. Note that there is a hole for the oilway in all the shells so they can't be incorrectly fitted. (Some bearing shells only have holes for the oilways in half of them, to align with the oilways in the head, and solid ones for the bearing caps without the oilways. It's been known for the solid shells to be accidentally fitted in the wrong place, so blocking the oilway. Kawasaki, as ever, has made sure that things are as foolproof as possible.) Also note that the tappet buckets have all been fitted with the gap towards the top,

28.1 Refitting the tappets with shims on the top.

which makes prising out shims a lot easier later on. (Although the buckets spin round quite quickly when the engine's turning so the gap can easily move out of sight. To remedy this keep turning the engine over until the gap comes round to the top again.)

In preparation for fitting the camshafts I rotated the engine (by means of a 17mm spanner on the advance and retard nut on the end of the crankshaft) so that the 'T' mark on the 1 and 4 side of the advance and retard mechanism was directly in line

113

HOW TO RESTORE KAWASAKI Z1, Z/KZ900 & Z/KZ1000

28.2 Fitting new camshaft bearings- note the tappets are turned so that the gaps are facing upwards to facilitate shim removal later.

28.3 Engine turned so that the 'T' mark on the advance and retard unit aligns with the mark on the crankcase.

28.4 Loosely fitting the cams – the right way round!

28.5 The arrow on the edge of the exhaust camshaft sprocket.

with the mark on the crankcases. See photo 28.3. This set the valve timing to factory standard.

I then slid the camshafts under the loose cam chain so that they were roughly in position. Note that the exhaust camshaft is the one with the worm drive on it for the tacho drive. Also note that Kawasaki seems to have considered the experience of the mechanic who might work on these engines and also stamped the shafts 'L' and 'R' to ensure they aren't put on the wrong way round. It really has thought of just about everything! See photo 28.4.

28.6 Aligning the mark on the exhaust camshaft with the top edge of the cylinder head.

I then found the small arrow stamped on the exhaust camshaft sprocket which is used to set the valve timing. See photo 28.5. I highlighted this with Tipp-Ex so that it was easy to see. I then engaged the cam chain and aligned the arrow on the camshaft with the top of the cylinder head. See photo 28.6. I counted round 28 pins on the cam chain, starting from the pin above the mark on the exhaust camshaft, until I reached 28. That pin aligns with the number 28 clearly stamped on the side of the inlet camshaft (amazing coincidence!). I had also highlighted the number on the inlet camshaft and the 28th pin on the chain so it was easy to see that everything lined up okay. See photo 28.7. That was the valve timing sorted – or was it?

It's important to note that I actually got the timing slightly wrong to begin with. If you look again at photo 28.7 you can see that I'd originally highlighted the pin to the left of the correct one on the cam chain as the right one, so had to scratch off the Tipp-Ex before marking the correct one next to it. The reason for this is that the cam chain was quite slack between the crankshaft and exhaust camshaft, and when I had originally lined up the exhaust camshaft, unbeknown to me, it was

28.7 Counting round 28 pins on the cam chain and aligning the 28th pin with the mark '28' on the inlet camshaft.

CAMSHAFTS, TAPPETS & OIL PRESSURE SWITCH

28.8 Fitting the camshaft bearing caps.

28.9 The top cam chain tensioner fitted – facing the same way as it was prior to removal.

one link out relative to the crankshaft. It was only when I applied tension on the cam chain that the exhaust camshaft turned, taking up the slack, and revealing that it was actually a link out. I therefore had to move the cam chain round a link on the exhaust camshaft to remove the slack, do the same for the inlet camshaft position, and re-mark the 28th pin. If I'd not noticed this the entire valve timing would have been one chain link, or about 10 degrees, out!

Note that the valve timing was now set as it left the factory – standard factory setting. However, this is almost certainly not the optimum setting as it is only a general setting. Due to tolerances in manufacture and assembly, etc, most engines won't have the valve timing at the optimum setting, just pretty good (standard factory setting) – it's a bit of a lottery; some engines will be better than others. You can buy new camshaft sprockets that are adjustable to allow you to turn the sprockets very slightly to set the valve timing to the absolute optimum position. To do this you will also need a couple of dial gauges and a timing disc for the crankshaft. I was thinking of doing this but, to be honest, I just couldn't be bothered! I wasn't going to race my bike or do burn-outs, etc, and, as far as I was concerned, the standard factory setting on the valve timing was fine. Anyway, I was running out of time and money (again), and that was as good an excuse as any. If you do wish to fine-tune the valve timing you can find details of stockists who specialise in performance upgrades at the back of this manual.

With the camshafts now correctly timed (hopefully), I fitted the bearing caps, torqueing them in order as per the workshop manual. See photo 28.8. After this I fitted the top cam chain tensioner to the top of the head. See photo 28.9. With this in place, I again checked the valve timing and all was well. Gingerly, I also turned over the engine several times to check that the valves weren't hitting each other or the pistons, etc. All seemed well.

Note that the original valve timing marks on the cam chain and camshafts only line up something like every 90 turns of the engine (It's true – honest!), so if you want to keep the marks you made in the right place, turn over the engine forwards and backwards so you can check them again if needs be, but be careful when turning over the engine backwards before the cam chain has been tensioned.

At this point I fitted the cam chain tensioner along with the oil pressure switch and engine breather at the same time, as I thought this would be best and easiest in terms of order of assembly (no carburettors, etc, in the way).

First off I fitted the oil pressure switch body to the engine, having fitted two new 'O' ring seals to where the assembly mounts to the crankcases – and a further one under the inspection cap. See photo 28.10. I also fitted the base of the engine breather to the crankcases. See photo 28.11. I fitted a new 'O' ring to the oil pressure switch body and screwed it into position. See photo 28.12. After this I cleaned and checked the cam chain tensioner – which is a fiendishly simple piece of kit: a rod with a spring behind it. See photo 28.13. I fitted the cam chain tensioner to the engine together with

28.10 Oil pressure switch base being fitted, with new 'O' rings.

28.11 Engine breather base plate fitted.

HOW TO RESTORE KAWASAKI Z1, Z/KZ900 & Z/KZ1000

28.12 Oil pressure switch fitted with new 'O' ring.

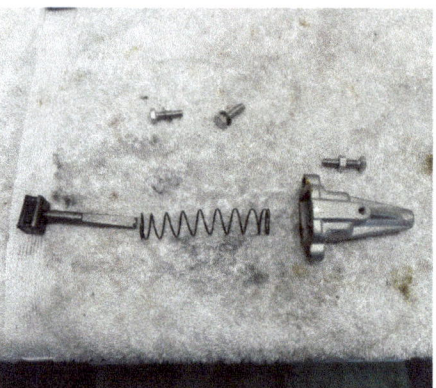

28.13 Cam chain tensioner mechanism checked ready for reassembly.

28.14 Engine breather, oil pressure switch and cam chain tensioner in place.

the engine breather cover (with new 'O' ring underneath it). See photo 28.14. I then rotated the engine a few more times to check that all was working properly. All still seemed well. (Don't forget to turn the engine at every step in case something is wrong.) I then set the camchain tension by loosening the lock nut on the side of the tensioner, turning the engine over a few times, and then retightening it – the spring inside the unit pushes the rod tight against the cam chain with just the right amount of pressure.

Next up it was time to adjust the tappets. To begin with I had to measure the existing gaps, and, from these, work out what size shims were required to achieve the correct gaps. Unfortunately, I quickly discovered that there were no gaps at all on any of my tappets. I'd had the valve seats re-cut and this had closed up any gap there might have been. I couldn't measure the tappet clearances as there weren't any – damn! I had to order a few very thin shims (2.20, 2.30 and 2.40mm thickness) so that I could insert them, one at a time, in place of the existing, much thicker shims, to give me a clearance to measure, from which I could order the correct size shims and then insert them. This meant I had the very laborious job of removing each shim in turn, replacing it with one of the thin shims, measuring the gap, removing the thin shim (so it could be used to measure another tappet), replacing the old shim (you will damage the camshafts if you turn over the engine without a shim in place), before ordering the correct size shims and replacing all of the original shims with the correct ones: phew!

I had thought of maybe checking the tappets on the bench before fitting the cylinder head, temporarily fitting the camshafts to check clearances and changing shims by then removing the camshafts, and I rather wished I had done at that point!

Anyway, undeterred, I set about the job. I'd bought a 'special tool' for removing shims which duly arrived not looking very special at all and with no instructions. Hmmm. The 'special tool' was in two parts: one was to hold down the tappet whilst the other was used to prise out the shim from the top of the tappet. The method I adopted was to open the valve in question by rotating the camshaft, slotting the wedge in to hold the tappet, then turning the camshaft to move the cam out of the way before prising out the shim with the special tool, and finally pulling it out with a small magnet. See photo 28.15. This may sound pretty straightforward, but the wedge to hold the tappet must be placed on the very edge of the tappet, not on the shim itself (otherwise the shim won't come out), and the edge of the tappet is really thin. Trying to get that wedge to sit just on the edge without catching the shim was very difficult. I also realised that, as the engine was turned over, the tappets had a tendency to turn in their housings – quite rapidly – which

28.15 Removing one of the shims with special tools and a small magnet.

CAMSHAFTS, TAPPETS & OIL PRESSURE SWITCH

meant that the little groove in the tappets (there so that it's possible to prise out the shims with the special tool) are often no longer at the top where you set them, but out of sight down at the bottom. You therefore have to try and rotate the tappet to get the groove back to the top – not easy.

Halfway through this little exercise I made a discovery that helped no end. It suddenly dawned on me that the little metal W-shaped removal tool was, in fact, asymmetrical, with one side much wider than the other, and that, if I used the thinner end, the whole process was much easier. Dear special tool manufacturer, thanks so much for the instructions – not! See photo 28.16 of the tool with different thicknesses on each side (the damage you can see was caused by me trying to tap the wedge sideways when in place to get it off the shim and just on the tappet!).

Only later on did I discover that the original factory tool for removing and fitting shims is still available, and is such a better tool! See photo 28.16A. Once the valve has been fully depressed by rotating the camshaft to open the valve, the tool is clamped to the side of the cylinder head with the tip resting on the edge of the tappet bucket. The camshaft is then turned again to move the cam lobe out of the way, and with the tip of the tool still holding down the tappet, the shim can be removed or replaced. See photo 28.16B

Eventually, all of the old shims

28.16B The tool is clamped to the side of the cylinder head and holds down the tappet.

28.17 A selection of different sized shims.

were removed one-at-a-time and replaced with thin shims (between 2.20 and 2.40), thin enough to provide a gap to be measured. See photo 28.17. From these measurements I was able to order the correct size shims and go through the process of inserting the final shims. Having done so, I checked the tappet gap with my feeler gauges. You are trying to achieve a gap between 0.05 and 0.10mm. Shim sizes go up by 0.05mm, so if the gap is, say, 0.04mm, and you have a 240 shim fitted, fit a thinner 235 shim, which will take the gap to 0.09mm, which is within tolerance. If the gap is 0.12mm with a 260 shim fitted, fit a 0.05mm thicker shim (265) to take the gap down to 0.07mm, again within tolerance. See photo 28.17 of a selection of shims, and photo 28.18 of the gaps being checked. In the photo, note that the tip of the cam is directly opposite the shim, which is where it should be for measurement (not just off-cam, but 180 degrees round). Having said this I later discovered that some engine rebuilders measure the widest gap, wherever that may be, and take their reading from that.

With the tappets set (at last!) it was time to fit the cam cover. This appeared symmetrical but, when I trial fitted it, for some reason it fitted much better one way round than the other, so that's how I assembled it. See photo 28.19 of the cam cover not mating properly with the head when fitted one way round. I then fitted the little half-moon rubber seals

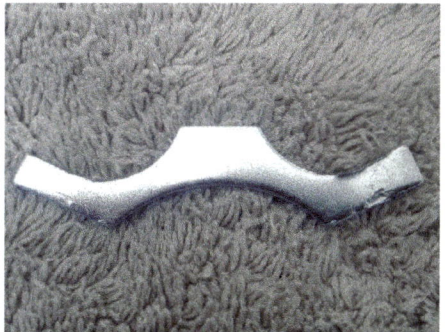

28.16 The wedge has one side wider than the other – as I eventually discovered!

28.16A The factory shim removal tool – so much better!

28.18 Checking the tappet gap.

HOW TO RESTORE KAWASAKI Z1, Z/KZ900 & Z/KZ1000

28.19 Cam cover should go on either way, but it didn't seem to fit one way round.

28.20 Rubber seals fitted with Wellseal, but gasket fitted dry to enable easy removal to check tappets after running in.

28.21 Cam cover fitted!

to the ends of the camshaft bores, and sealed them with Wellseal. The manual recommends plastic gasket but I thought I'd trust to Wellseal (as always). I fitted the gasket dry so that I would be able to remove the cam cover without too much problem to check the tappets after running in. I later discovered that the cam cover should be fitted dry anyway, as it doesn't generally leak and it's a lot easier to remove at a later date. See photo 28.20.

I was then finally able to bolt on the cam cover and torque the bolts. (Don't forget to fit the 4 HT cable clips under the four bolts to the front of the inlet cam. See photo 28.21.) After much struggle it was finally job done. Putting on the cam cover and effectively 'closing' the engine was another big milestone.

LESSONS LEARNT

- Camshaft bearings are a universal fit.
- Camshafts are stamped 'L' and 'R' to ensure correct orientation.
- The inlet and exhaust camshafts aren't stamped as such but the exhaust cam has the drive on it for the tacho, so is easy to identify.
- Fit the oil pressure switch and engine breather at this point as they're easy to get at, together with the cam chain tensioner.
- I set the camshaft timing without the tensioner, but then checked it with the tensioner tightened to make sure it was all in-line.
- Basic valve timing is easy to set. Align the arrow on the exhaust cam with the top of the cylinder head, then count round 28 pins on the cam chain and align that with the number 28 on the inlet cam shaft. First check that the cam chain is taut between the crankshaft and exhaust cam shaft.
- You can set the valve timing to its optimum position by using adjustable camshaft sprockets and a dial gauge and degree disc to exactly set the valve timing. The amount this will improve performance varies from engine to engine – but it nearly always improves it to a degree. You can, of course, fit high-lift cams, lighter valves, stronger valve springs, etc, too, but, for me, the engine is fine as it is in standard form. If I ever go over the ton again it's because the throttle's jammed ...
- If you recut the valve seats, all of the old shims will be too thick to even get a reading.
- The 'Bat Wing' shim removal tool I used was okay, but the factory one is far better. Available from suppliers such as Z-Power (see page 218).
- Note that shims fitted to very early bikes were prone to breaking and were soon upgraded.
- Trial-fit the cam cover to check whether it fits better one way.
- I fitted the cam cover gasket dry and this seems to be the standard way of doing it – as a British biker I still can't get over fitting cam covers without Wellseal.
- Refitting the cam cover is a great feeling!

Chapter 29
Reassembling the gear change & gearbox cover

Next on the agenda were the gear selector mechanism and gearbox cover. My first job (as ever) was to run a tap down the threads which I had neglected to do before – when it would have been so much easier. See photo 29.1. After this I inserted the pins in the gear change drum, with the long pin in the position shown in photo 29.2. I was a bit confused because I was pretty sure the long pin and the gear change drum itself were in the correct position, but a diagram in the *Kawasaki Workshop Manual* clearly shows it being in a different position. Eventually, I found another diagram in the same manual which suggested that the position I had the drum and long pin in was correct so I went with it. Not very reassuring, though. Note that the longer pin is what operates the neutral switch, so it should align with the neutral switch in the outer cover.

With the pins inserted I fitted the small detent lever and its spring (which I had checked to see if it had stretched beyond recommended limits, as per the workshop manual), to the left of the gear change drum, ensuring that the lever was free to move on its shouldered mounting bolt. See photo 29.3. This photo also shows the correct position of the spring, with the end of the spring to the outside of its retaining pin, not the inside.

I cleaned and checked the gear shaft and pawl mechanism and gear change drum cover plate. See photo 29.4. Having already fitted the return spring pin that the hair spring on the mechanism engages with (see photo 29.2 again), I fitted the pawl mechanism to the casing. The long arms of the pawls engage with the pins in the gear change drum and

29.1 Tapping out the threads in the gearbox casing.

HOW TO RESTORE KAWASAKI Z1, Z/KZ900 & Z/KZ1000

29.2 Refitting the pins in the gearbox drum. The return spring pin was also fitted and locked.

29.3 Detent lever and spring in position.

29.4 The gearchange shaft and pawl mechanism.

29.5 Gearchange shaft in place, along with the 'O' ring on the main shaft.

29.6 Gearbox casing with set screws and seals ready to be inserted.

turn it to change gear. I also fitted the drum cover plate to the gear change drum with the protrusion in the cover over the long pin. This protrusion is what presses on the neutral switch. I also fitted the 'O' ring seal on the gear shaft just in front of the bearing, without which the gearbox will leak. See photo 29.5.

I then assembled the new crosshead screws and oil seals for the gearbox cover (see photo 29.6) before inserting the seals in the cover using my normal method of heating the casing slightly, lubricating the outside edge of the seal, and driving it home with a suitably sized socket and lump hammer (NB oil seals always fit with their innards toward the oil and their flat faces outward), applying Wellseal prior to

REASSEMBLING THE GEAR CHANGE & GEARBOX COVER

29.7 New seals fitted and cover ready to be fitted.

assembly. I fitted a new gasket and then screwed the cover into position. See photo 29.7. After this I screwed in the neutral indicator switch and the cover was ready to accept the gearbox sprocket collar (which slides inside the oil seal), and the gearbox sprocket itself. See photo 29.8.

LESSONS LEARNT
- Even the best manuals can be misleading at times.
- You can't really test the gearbox until the bike is moving, due to the ball bearings in the main shaft preventing the selection of any gears apart from first when stationary.
- Don't forget to fit the 'O' ring to the main shaft before fitting the casing.
- The protrusion on the gear change cover operates the neutral indicator switch.
- Oil seals are fitted with their open sides to the oil and their flat sides outwards.

29.8 Cover fitted ready for the sprocket collar and sprocket to be fitted on the main shaft.

Chapter 30
Fitting the generator & starter motor

So to the generator and starter motor. To begin with, I think it's worth looking at how the whole thing works. The generator (alternator) works much as usual, with a rotor full of magnets spinning within coils of wire to generate a current. The starter motor, however, is a bit different. Most starter motors only engage when they are in use and then disengage afterwards, but the Z900 starter is continuously engaged, so requires some form of clutch/disengagement system in order to disengage it when the engine is running. Kawasaki came up with a clever solution.

The starter gear drives directly onto the starter clutch gear sprocket (the large sprocket behind the rotor), and this large sprocket is connected in turn to the crankshaft via a clutch system in the back of the rotor. This clutch system consists of three rollers that are ingeniously spring-loaded so that, when the large clutch gear sprocket turns anti-clockwise (driven by the starter motor), they lock solid, the clutch gear sprocket is engaged with the crankshaft, and the engine is turned. When the rotor then turns anti-clockwise (when the engine fires), the rollers disengage, as does the clutch gear sprocket, so the sprocket stays still and so does the starter motor. Very clever and very efficient.

For all of the above to work properly, a damper rubber behind the starter clutch gear sprocket is required to prevent the sprocket rattling around in the casing when the engine is running and the sprocket is disengaged. This damper rubber is supplied in three different sizes, depending on the gap between sprocket and crankcases, so I needed to trial-fit the sprocket to enable me to measure the clearance behind it, and thus determine what size damper rubber was required as my original one was damaged.

To begin with I fitted the large

30.1 Trial fitting the thick thrust washer (chamfer inwards), roller bearing, and starter gear sprocket.

thrust washer with the chamfered side facing inward, followed by the starter clutch gear sprocket on its roller bearings. See photo 30.1. I then used a Vernier calliper to measure the gap between the sprocket and the crankcase (see photo 30.2), and this showed a gap of 6.44mm. I therefore knew I required the medium-size

30.2 Measuring the gap between the starter clutch gear sprocket and the crankcase.

FITTING THE GENERATOR & STARTER MOTOR

damper rubber as stipulated in the *Kawasaki Workshop Manual*, which was the same size as my old, damaged one. The damper rubbers come in three widths – 6.3mm, 7.3mm, and 8.3mm – and the manual states that any gap between 6.05mm and 7.05mm requires the middle size. Although my old damper rubber was the correct thickness, it was damaged, so needed replacing.

Unfortunately, I then discovered that the damper rubber was one of the few parts that were NLA (No Longer Available), so I was snookered. I searched the net and eventually found one of the correct size on sale in the States – at an unsurprisingly high price. Relieved that I could actually get one at all, I paid the high purchase price, then the high postage cost from the US, then the expected import tax duties and associated additional postage charge. All-in-all it cost me around £50, but I had one. See photo 30.3 of the old and new replacement damper rubbers.

I fitted the new damper rubber to the back of the clutch gear sprocket (see photo 30.4), and slid this onto the crankshaft followed by the thin thrust washer. See photo 30.5. I then checked that all was well with the three rollers in the back of the rotor

30.5 Starter clutch gear installed followed by the thin thrust washer.

30.6 The rotor with the three roller bearings that work the starter clutch.

that form the clutch, which allows the sprocket to engage in one direction only. The three rollers are held in position by a set of small springs and plungers, and all seemed well

with mine. See photo 30.6 of one of the rollers and springs removed for inspection.

I fitted a new woodruff key to the crankshaft that mates with a groove in the rotor,* and then slid the rotor onto the crankshaft (you have to jiggle it a bit to get the rollers on), then fitted and torqued the rotor retaining bolt on the end of the crankshaft. See photo 30.7. How did I lock the engine to torque the nut? If you look again at photo 30.7 you will see the heinous workshop crime of me locking the crankshaft by means of temporarily fitting the starter motor and then locking the gears with the wooden end of the shaft of a hammer. Any proper mechanics reading this will either have a heart attack or ceremoniously burn this book for reasons of heresy. It's really not good practice to do this as you risk damaging so many parts but, as the special locking tool referred to in the manual is now just a legend, I thought 'bugger this' and reached for the hammer shaft. I gently torqued the nut just to check I wasn't putting too much strain on the sprockets and, to

---

* Note that later model Z1000s didn't use a woodruff key; instead, the rotor was held in place by friction on the tapered crankshaft.

30.3 The old and new damper rubbers.

30.4 Damper rubber on the back of the starter clutch gear sprocket.

30.7 Rotor installed and rotor nut being torqued up using non-recommended locking method!

HOW TO RESTORE KAWASAKI Z1, Z/KZ900 & Z/KZ1000

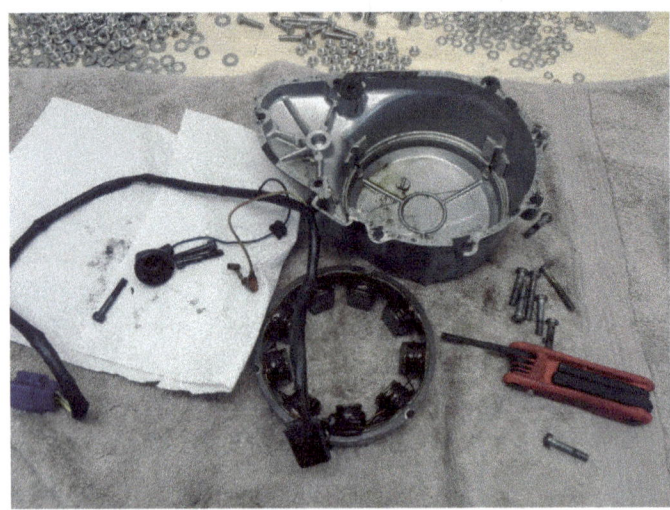

30.8 Removing the alternator wiring from the outer housing.

30.9 New wiring loom – but with three yellow wires instead of the three differently coloured ones.

my amazement, it torqued easily and without any visible damage to any components. I have to say it's not a great idea and I wouldn't recommend it – but, hey, I'm a grown-up and I can do what the heck I like!

I then looked at the wiring inside the alternator cover and removed it by unscrewing the three Allen screws that hold it in place. See photo 30.8. One problem that these bikes often suffer from is oil leaking from the grommet where the alternator wires exit the casing, and mine was no exception: oil was dripping from it even when just standing in the garage. I had already decided to change the grommet, but then discovered the real problem – you can't replace the grommet without first removing the wiring from the main alternator. These wires are soldered on and are very hard to remove and replace. I now know why so many grommets leak – replacing them is a total nightmare.

I therefore had two choices: re-use the old grommet with a dollop of new sealant and hope it didn't leak, or replace the grommet and the wiring with it. In the end, I bit the bullet and decided to replace the grommet and the wiring. I bought new wiring only to discover that the three wires were all coloured yellow, unlike my original wires which were all different colours, and, once again, there were no instructions. See photo 30.9. So which one went where? After some investigation I found that all three wires were inter-connected, so it shouldn't matter which went where (at least I hoped so!). I gingerly cut off the old wires and soldered the new ones in place on the short bits of wire coming off the alternator that were all that was left to solder onto. I checked my connections at every step in the knowledge that my soldering is very suspect. See photo 30.10. Time would tell whether or not it had been a success. (Having started the engine the alternator was working well – much to my surprise.)

I then got ready to insert the alternator coils into my new casing. See photo 30.11, from which you can see that my old casing was so badly scratched and damaged that I thought replacement was the only viable option. If you're a real stickler for originality, maybe the old one could be saved after extensive work – but I'm not, so I replaced it. I sealed the grommet in place with copious amounts of black, high temperature RTV sealant. At this point I discovered that the main cause of leaks in this

30.10 Soldering the new wiring loom to the alternator.

FITTING THE GENERATOR & STARTER MOTOR

30.11 The old and new generator covers.

area appears to be from where the wires go through the grommet, not from round the edge of the grommet itself, and if you seal the wires where they pass through the grommet properly then you shouldn't really need to replace the grommet itself to make the engine oil-tight.

Next up was the starter motor. Before stripping it I checked the alignment marks on the body which enable it to be replaced in the same position. However, I realised that, although there were marks on the body, there were no corresponding marks on the end caps, so I used a marker to ensure everything went back in the same position. See photo 30.12. I then took apart the motor by removing the two outside bolts clamping it together. Photo 30.13 shows the motor stripped. Everything seemed to be in order so I just cleaned the brushes with WD40 (note all the dust in photo 30.13 that came out of the motor), and then used fine emery cloth and Scotch-Brite on the commutator which was quite dirty. (Be careful cleaning the commutator, as doing this too aggressively can damage it.)

I reassembled the starter motor and prepared to fit it into the back of the alternator cover. I decided to change the 'O' ring on the front shaft of the motor that keeps it oil-tight where it mates with the crankcases, and took one out of my box of spare 'O' rings that was nearly the same size. However, when I removed the old one I found that my replacement seal was thicker than the original (see photo 30.14), and wouldn't work as, when I tried to refit the motor, the shaft wouldn't go back in the crankcases without scalping the top of the seal. I ordered a correct new one (for some reason it doesn't come with the gasket set and nor does the one for the tacho drive) and the starter slotted home nicely. See photo 30.15.

Also, if you look at photo 30.15 again, you can see that the clutch gear sprocket sits further out than the starter motor gear, which makes me think that I may have had the wrong rubber damper, and should have used the thinner one? Not sure, but I didn't think it mattered too much.

Having checked that the clutch gear sprocket wasn't fouling on my wonderful new wiring due to the above (it was close!), I fitted the casing to the engine using a genuine Kawasaki gasket rather than the pattern one in the gasket set (which I had been told was a good idea in order to prevent leaks from the wiring grommet), and Wellseal. I also put some threadlock on the long mounting screw at the top as per the manual. See photo 30.16.

The job was completed by connecting the wiring to the neutral switch behind the gearbox sprocket, and to the oil pressure switch. See photo 30.17. The wiring from the alternator and starter motor was then routed back toward the main loom in the channel above the gearbox sprocket. See photo 30.18. Note that I had actually already fitted the gearbox sprocket and chain by

30.12 Marking the starter motor cover before dismantling it.

30.14 The old 'O' ring seal for the starter motor shaft and a new one that didn't fit.

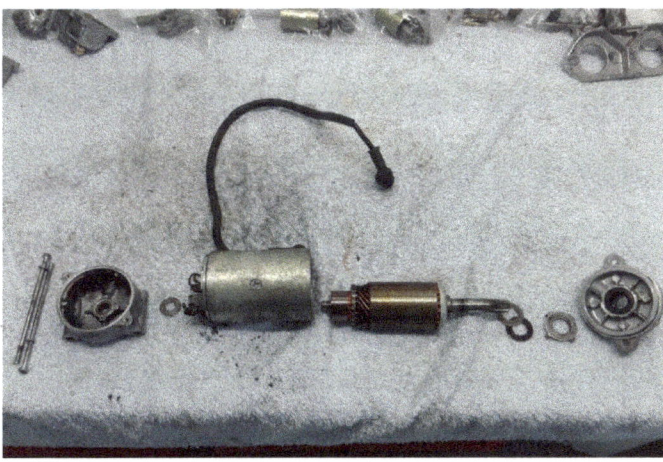

30.13 The starter motor dismantled and commutator cleaned.

30.15 Starter motor fitted. Note gears not meshing perfectly suggests incorrect size of damper rubber fitted.

30.16 Generator outer cover fitted and wiring being routed.

30.17 Wiring up the oil pressure switch.

this time, but for various reasons (I got confused!) fitting the gearbox sprocket is covered later on.

LESSONS LEARNT
• The starter motor engages and disengages via an ingenious clutch system in the alternator housing.
• You can't replace the rubber grommet for the alternator wiring without changing the wiring, too.
• A damper rubber behind the clutch gear sprocket comes in three sizes – all currently unobtainable.
• Use a high-temperature RTV sealant around the grommet, especially where the wires go through it.
• Use a genuine Kawasaki gasket on the alternator casing.
• Starter motors are generally in good condition but require cleaning, lubricating, and the commutator gently rubbing down.

30.18 Everything fitted and wiring routed above the gearbox sprocket towards the rear of the bike.

Chapter 31
Dismantling the carburettors

If there's one part of any restoration that is the most important to get right, it's the carburettors. If these are right, the bike will run right. If they're wrong, it'll always run like a dog, no matter what you do to the rest of the engine.

Before the carburettors could be vapour blasted and refurbished, they had to be fully dismantled. I removed them from the engine by pulling them off the rubber intake manifolds and disconnecting the two accelerator cables – which was a fiddly job but eventually completed. See photo 31.1 of the carbs on the bench. You can compare these carbs from my Z900 with some earlier carbs from a Z1A. See photo 31.2 of a set of Z1A carbs that I bought in very good condition, and then rebuilt and further refurbished with the intention of putting them on my Z1A, before I had to sell them to try and finance the restoration of the Z900 – along with my cherished Hinckley Triumph Thunderbird 900 – and I'm still in debt as the restoration costs are just so high. Hey-ho.

If you compare the two photos you can see that the carbs are essentially the same in how they operate, although do so in slightly different ways. The main difference is that, although both of them have an operating shaft that runs along the top of the carbs that serves to raise and lower the throttle slides, the earlier Z1A carbs have the shaft exposed, and the later carbs have the shaft and associated adjusting screws enclosed.

The first thing I noted was that the rubber inlet manifolds on the engine were badly cracked and needed replacement (not mending

31.1 Carbs removed from the engine.

31.2 Comparison with Z1A carbs.

HOW TO RESTORE KAWASAKI Z1, Z/KZ900 & Z/KZ1000

with brown sealant as a previous owner had attempted!) See photo 31.3. Luckily, these parts, as with most, are readily available.

I then removed the float chambers from the bottom of the carbs as I was desperate to see what they were like inside, and, as suspected, they were a real house of horror. See photos 31.4 and 31.5 of all the crud in one of the float chambers. This was entirely to be expected in an old bike that had not been used for a while. The root cause of this is the fuel which sits in the carburettors slowly turning to gum, and solidifying over time. This combination of gum

31.3 Cracked and damaged carb inlet manifolds.

31.4 Crud in the bottom of the float bowls.

31.5 More crud in the top of the float bowls!

31.6 Beginning the removal of the main shaft.

and hard crud combines to effectively block up any carburettor and render it unserviceable, which is why it is essential to fully clean out the carburettors as part of any restoration project.

I must also add that, with the increased use of ethanol in fuels, the tank life of petrol is becoming increasingly shorter, and even bikes laid up over winter can suffer from severe carb blockages unless some form of fuel stabiliser is used – and even then that's not fool-proof. Beware.

Having removed the carb tops the first job was to remove the operating shaft, connected to the carbs via four short locating bolts, one on each carb, plus one holding the throttle cable pulley and spring. To begin with I removed the large spring on the cable pulley to release the tension on the shaft, and then removed the locating bolt from the pulley, followed by the four on the carbs. See photo 31.6. After this, I removed the small locating plate from the left of the gantry. See photo 31.7. The shaft could then be withdrawn. See photo 31.8.

With the shaft out, the throttle slides and needles can be removed. See photo 31.9. I then removed the carbs from the gantry by undoing the crosshead screws that hold them

31.7 Removing the small locating plate or shaft stopper.

in place. The carbs stayed in pairs, held together by the fuel T-pieces and short rubber connecting pipes. See photo 31.10. The paired carbs were then pulled apart releasing the T-pieces and rubber connectors. See photo 31.11.

I was then able to strip the carb bodies. First of all, I used a small punch to drift out the float pin. See photo 31.12. Note that the pin has a crimp at one end that holds it in place, so the pin has to be punched out crimped end first – but take care not to damage or break the pillars that hold the pins. Also note in this photo the special grommets in the top of the carbs that fit round the main shaft – these are currently unobtainable, so treat these with great care. After this, I unscrewed

DISMANTLING THE CARBURETTORS

31.8 Withdrawing the shaft.

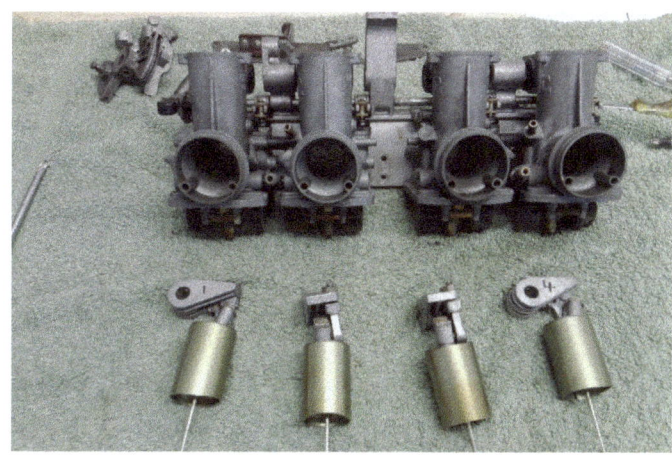
31.9 The carburettor slides and needles.

31.10 Carbs removed from gantry.

31.11 Fuel inlet T pieces and connecting rubbers removed from between pairs of carbs.

31.12 Removing the float by tapping out the pin – from the correct side.

31.13 Main jet, pilot jet and choke unit removed.

31.14 Air screw and spring removed.

and removed the main jet, pilot jet, and choke operating assembly. See photo 31.13. I then removed the long, thin starter pipe (only fitted to some models) which is a push-fit. This can be seen still in the carb body in photo 31.13, together with the float valve seat that was also later removed. Next, I removed the air screw and its spring. See photo 31.14.

Having removed the float valve assembly, the carb was now fully stripped and ready to be vapour blasted. See photo 31.15. The only part not removed was the needle jet at the bottom of the throttle body (see photo 31.16), but it's the one part on a carb I've never taken out before having it cleaned, without any problems, so I left it in situ.

However, note that replacing the

129

HOW TO RESTORE KAWASAKI Z1, Z/KZ900 & Z/KZ1000

31.15 Carburettor body fully dismantled and ready for vapour blasting ...

31.18 The locking nut and carb synchronisation screw removed.

31.21 The needle removed from the throttle slide.

31.16 ... apart from the needle jet.

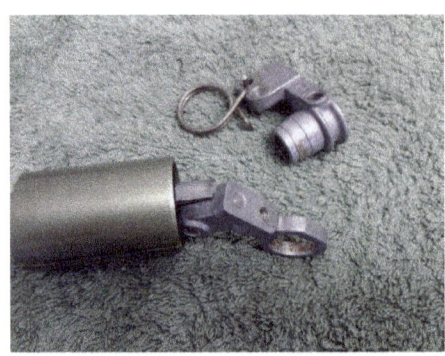

31.19 Spring loaded mechanism dismantled – rather unnecessarily.

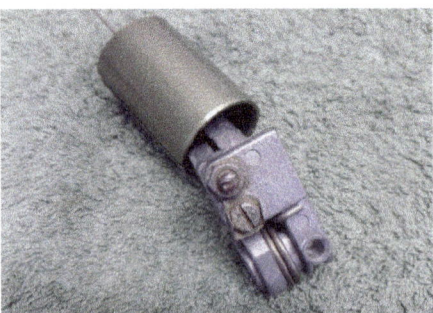

31.17 Throttle slide and needle assembly ready to be dismantled.

31.20 Removing the two screws holding the needle in place.

needle jet is recommended. It is an interference fit and can be removed by careful use of a suitable drift, and a new one tapped in.

With the carb bodies, tops, and float chambers ready to go to the vapour blaster (it's important to have the carbs vapour blasted only, as they're made of very soft alloy and will be damaged by a more aggressive blasting process), I turned my attention to the throttle slides and needles. See photo 31.17. As can be seen from the photo, on the top of the assembly is the adjusting screw, used to synchronise the carbs and associated lock nut. I duly removed these (see photo 31.18), and then dismantled the rather complicated, spring-loaded mechanisms above the throttle slides. See photo 31.19. This proved rather unnecessary as there are no serviceable parts, and later discovered that trying to reassemble them is a nightmare. Finally, I removed the two screws at the bottom of the throttle slide that released the needle. In order to remove these two very, very tight screws, I found it easiest to replace the slides in the carb bodies, preventing them from turning, and then applied a lot of pressure to release the screws without worrying about damaging the needles. See photo 31.20. The needles were now released from the throttle slide ready for inspection. See photo 31.21. Disassembly of the carbs was complete.

LESSONS LEARNT
- Although different models have different types of carburettor, they are all fairly similar, and operate on the same principles.
- Carbs are nearly always badly gummed up and blocked, and require thorough cleaning.
- The secret to a nicely-running engine is in the carburettors.
- The grommets for the main shaft (where fitted) are currently unobtainable.
- There's no need to dismantle the spring-loaded mechanism on top of the throttle slides.
- Have carbs vapour blasted only as the alloy is quite soft.

www.velocebooks.com
New book news • Special offers • Newsletter • Details of all Veloce books • Gift Vouchers

Chapter 32
Rebuilding the carburettors

Time to rebuild the carburettors. To begin with, I assembled all of the component parts after they had been vapour blasted and polished (see photo 32.1), and gave them a thorough clean. For carburettors to work properly, all of the various jets and drillings have to be scrupulously clean. I generally use a foaming carb cleaner so that I can see it coming out of the various holes, and know they're clean and unblocked, but on this occasion I'd misordered and had two cans of carb cleaner, neither of which was the foaming type. I should have used foaming oven cleaner or similar instead.

I cleaned the carbs as fully as possible, although it was hard to tell whether all of the tiny airways were clear (which caused a problem later on). One tiny airway exits just near to the needle jet in the main carb body: it's only about 0.5mm wide but is an essential part of the carburettor, and must be completely clear for the carb to run properly. See photo 32.2. Foaming carb cleaner is great, as you can see it coming out of the airway quite clearly. Otherwise, to check that this very small airway is clear, insert the nozzle of an aerosol carb cleaner into the opening for the pilot jet in the float chamber. If you squirt some cleaner up here you should see it coming out of the small airway, showing that it's clear.

As part of the cleaning process I discovered a blocked jet that I wasn't expecting, and nearly didn't find as it was in the float chamber bowl, not the main body of the carb. If you look at photo 32.3 you can see the drilling for the starter pipe, which was completely blocked on one carb and would have caused problems with choke starting if I hadn't discovered

32.1 All carb parts ready for reassembly.

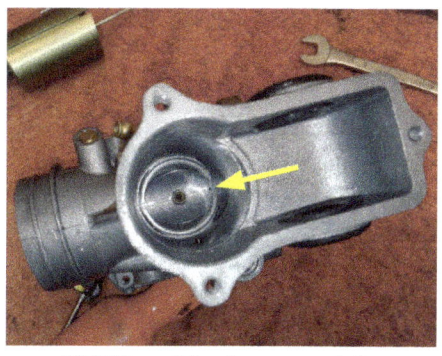

32.2 Clean this airway carefully.

HOW TO RESTORE KAWASAKI Z1, Z/KZ900 & Z/KZ1000

32.3 Blocked starter pipe passageway.

32.4 Ready to assemble the throttle slide and needle assembly.

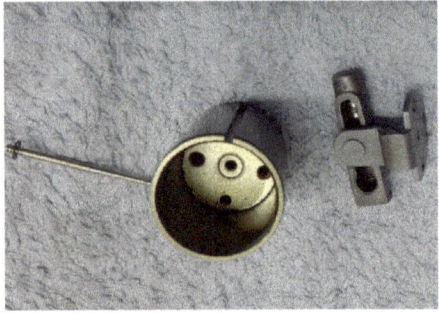

32.5 Ready to insert the needle and lower spring loaded mechanism.

it. I managed to clear it with a piece of wire, as carb cleaner and compressed air wouldn't shift it.

With the carbs thoroughly cleaned (or so I thought), I began to reassemble the throttle slide and needle assembly. See photo 32.4. I checked the needles for straightness and for any scratches, etc, and ensured that the throttle slides ran smoothly in the bores of the carbs without being too loose. Bent or scratched needles can cause erratic running, and worn throttle slides and/or carburettor bodies can let in air round the sides, and will make the bike run like a complete dog. In either case, replacement is the only solution – although availability of new carbs is poor. Some owners fit the later flat slide carburettors which can improve running at the cost of originality. Not an easy one.

With everything checked and given the thumbs-up, I began reassembling the slide assemblies which I didn't really need to dismantle in the first place. The first job was to insert the needle into the throttle slide. See photo 32.5. Note that the specifications in the workshop manual provide a reference number for your jet needle (make sure you have the correct specifications as there were many changes along the way for different models): in my case, the correct needle was a 5DL31-3. The last digit of that number tells you which groove the clip should sit in on the needle. Most needles have five grooves counted from the top, so the number three tells you that the clip should be in the third groove down. This is definitely worth checking as carbs have so often been messed about with over the years, and one such change could have been someone moving the position of the clip on the jet needle. I then screwed the first part of the spring-loaded mechanism into the slide, holding the needle firmly in place. See photo 32.6.

After this I assembled the rest of the spring-loaded mechanism, see photo 32.7, but then had to dismantle it again when I realised that the only way I could reassemble the upper section, with its very strong hairpin spring, was to do this first. I finally found a way of slotting these back together, but it was a real struggle. See photo 32.8. Note that you really don't need to dismantle this entire assembly as you can simply unscrew the whole thing from the throttle slide in order to get to the jet needle, which you do need to inspect.

With the throttle assemblies finally reassembled, I turned to the main carburettor bodies and various jets. I discovered that the main and pilot jets in my carbs had both been changed over the years. This is quite usual as Z900s (mine included) have often had 4-into-1 exhaust systems and sports air filters fitted at some point in their lives, and carbs are often rejetted to suit. I had ordered refurb kits which came with new main and pilot jets, so I replaced the old (larger) jets with the new, standard ones as I was returning

32.6 Needle inserted and bottom section of spring loaded assembly screwed on top.

32.7 Top half of assembly slotted in and screwed together.

REBUILDING THE CARBURETTORS

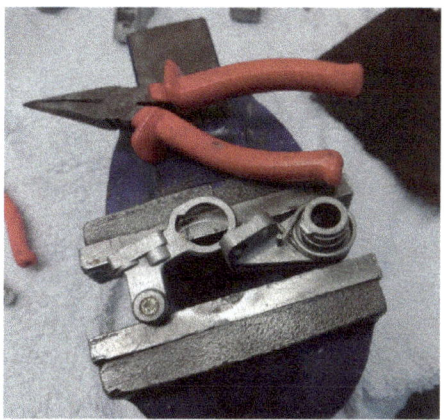

32.8 Top half of assembly removed again to assemble the strange spring loaded assembly above the throttle slide.

32.9 The old and new main jet.

32.10 Starter pipe (1), pilot jet (2), new main jet (3), and float valve (4) inserted.

32.11 Floats in place.

the bike to largely standard spec, including fitting the original air filter and exhaust system. In my case, this meant 115 main jets and 17.5 pilot jets. See photo 32.9 of the old and new jets, together with the air pipe it screws into.

I then fitted the various jets into the carb body. See photo 32.10 which shows the following: 1, the starter pipe (only on some carbs); these are just a push-fit; 2, the pilot jet; 3, the main jet; 4, the float needle valve. I then checked the floats to ensure they were in good condition, but as they are of solid construction as opposed to hollow, there's no chance of them leaking and not floating properly, as is the case with hollow ones. I refitted them by gently tapping home the float pin. See photo 32.11.

Turning over the carb bodies I fitted new air screws, and refitted the original choke assemblies, complete with new 'O' rings. See photo 32.12. Note that on some carbs there is a mark next to the air screw to show where the screw slot should align when correctly set. However, when using replacement parts, this doesn't always work: the air screws on my carbs should be set at $1\frac{3}{8}$ turns out, and none of them aligned with the aforementioned mark.

I then fitted new gaskets to the bottoms of the carb bodies, and screwed the float chambers back on. See photo 32.13. As well as polishing these, I also fitted new brass drain screws, which don't

32.12 New air screw and choke assembly in place.

32.13 Polished float chambers in place with new drain plugs fitted.

32.14 Throttle slide assembly inserted.

32.15 Carbs ready to be mounted on the gantry with the original grommets inserted for the main shaft.

133

HOW TO RESTORE KAWASAKI Z1, Z/KZ900 & Z/KZ1000

32.16 Old and new fuel pipe T pieces.

32.16A The new upgraded T-piece that doesn't leak.

32.17 Checking the holes in the shaft to ensure it's inserted the correct way round.

32.18 With the bolts to the carbs in place the bolt holding the throttle pulley was inserted whilst tensioning the spring.

32.19 Inserting the small locating plate to hold the shaft in place.

come in the refurb pack, and have to be bought separately. (I think they make the carbs look just that bit better.)

I then slid the throttle valves into the carb bodies, locating each in its original position. See photo 32.14. I then refitted the original rubber grommets in the top of the carb bodies to take the mainshaft. See photo 32.15. Note that new grommets are currently unavailable, so try and re-use the originals. If all else fails, you might get away with using standard rubber grommets, although I think this would be a last resort.

Before fitting the carbs to the gantry I had to reconnect the relevant left and right pairs with the short rubber breather tubes and T-piece fuel pipes. I trial-fitted the original T-pieces but, as I suspected, they were a very loose fit in the carb bodies, and would definitely have leaked. I therefore fitted new replacements which were a reassuringly tight fit. See photo 32.16 of the old and new T-piece connectors.

Note that after the bike was finished the T-pieces continued to leak slightly from where they joined the carburettors, and I discovered that improved brass ones with better seal were available. I fitted a pair and they have never leaked since. See photo 32.16A.

I prepared to fit the mainshaft, laying it across the tops of the carbs and aligning all the relevant bolt holes to ensure I was fitting it the right way round. See photo 32.17. I then slid the mainshaft into position, not forgetting to slide it

REBUILDING THE CARBURETTORS

32.20 The throttle cable bracket in place, with odd spring behind it.

adjustment screws had seen better days. This was for two reasons: new replacements are unavailable so I had to use the original ones, and synchronising the carbs is one of those jobs that has almost certainly been done way too often in the past by previous owners who may have neglected to first loosen the lock nuts! I then placed a piece of 0.75mm thick locking wire under the throttle slide of each carb from the engine side. In the middle of the slide is a very small notch which the wire sits under. See photo 32.23. I then adjusted the height of the throttle slides using the adjusting screws so that the wire was a sliding fit. If you look at photo 32.24 you should hopefully be able to see that all of the throttle slides are now at exactly the same height. The carbs

32.21 Opening the tickover screw to give the correct gap.

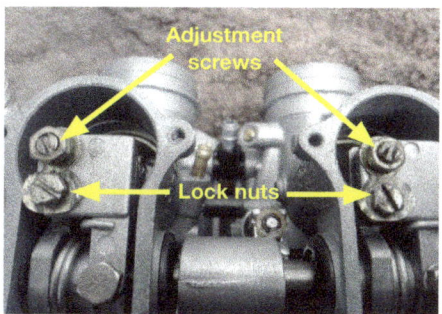

32.22 Loosening the adjusting screw and locknut on top of the carbs.

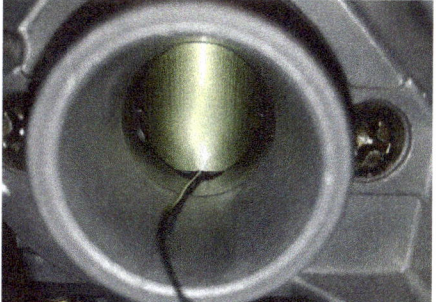

32.23 Using a 7mm diameter piece of locking wire to synchronise the carbs.

through the throttle butterfly also. I bolted the top of the throttle slides into the mainshaft before attaching the butterfly spring mechanism; bolting the butterfly to the shaft whilst tensioning the spring. See photo 32.18. I then screwed the little locating plate to the left side of the carbs. See photo 32.19. After that I attached the cable bracket to the gantry via the small spring behind it, which is there for reasons known only to the fiendishly clever engineers at Kawasaki – so for a good reason! See photo 32.20

With the carbs assembled it was time to synchronise them. The first job was to screw the tickover adjustment screw so that the gap between the end of the butterfly and the end of the throttle cable holder was about $\frac{1}{16}$in. See photo 32.21. Then I loosened the lock nuts and the adjuster screws on top of the carbs. See photo 32.22. Note that the

32.24 Carbs synchronised.

HOW TO RESTORE KAWASAKI Z1, Z/KZ900 & Z/KZ1000

were now synchronised. (They would be fine tuned later on, when the engine was running.)

I replaced the carb tops together with the strengthening plate that was added to this particular evolution of carburettor. See photo 32.25. After this, I screwed the throttle stop screw into the back of the gantry, which should be set so that the throttle slides stop when they have reached full opening. See photo 32.26. I also inserted the choke lever and its long shaft, and added the little actuation levers to it as I slotted home the choke shaft, engaging them with each choke mechanism. I then checked the choke operation and found it terrible: it didn't open properly and just kept jamming. Eventually, I realised I'd fitted the little actuation levers upside down. I turned around the levers – and the choke worked perfectly: smooth and precise! See photo 32.27. I couldn't believe that such a little thing could make such a huge difference. There's a lesson in there somewhere. Anyway, the carbs were now finished and ready to be fitted to the engine.

LESSONS LEARNT
- Check, check, and then check again that all passageways are free and unblocked.
- Use foaming carb cleaner (or similar) to check that all airways are clear (I should definitely have taken my own advice on that one!).
- Check the needles for straightness and scoring, etc. Check throttle slides for a good fit in the carb bodies.
- Check the specifications for your carburettor for info on jet sizes and needle clip position.
- Don't dismantle components that don't require it.
- Synchronise the carbs on the bench.
- Fitting any part upside down isn't a great idea, and even simple mistakes can have major consequences.
- The secret to a sweetly running engine is in the carburettors.

32.25 Carb tops replaced with the strengthening plate.

32.26 Throttle stop screw in place – note the upside down choke actuation levers

32.27 Choke actuation levers now the right way up.

www.velocebooks.com
New book news • Special offers • Newsletter • Details of all Veloce books • Gift Vouchers

Chapter 33
Carburettor tuning

Tuning carburettors ... tuning bloody carburettors! I've spent most of my life tuning flaming carburettors – or, more accurately, I've spent most of my life (unsuccessfully) sorting out the problems that others (and myself) have created when messing about with their carburettors in an effort to tune them.

Tuning carburettors falls into two categories –
- **Basic tuning:** Synchronising the carburettors and adjusting the air screws (and possibly checking the float height) – generally after an engine rebuild. 'Note that 'synchronising' simply means adjusting the caburettors so that they all open and close at the same time and by the same amount, they will therefore work at exactly the same power as each other.'
- **Retuning:** Rejetting the carburettors, and/or adjusting or replacing the jet needle, and/or changing the throttle slide – when the engine has been modified.

The main advice I can give anyone regarding tuning carburettors is that, unless you really have to, don't! The chances are that you'll end up in a complete mess with a bike that runs like a complete dog. Tuning is only really necessary when you set up the carbs for the first time after a rebuild, or when you change something major on the bike such as the exhaust system or air filters, or camshafts or the carburettors themselves. Otherwise, leave well alone.

If your bike is standard, you should only need to carry out basic tuning, and even then only very occasionally. If the bike isn't running right it's almost certainly not a problem with the tuning, but a fault with the carburettors themselves, so you can tune to your heart's content without curing anything. In other words the reason the bike's not running properly probably isn't because the carbs aren't tuned, but because they're faulty, eg, a blocked airway, the wrong jets fitted, an air leak from the inlet manifolds, wear in the throttle slide, a bent or scratched needle or a needle clip set in the wrong groove etc.

BASIC TUNING

Synchronising the carbs needs doing very infrequently, and is best done with the carbs off the bike, as in my case (see previous chapter on this procedure). When the engine is then back up and running and you want to check the carbs are synchronised, start by attaching a set of vacuum gauges to the take-offs on the inlet manifolds. The readings should all be the same, and if they're not then one or more carb will require fine adjustment to achieve perfect synchronisation, following the basic synchronisation you already did with the carbs off. The main item to note is that some of the vacuum gauge sets sold aren't great quality (mine included) and give false readings. In my case I spent ages trying to synchronise the carbs on my Z1A when I bought it, only to discover that the gauges were faulty – I connected them all to the same carb in turn and they all gave different readings! I now just use one of the four gauges and connect it to each carburettor in turn to ensure the correct reading. If you look at photo 33.1 you can see the bike having the carbs synchronised with gauges after it was finished and the teething troubles were ironed out.

First of all I ran the engine until it was up to temperature and the choke was fully off, then checked the synchronisation with my set of gauges. I only used one of the four gauges, fitting it to each carb in turn as I discovered that different gauges gave different readings and their readings weren't to be trusted.

HOW TO RESTORE KAWASAKI Z1, Z/KZ900 & Z/KZ1000

33.1 Synchronising No 4 carb by removing the petrol tank and turning the adjuster in the top until the gauge read the same as the for the other carbs.

When the gauge is attached you just adjust the little valve in the pipe under the gauge to stop the needle from flickering and then check each carb in turn. In my case my bench synchronisation was pretty accurate and carbs 1, 2 & 3 gave almost exactly the same reading on the gauge, only carb No 4 was slightly out. I therefore removed the fuel tank and replaced it with two slightly adapted funnels to hold petrol so I could run the engine without the fuel tank in the way. I then removed the top from carb No 4 and synchronised it by loosening the locking nut and then screwing the adjuster in or out (see photo 32.22 in the previous chapter) until the gauge read the same as the other carbs. Job done.

It's also worth noting that there are various sections on the face of the gauges telling you how the engine is running – but I completely ignored these as my gauges were so inaccurate they weren't to be trusted, and I just set mine so that the needle was in the same place for each carb regardless of where it was on the gauge. The rule here is 'Never buy cheap.' My gauges are worse than useless because they actually give false readings which caused no end of problems until I realised what the problem was. See photo 33.2.

Checking float height. Again, this is only ever usually done after a carb rebuild to check that the floats in the carbs are shutting off the fuel at the correct level. Incorrect levels can cause poor running. However, I have to admit that I have never reset the float levels on a carburettor. I checked a few, years ago, but as I never found one that needed adjustment I've not bothered to check them since – as it's such a pain of a job and they all seem to be within tolerance. So, again, my advice is to leave well alone. That said, I know some people who swear by adjusting the float height – such is the nature of motor mechanics.

The air screws on the carbs should be set as per the manual to begin with – in my case 1⅜ turns out from closed. Fine tuning is then carried out with the engine warm and on tickover. Adjust each air screw in turn to achieve the fastest tickover. Job done.

That's it for basic tuning. Finito: there is no other way to tune the carbs.

If your bike is standard but still running like a dog after basic tuning, there's a problem somewhere else (see below), not with the tuning. End of.

RETUNING

If you've changed something major on the engine, such as fitting a sports exhaust system or high-performance camshafts, increased the engine capacity, or fitted high compression pistons etc, then, and only then, do you need to consider retuning the carburettors in terms of changing the

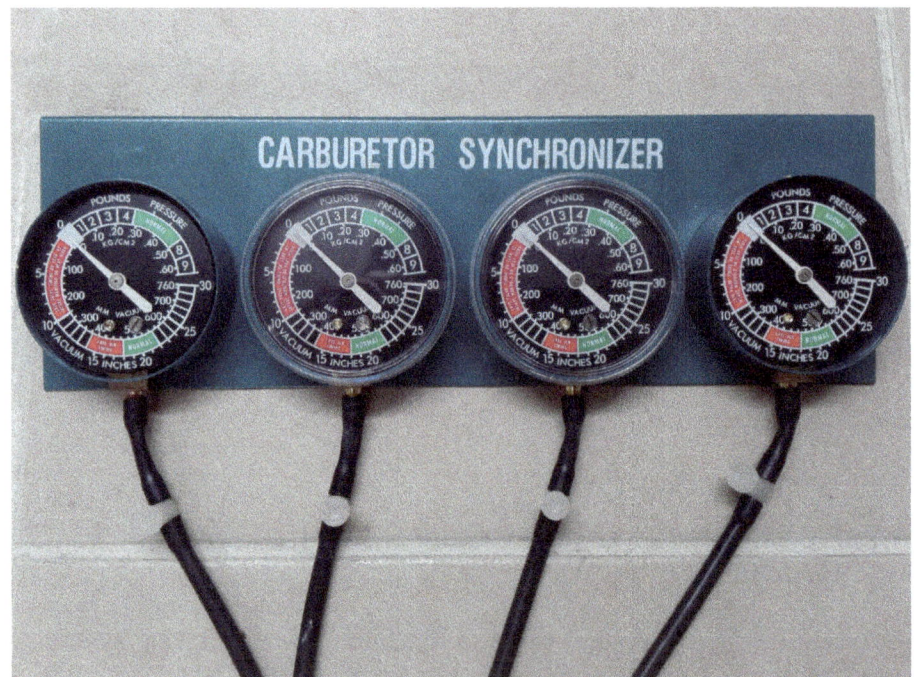

33.2 My gauges with different sectors showing engine condition – or at least they should – never buy cheap!

CARBURETTOR TUNING

original jet sizes, and/or needle, and/or throttle slide.

The problem is, what do you change and by how much? It is very, very easy to start changing things willy-nilly, and get in a complete mess that's hard to get out of because you've messed about with so many things you don't know what's causing what to happen. The bike that you spent a shed-load of money on modifying is now running like a complete dog, and is far worse than it was before you started.

My advice is to consult the manufacturer of any engine tuning item you buy (eg exhaust systems or high lift camshafts, or big-bore conversions, etc), and check what adjustments it recommends. If it's something like 'rejet to suit' then I would leave well alone unless you are willing to pay for something like a rolling road tune where they can sort it for you – but it won't be cheap. Ideally, you should be given clear, precise instructions on what changes are needed to the carburation when buying engine tuning parts. I recently spent 18 months trying to get a bike to run properly after simply changing from standard air filters to open bell mouths – it was infuriating!

If you do want to retune your carbs as the engine's been modified, but have no means of accessing recommended tuning adjustments, be aware of what parts of the carburettor affect what throttle openings. Here are the basics –
• Up to $1/8$ throttle opening: the size of the pilot jet.
• From $1/8$ to $1/4$ throttle opening: the size of the throttle slide cut-away.
• From $1/4$ to $3/4$ throttle: the jet needle position and/or size of the needle jet.
• From $3/4$ to full throttle: the size of the main jet.

Try to run the bike first to check for problems, and at what throttle settings these are, and take it from there as to which parts may need changing.

Another way forward is to fit some newer, uprated carbs such as Mikuni flatslides. These carbs are designed for racing and fast road use, so may be a better option. They are also designed to be easily adjusted to suit different bikes. However, they're expensive and, whilst you may well gain in top end performance, you may lose low end smooth running and mid-range grunt.

POOR RUNNING? POSSIBLE CULPRITS

Rather than carburettor tuning problems, there are likelier culprits when it comes to an engine that's running rough, and the main one is usually … the carburettors! What? Yes, I find that most poor running problems are caused by the carburettors; not their tuning but faults with the carbs themselves, as follows –
• Blockages in the carbs. A very common problem and by far the most likely. Carbs suffer badly from blockages, especially in their tiny passageways – bad news for carbs. Blocked carbs simply won't run properly.
• Air leaks. Cracks or holes in the inlet rubbers or loose jubilee clips can let in air, and throw the carbs out of kilter.
• Worn throttle slides. The throttle slides on higher mileage bikes can wear the throttle bodies and/or slides, again causing air leaks and erratic running.
• Bent or damaged jet needles causing erratic fuel delivery and erratic running, usually with an associated flat spot in the rev range.
• Leaking carb floats causing flooding, usually associated with petrol coming out of the overflow tubes.
• Leaking float needles. Sometimes these won't seat properly, and cause the carburettor to flood, as above.
• A blocked fuel tap. So often an apparent carb problem has been found to be not the carbs at all, but a blocked or partially blocked fuel tap.

There are many causes of poor running that are nothing to do with the carbs: electrical problems involving the ignition system (sparkplugs, points, condenser, HT caps, HT leads, ignition coils, ignition timing, wiring connectors, electronic ignition modules, etc), and mechanical problems (leaking valves, poorly adjusted valve clearances, a holed piston, broken piston rings, blown head gasket, leaking exhaust system, etc). Jumping to conclusions is an easy trap to fall into, but if the bike is generally healthy and poor running continues, then suspect the carbs.

To sum up. Do as little as possible to the carbs other than thoroughly clean them, and check for damage and incorrect jets, etc, fitted by previous owners. Synchronising carbs is the job most often completed unnecessarily (see the state of the adjustment screws on my carbs in the previous chapter!) If you do need to retune following engine upgrading, don't just dive in; find out what the recommended changes are and follow this advice. Sometimes, what is gained in top end power is lost in terms of around-town usability. Above all, appreciate that poor running is only very occasionally due to poor carburettor tuning.

LESSONS LEARNT
• There are two types of carb tuning: basic and retuning.
• Basic tuning only allows for very limited adjustment.
• Retuning is only required after major engine upgrades.
• Synchronising is the most over-performed adjustment on carbs.
• 90 per cent of carb problems are due to faults with the carbs, not their tuning.
• 90 per cent of problems with carbs is due to jet and airway blockages.
• Meddle at your peril.
• You can quite easily upgrade engine performance on Z900s (there are plenty of engine power upgrades available), but this can come at the cost of poor low- and mid-range running.
• Whilst carbs are often the cause of most running problems, other factors such as the ignition system and mechanical parts can also be the source of the problem.
• The next time you buy a bike and the vendor says: 'It's all been rebuilt – it just needs the carbs tuning a bit,' you know that means there's a considerable amount of work to be done, and at least a full carb rebuild. (I think vendors have said that to me nearly every time I've bought a bike!).
• Good luck!

Chapter 34
Refitting the clutch

I had already checked the various components parts of the clutch basket for signs of excessive wear, and all seemed well. I now also checked the clutch plates for thickness, warping and damage to the teeth, length of the springs in the pressure plate, and the teeth of the clutch hub where the clutch plates sit to check for pitting caused by the edges of the clutch plates – no problems; I didn't even replace the clutch friction plates. (I didn't think they required replacing, and if they do in the future, then it's not that big a job.)

First of all I slotted the large distance washer onto the gear shaft that sits behind the clutch hub. See photo 34.1. This was followed by the clutch hub itself, which is held in place with a dished locking washer and nut. The washer is clearly marked as to which way round it fits. See photo 34.2. I then loosely fitted the washer and nut ready to torque them. See photo 34.3.

I had been very worried about how to lock the clutch hub in order to torque the hub nut as I'd had such a torrid time removing it. As a result, I ordered a new locking tool from eBay, which looked a bit like the original Kawasaki item, but it took ages to

34.1 Fitting the distance washer that sits behind the clutch hub.

34.2 Sprung washer holding the clutch hub in position is sided – and clearly marked.

arrive so I had another think. I again tried using my original locking tool and found that I had been using it incorrectly. Instead of trying to jam it between the inner and outer teeth

34.3 Clutch hub in position with sprung washer and self-locking nut loosely fitted.

of the clutch, I realised that it should only fit into the teeth of the clutch hub (and not the clutch basket as well), and then the arm of the tool could be locked against something else. I therefore loosely inserted the swinging arm spindle and the tool locked the clutch hub really well, and the high torque required to tighten the clutch hub nut was achieved without incident. See photo 34.4. You learn from your mistakes.

With the hub now successfully fitted, I slid the clutch plates into place – with alternate friction and plain plates, the odd thing being that they began and ended with a friction plate, not a plain plate. See photo 34.5. I then inserted the ball bearing

REFITTING THE CLUTCH

34.4 Torquing up the clutch hub nut by spragging the clutch properly!

only pressing fairly lightly on the springs I thought that was fine. If they were any looser then I would worry that the clutch might slip. After this I fitted a new glass oil sight level in the outer casing, easing it into position with a suitably-sized socket, a soft-faced hammer and some

34.7 Beginning to fit the pressure plate.

and mushroom-headed pushrod in the centre of the gear shaft (having already inserted the long clutch rod from the other side of the engine). See photo 34.6. (You can also see the mushroom-headed pushrod and the ball bearing waiting to be fitted in photo 34.5, sitting on the bike lift.) The ball bearing helps reduce wear on the mushroom-headed pushrod, that goes from a standstill to several thousand revs in an instant as you engage the clutch. Note that I also liberally oiled the face of the pushrod for this very reason. Upgrades to the mushroom-headed pushrod are available, but are only really necessary for high speed racing.

Next up was the pressure plate that pushes on the clutch plates via five springs. See photo 34.7. I then fully tightened the bolts holding down the springs. See photo 34.8. The Clymer manual gives a torque setting for these bolts, but I could find no reference to any such setting in the Kawasaki manual, and as when they're fully tightened the bolts are

34.8 Pressure plate fitted.

34.9 Drifting out the old sight glass from the clutch cover.

34.5 Clutch plates slid into position.

34.6 Mushroom headed push rod and ball bearing in situ.

34.10 Oil level glass fitted to the outer cover – with the aid of some soap

HOW TO RESTORE KAWASAKI Z1, Z/KZ900 & Z/KZ1000

34.11 Outer clutch cover fitted.

34.12 New clutch spragging tool that I never used.

soap. See photo 34.9 and 34.10 of the removal and refitting of the sight glass.. You do have to be careful with this as it is easily damaged whilst installing it. I used soap because this hardens when it dries, unlike oil that stays liquid, so can provide good lubrication and a better seal.

I then applied the usual Wellseal to both faces and, after it had gone off, fitted a new gasket and then the outer casing. See photo 34.11. The clutch was in!

As soon as I'd finished the clutch the new locking tool arrived (of course), and although it looks like the original Kawasaki workshop one, I never got to use it so can't say how well it works. See photo 34.12. Note that this is available on eBay but that there are many different ones for various models. If you do buy one, make sure it's the right one for your bike.

The engine was really coming together now! See photo 34.13.

34.13 Engine coming together.

LESSONS LEARNT
- Check all parts of the clutch before reassembly.
- It wasn't the locking tool that was the problem, it was the guy operating it ...
- Don't forget to insert the ball bearing behind the mushroom-headed push rod.
- Ensure you put engine assembly lube on the face of the mushroom-headed pushrod.
- Be careful when fitting a new oil sight glass to the outer casing.
- That clutch casing is so iconic when it comes to Z900s, and getting it back on the engine makes you feel like you're getting somewhere – at last!

Chapter 35
Refitting the swinging arm & shock absorbers

My next job was to refurbish and refit the swinging arm, together with new shock absorbers. I had already removed the old bushes and bearings from the arm before having it powder coated, but I have included the process here for the sake of clarity.

Removing the old bearings and bushes from the swinging arm is never an easy job, as they are often pretty jammed in or rusted solid through years of neglect. I drove out the bearings from the bushes using a long screwdriver (don't tell the proper mechanics!): a hard job as they were very dry, but they came out okay. See photo 35.1.

After this I had the more difficult job of removing the bushes that are pressed into the swinging arm itself. Not only were the bushes very tight in the arm, but the first one was very hard to drive out. The problem is that a long spacer between the bushes prevents the bearings from sliding out of position, and this is in the way when you try to drive out the first bush, which has to be done from the opposite side of the arm. What you have to do is actually put a drift on the spacer itself, and then use this to drive out the bush, so the whole thing's very awkward. I heated the

35.1 Drifting out the bearings.

35.2 Drifting out the bushes.

35.3 Bush finally removed, with spacer now emerging.

HOW TO RESTORE KAWASAKI Z1, Z/KZ900 & Z/KZ1000

arm with a blowtorch, and then used a thick drift (an old socket extension bar) on the edge of the spacer: eventually the bush came out. See photos 35.2 and 35.3 of the first bush being pushed out by the spacer.

The second bush was easier to remove as, with the spacer out of the way, the drift can be placed directly on the back of the bush. All the old bearings and bushes were then out of the swinging arm, together with the long spacer tube that separates the bearings. See photo 35.4 of the assembly on the bench. With bushes and bearings removed, all I had to do was remove the grease nipple from the top of the arm, and then send the swinging arm with the other frame parts to be powder coated.

Having been powder coated the swinging arm was ready for reassembly, but I didn't know whether or not to upgrade the bearings. As with the head races for the front forks, upgraded roller bearing kits are available to replace the original plain bearings. See photo 35.5 of such a kit as advertised on eBay. After a bit of thought, I decided against this particular upgrade for the following reasons –

- It was an expensive upgrade and I was running out of cash – again – despite having sold my Triumph Thunderbird to raise funds.
- I was planning on using the bike only for Sunday morning jaunts around Derbyshire, so probably wouldn't notice the difference, anyway.
- The upgrade was from an unknown supplier and of unknown quality.
- Properly fitted new standard bushes should work fine.

So I bought a new set of standard bushes and bearings. See photo 35.6 of the old and new bushes.

To begin reassembly I gave the grease nipple a good clean before refitting, as it was full of old grease. If you don't clean this out, when grease is first pumped through it, the old grease is pushed into the bearings, not the nice, new fresh grease. See photo 35.7.

I then fitted the new bushes – which was a lot harder than it sounds! I again heated the swinging arm, and put the new bushes in the freezer (to expand the former and shrink the latter), and then tried to knock them in. They did not want to go. Halfway through trying to hammer them home (with a lump of wood and a hammer) they both jammed, and I had to hit them much harder than I would have liked to drive them home, but finally they were in. See photo 35.8. Note It's important to drive the bushes fully home as otherwise they'll sit slightly proud and the swinging arm won't fit inside the frame.

I was relieved to get the bushes in, but my relief was short-lived when I discovered that the bearings that run inside them no longer fitted; they were just too tight. See photo 35.9. This confused me as I'd tried them before and they were a perfect fit. And they weren't just a bit tight now – they were way too tight. I took the swinging arm and bearings to the engineer to see if they could ream out the bushes sufficiently for the bearings to fit snugly and smoothly. This they did, and when I went to collect the parts they said they thought the bushes had distorted slightly during fitting, which was why they needed reaming. You live and learn.

Whilst the swinging arm was away being sorted, I cleaned the bearing caps for the outside of the bushes: these have an 'O' ring to

35.4 The old bearing assembly with bushes, bearings and the long central spacer.

35.6 Old and new swinging arm bushes.

35.8 New bushes installed – after a fight.

35.5 A roller bearing swinging arm upgrade kit.

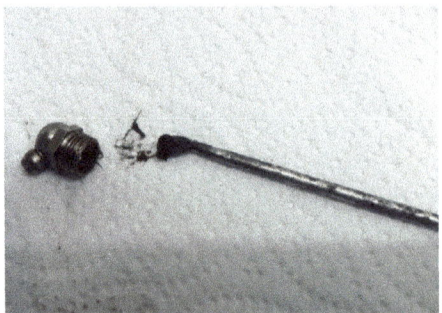

35.7 Removing the old grease from the grease nipple.

35.9 Now the new bearings won't fit anymore.

REFITTING THE SWINGING ARM & SHOCK ABSORBERS

35.10 Cleaning up the end caps and 'O' ring seals.

35.11 Damn! The spacer goes in first!

35.13 With my 'bespoke' spacer inserted, the bushes were liberally greased and then also inserted.

prevent grease seeping out. See photo 35.10.

The swinging arm came back from the engineer, and I prepared to fit it to the frame, at which point I realised I should have fitted the long spacer *before* fitting the second bush, as it couldn't be inserted afterwards: 'Damn and Blast!' See photo 35.11. I knew that there was no way those bushes were going to come out again without an awful lot of persuasion, probably using the engineer, and that the bushes would almost certainly become scrap in the process (they were very, very tight!). Hmmm.

In the end I realised that the spacer isn't under a huge amount of pressure, and is there to prevent the bearings from slowly working their way out of the bushes toward the inside of the swinging arm. I had some spare 22mm copper pipe for plumbing and tried this – it was almost the exact size of the bush; just a little too big. I cut the pipe to the exact length required (important), and then cut it along its length. See photo 35.12. This meant that I could squeeze it enough to slide it through one of the bushes before it sprang open again when inside the swinging arm, enough to prevent the bearings from sliding inward (hopefully). Time will tell (so far, so good).

With my bespoke (ahem) spacer in place, I liberally greased both bushes and inserted the two plain bearings. See photo 35.13 of one of the bearings nearly home. I then 'stuck' on the end caps with grease, and was ready to insert the swinging arm into the frame. The first thing I did was determine that I had the swinging arm the right way up by checking that the grease nipple was on the top. The

35.12 Cutting down the length of some 22mm copper tubing.

swinging arm will fit either way up, so check you've got it right.

With the swinging arm the right way up I tried to insert it into the frame, but, needless to say, it was a very hard job with the frame initially seeming far too narrow. After much time, effort, and becoming increasingly covered in grease, I finally got it into position and knocked home the spindle. Job done – see photo 35.14 – or so I thought ...

What I hadn't realised was that the swinging arm is too wide near the back to clear the bottom section of the frame (where the silencers bolt on). I had fitted the swinging arm with the rear end downward (due to its weight), and now it was too wide to be pulled up, past the silencer mountings, into its usual position. See photo 35.14 again. Bugger! Needless to say, I had to take it off again, and this time fit it with the rear end above the silencer mountings,

35.14 Success! It's in at last! But it's too low and will have to come out again!

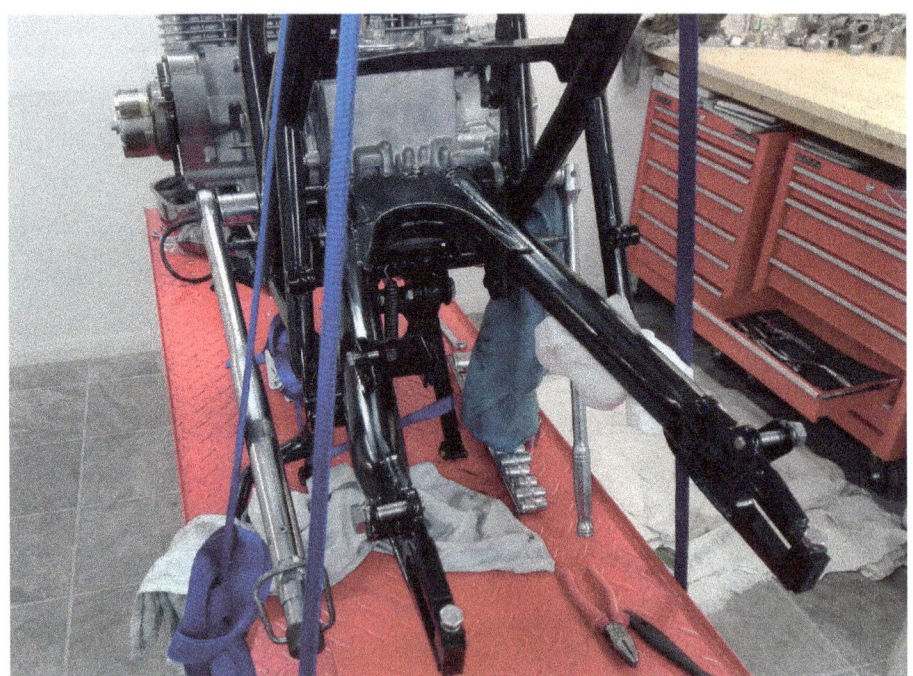

35.15 Swinging arm now fitted above the lower frame and with the spindle being torqued up.

which was twice as hard as I had to hold it up as well as fit it. Eventually, it was done (again) – see photo 35.15 – with rags between the arm and the silencer mountings to protect both. And I thought I'd been so clever by ensuring I had it the right way up. Pride comes before a fall, as my mother would often say.

At this point I think it's worth mentioning Robert M Pirsig's classic novel, *Zen and the Art of Motorcycle Maintenance*. If you haven't read it, but intend to work on bikes, it's a must (although there is some pretty heavy philosophy in there, too!). One of his mantras is that, if you have to do anything twice, the second time round you will do it much faster and learn far more about it, and get to understand it more, than if you'd done it once – it's a double whammy! I can't tell you the number of times I've had to repeat this mantra to myself as I've been forced to take off some or other part that's taken me ages to put on because of some stupid schoolboy error. The thing is, he's right! You learn so much more about it and complete the job far more quickly the second time round.

With the swinging arm finally in (the correct) position, and the spindle inserted, I torqued the spindle nut. I locked the other end of the spindle with a long-handled socket that jammed against the bike lift, and used the torque wrench on the nut. See photo 35.15 again. I was rather confused to begin with as the manual gives a very wide range of torque settings on this nut: between 58 and 87ft/lb. Usually when a range is given I err toward the top end to ensure that everything is good and tight, so this is what I decided to do. However, when I tightened the nut to near 87ft/lb, I realised that the swinging arm was doing anything but swinging – it was pretty much locked solid. I loosened off the nut a little and the arm suddenly became loose. In the end, I almost ignored the actual torque setting (although stayed in range), and tightened the nut until the swinging arm was tight but moved smoothly, slowly going down under its own weight, which I've always believed to be the correct setting. I now know the reason for the wide range of torque in the manual: it will differ, bike-to-bike.

I then fitted my new shock absorbers. I'd agonised over these for quite some time. There had been many options –
• Modern shocks that don't look original but are vastly superior.
• Classic-looking Hagon shocks that look period but are much better than the originals.
• Period-looking repro shocks that are relatively cheap but don't work too well.
• Reflector on the top or not?

I didn't want modern-looking shocks on my standard bike, so

35.16 New rear shocks fitted to my preference – and wallet!

REFITTING THE SWINGING ARM & SHOCK ABSORBERS

they were out. I did want the Hagon shocks, but they were about three times the price of the cheaper copies. In the end I had to go for the cheaper copies for budget (or lack of) reasons, my reasoning being that, if in the future I do decide to upgrade, it's only a ten-minute job to change them. I can clearly hear my dad's voice: 'Buying cheap is the most expensive thing you can ever do,' as you know that the cheap items will always need replacing for one or other reason, so you'll end up buying the expensive ones and paying twice. Best just to buy the expensive ones straight away – but when did I ever listen to my father's advice?

Shocks in the USA had reflectors on the top (KZ) but European ones didn't (Z). I chose to have ones with reflectors because I like them.

With the choice finally made and the cheaper shocks purchased, I duly fitted them after spending ages looking for the top mounting bolt, before realising that they're already mounted to the frame! Durr! See photo 35.16.

The final job was to grease the bushes and bearings. I used my trusty old grease gun for this and pumped about three guns' worth into the arm, filling the void around the long spacer and forcing grease down the bearings. I kept pumping until the pressure built, indicating that the grease was now under slight pressure and would force itself between the bush and the bearing. See photo 35.17.

LESSONS LEARNT
• Drifting out the old bushes and bearings isn't easy, but at least you don't have to worry about damaging them in the process.
• Uprated swinging arm bushes are available, but do you really need them? (Other than when you vie for bragging rights at the local bike meet.)
• It's possible to distort swinging arm bushes when you fit them.
• Don't forget to insert the long spacer before fitting the second bush.
• Don't fit your swinging arm upside down (or hanging below the silencer mountings!).
• Remember Robert M Pirsig's mantra about having to take apart something that you've just assembled incorrectly ...

35.17 Greasing the bushes with a grease gun.

Chapter 36
Refitting the rear wheel

With the swinging arm finally in position I could turn my attention to the rear wheel and rear brake assembly. Although the back wheel itself was finished, together with the brake plate, the rear sprocket carrier wasn't ready, and had to be assembled. The first job was to fit my new standard rear drive sprocket (sprockets and rear chains wear out so quickly on these bikes that replacement is virtually always required) to the carrier, and insert the special bolts from the rear that engage with blocks on the carrier, and prevent them from turning when being tightened. See photo 36.1. I tend to find that sprockets on imported US machines are often not standard, as it's all about acceleration and the standing ¼ mile there, so bikes tend to be geared very low so as to provide maximum acceleration. In my case, I think the sprockets were standard, though I didn't really check as I knew I was going to be replacing both – but it's worth knowing.

I then turned over the carrier and fitted the new sprocket onto the bolts with new nuts and locking tabs. The nuts needed torquing to around 30ft/lb, but, I could only do this together with the gearbox sprocket when the wheel was in situ and could be locked with the rear chain (see photo 36.2). I therefore just tightened them a bit and left torquing them until after the wheel was fitted. I also made another schoolboy error, clearly visible in this photo – can you spot it? Answer below. (If only I had a brain!)

I loosely assembled the sprocket carrier and its two spacers on the rear wheel spindle to check how it all went together. See photo 36.3. Note that the thinner spacer goes on the outside and the much longer spacer with a flange in the middle goes on the inside, and sits inside the bearing. Note also that I'd got them muddled up, and had had the inner spacer chromed (which is completely invisible when the wheel's on), rather

36.1 Inserting the special sprocket bolts in the back of the carrier.

36.2 Bolting the new sprocket to the carrier.

36.3 Refitting the back wheel – spacer, then carrier, then large spacer.

REFITTING THE REAR WHEEL

than the outer one which is visible. I was having a bad day.

Next up were the rubber shock absorbers that fit between the sprocket carrier and the rear wheel. If they're damaged power delivery will be juddery, often accompanied by noises from the rear end. I checked mine and they seemed okay. They're expensive to replace (as with everything!), and, as they looked more than serviceable, I cleaned them thoroughly (grit and dirt will considerably shorten life), and put them back into service. See photo 36.4.

Having inserted them into the rear wheel cavity (see photo 36.5), I then tried to fit the rear wheel with the sprocket carrier already on the spindle (as in photo 36.3), but there was no way it wanted to go in, so I fitted the sprocket carrier to the wheel and fitted the whole lot together. Even then it was really difficult as the swinging arm was narrower than the wheel – why isn't it ever the other way round? I removed the end caps on the swinging arm and slotted it in, but it still didn't want to play ball. In the end I fitted the wheel, together with the long 'cotton reel' shaped spacer on the outside of the brake plate (see photo 36.18 for reference), but without the right-hand adjusting plate. With a big screwdriver I then carefully prised apart the swinging arm enough to allow me to get the adjusting plate in position (not easy). How you're supposed to change a rear tyre on the open road I've no idea. So much for quick release! Anyway, it was finally fitted, see photo 36.6.

Next up was the rear brake as I wanted to use the brake to help lock the rear wheel when I tightened the gearbox sprocket (the gearbox sprocket is torqued to 100ft/lb, and the more resistance there is to lock it, the better). I retrieved my brake torque arm (which I hadn't had rechromed as it was still in good condition, and needed only a good polish) and the various special bolts to hold it in place. See photo 36.7. I then loosely bolted the torque arm onto the swinging arm mounting ready to be bolted to the rear brake plate.

Next, I took my rechromed brake lever and spring and slid them onto the brake spindle on the frame (see photo 36.8), the only issue here being which way round the spring went. Luckily, I could cheat and compared it with the one on my Z1A, which showed me that the U-shaped end went under the brake lever, and the other end went on top of the bracket on the frame.

I then loosely fitted the rear brake arm on the brake plate. See photo 36.9. I wasn't sure what was the best position for maximum effectiveness at this stage so didn't tighten it; it would be adjusted when the wheel was properly fitted with the chain on, etc.

Next, I fully fitted the brake pedal with its large washer and domed nut, together with the ferrule and

36.6 Rear wheel fitted.

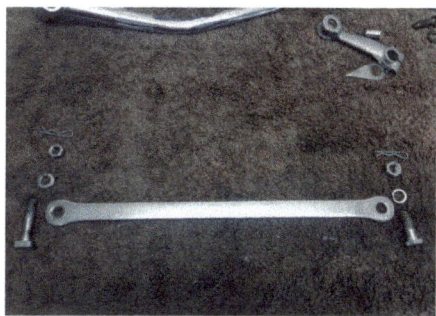

36.7 Rear brake torque arm ready for fitting.

36.4 Shock absorber rubbers.

36.5 Shock absorber rubbers fitted in the rear wheel hub.

36.8 Fitting the rear brake pedal.

149

HOW TO RESTORE KAWASAKI Z1, Z/KZ900 & Z/KZ1000

36.9 Fitting the rear brake arm.

36.10 Rear brake pedal fitted.

36.11 Rear brake arm assembly fitted

brake rod inserted into the fulcrum. See photo 36.10. I also fitted a new pedal stop nut and bolt to the frame. I then connected the brake arm, with the large spring in front of it and the knurled nut behind it. See photo 36.11.

I was nearly ready to fit the chain and finally tighten the engine sprocket – NOT! It was then, and only then, that I realised I had forgotten to fit one simple but essential component … the grease seal on the outside of the sprocket carrier. I don't know why, or how, but it had somehow escaped my notice, and I now needed to remove the rear wheel – again! All I could do was repeatedly mutter Robert's mantra through clenched teeth, and get on with it. I was having a really, really bad day.

With the wheel quickly removed and the sprocket carrier on the bench (yes, he's right about how much better you get at things), I started to remedy the situation. First of all, I packed the bearing with as much grease as I could (see photo 36.12), and then tapped in a new grease/oil seal. See photo 36.13. Turning over the carrier I packed more grease into the rear of the bearing before re-inserting my beautifully-chromed invisible spacer. See photo 36.14. I was then ready to re-refit the rear wheel.

One item of note is that this new bearing wasn't sealed. Most new bearings that I buy these days are, with grease already inside them and their own rubber grease seal, but not this one. I can only assume that this

36.12 Packing the carrier bearing with grease.

36.13 Oil/grease seal fitted.

REFITTING THE REAR WHEEL

36.14 Inside of bearing greased and long spacer fitted.

was either an old stock bearing or one that's an odd size that isn't available as a sealed item – does the same go for the front wheel bearings?

Now that the wheel was finally fitted, I slid the long spacer over the gearbox mainshaft and loosely fitted the gearbox sprocket and its nut. Note that I had already fitted the 'O' ring oil seal on the mainshaft. I then fed my new, gold-coloured chain with added bling round the sprockets. See photo 36.15. Note that later bikes (from Z1B onward) were fitted with these better, stronger chains, which have small, individual neoprene 'O' rings each side of each link to retain the grease and keep out the dirt, and are superior to the earlier chains (though still wear out quickly). You can convert earlier bikes to take these if you wish by putting spacers behind the sprockets to give the necessary clearance for the larger chains.

My chain was supplied with a closing link that was pressed on rather than the more usual horseshoe link, so I bought a small link-fitting tool and clamped the closing link in position. See photo 36.16. However, I wasn't that happy with the end result. The link was fitted nice and tightly and pushed fully home, but the ends of the link pins weren't peened over properly, so I was worried about the side of the link sliding off the end of the pins.

With the chain now fitted (at least temporarily), the last job before tightening the engine sprocket was to adjust the chain ... at which point I discovered yet another schoolboy error. On each chain adjuster is a little line that aligns with marks on the rear of the swinging arm, to ensure that the adjusters are adjusted by the same amount, so that the wheel is straight in the frame. When I came to look at the adjuster on the right, I discovered that I'd fitted it upside down so that the line which should have been at the top on the outside was now at the bottom on the inside, so didn't line up with the marks on the swinging arm. See photo 36.17. The only remedy was to semi-remove the wheel and

36.16 Inserting closing link into chain.

turn it over, but I'd had enough by this time, so the adjuster was left upside down, at least temporarily. You can only mutter a mantra so many bloody times.

Having left the adjuster where it was, I finished adjusting the chain and fitted the brake stay to the back plate, adjusting the angle of the brake arm so that it was pointing slightly backward, which I thought would give good leverage. I also ensured that the little brake wear indicator was pointing to the point of lowest wear as new shoes had been fitted. I then tightened the wheel spindle and inserted a snazzy, stainless steel 'R' pin through the castellated nut to hold it secure. Job done. See photo 36.18.

36.17 Schoolboy error on the chain adjustment cams.

36.15 Chain draped over sprockets ready for joining.

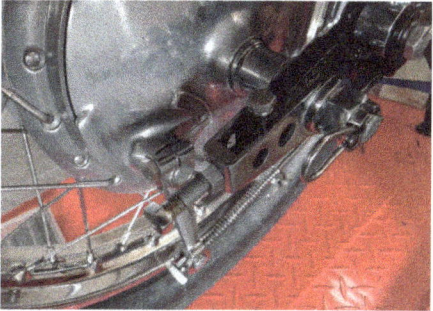

36.18 Fitting completed.

HOW TO RESTORE KAWASAKI Z1, Z/KZ900 & Z/KZ1000

LESSONS LEARNT
- Don't forget to fit the grease seal to the sprocket carrier.
- Don't fit your chain adjusters upside down.
- The Z1000 had a rear disc brake as opposed to the drum brake of earlier models, so assembly of the rear wheel and brake is slightly different to the above,
- Sometimes you just have to hold up your hand and say: 'I'm having such a bad day!'

Later on I ordered and then fitted a normal horseshoe link to the rear chain See photo 36.19. The manual says that these aren't usually fitted due to the bike's power causing immense strain on the chain. However, I think it's far better to have a horseshoe link that's fitted correctly than a closed link that might fall off at any moment.

I also bit the bullet and turned the chain adjuster the right way up as it would have just annoyed the hell out of me.

36.19 Horseshoe chain link fitted for peace of mind.

Chapter 37
Fitting the gearbox outer cover

With the rear wheel and rear chain fitted it was finally time to tighten the gearbox sprocket, which I'd been waiting ages to do. My chosen MO for this was the time-honoured and extremely hi-tech method of locking the sprocket with the wooden shaft of a hammer jammed in between the chain and the sprocket (again). See photo 37.1 of a hammer shaft bravely volunteering to sacrifice itself in the interest of motorcycle mechanics. Stirring stuff.

You do have to be careful locking a sprocket like this, as in some cases you risk bending the shaft or damaging the engine cases if things slip, but in this instance I think it was acceptable.

Note that I also locked on the rear brake as fully as I could to try and reduce the strain on the sprocket/hammer shaft. I did this by screwing down the small bolt that stops the brake lever from rising too high. I screwed the bolt down hard onto the lever so that it engaged the rear brake shoes as powerfully as possible.

With everything locked I tightened the gearbox sprocket to the required very high torque of 100ft/lb, and all went well; the nut tightened up without problem. After this I bent the locking washer over to lock it securely. I also slid the long clutch push rod into the gear shaft in front of the gearbox sprocket.

One item of note is that when I was assembling the sprocket, I noticed in the parts catalogue there was a small pin fitted inside the output shaft. I knew that mine hadn't had one fitted when I dismantled the bike and thought I'd better have one, so I ordered it. When it arrived I inserted it in the shaft through two holes drilled there for it, and it was then held in place by the nut which went on and covered the two holes

37.1 Locking the chain with the shaft of a hammer (a very brave hammer).

HOW TO RESTORE KAWASAKI Z1, Z/KZ900 & Z/KZ1000

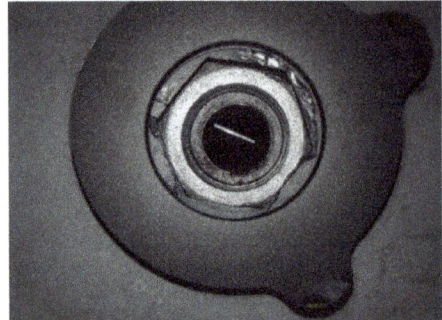

37.2 The confusing pin in the gearbox shaft.

37.3 The engine sprocket cover fitted.

to stop it falling out. See photo 37.2. But what was it for and why did I need it? I finally realised, after it was fitted, that it was the drive peg for the mechanical chain oiler fitted to Z1s and Z1As. I didn't need it at all.

So why was it still on the parts' list and why were the fitting holes still drilled in the gear shaft to take it? I can only assume that the listing was an error, and the machining for the gear shaft was simply left as it was before as it would have been more expensive to change it. Whatever the case I'd worried for no reason and didn't need it – but it's in there if I ever do! Anyway, moving on, I fitted the tin sprocket cover with its three retaining screws, and it was job done. See photo 37.3.

I then turned my attention to the outer gearbox cover and fitted the two oil seals that go over the gear change shaft into the cover. See photos 37.4 A and B. I realised that these oil seals have nothing to do with stopping oil coming out, but are simply there as a kind of soft bearing for the gear change shaft to run in, rather than fit a couple of small needle roller bearings – makes perfect sense.

After this I cleaned and inserted the clutch operating mechanism, which consists of a large nylon screw operating in a large nylon thread. By turning the screw (with the clutch cable) the screw runs down the thread and the push rod is pushed inwards. Simple. I screwed the outer thread into the casing and inserted the screw part with plenty of grease. The only point to note is that the screw can accidentally be inserted in the wrong position on the thread, as there is more than one 'start' for

37.4 Inserting the first oil seal on the gear change shaft (A) ... and the second one (B).

37.5 Incorrect positioning of the clutch operating mechanism.

37.6 Correct positioning of the clutch operating mechanism.

the thread. If you look at photo 37.5 you can see how the screw looks if inserted in the *wrong* position using the *wrong* 'start' and screwed down. The *correct* position is shown in photo 37.6. If yours looks like the one in photo 37.5, simply take the screw section out and re-insert it in a different position until it looks the one in photo 37.6. You can see that if you pulled on the arm (with the clutch cable) in photo 37.5 you wouldn't get much movement from the screw and the clutch would never

FITTING THE GEARBOX OUTER COVER

work properly, no matter how many times you adjusted it.

Also note that the empty housing next to the clutch actuating mechanism is for the chain oiler mechanism that was discontinued – no point in changing the tooling that makes the cases. Kawasaki did eventually change the outer gearbox casing on later Z1000 models, and also fitted a new clutch operating mechanism with ball bearings, which can be retro-fitted to earlier models if desired.

With the operating mechanism correctly fitted I attached the bottom of the clutch cable to the operating arm. See photo 37.7. Note the spring, the fact that the cable goes through a hole in the casing and that there's a small split pin to prevent the cable from popping out of the operating arm when slack.

With the clutch cable fitted it was time to fit the outer cover. This casing really is just a cover and so there's no gasket etc, as there's no oil behind it. You just need to check that you have inserted the long clutch push rod that the operating mechanism pushes on, and that you have slackened the actuator adjustment right off, to ensure that it doesn't press against the push rod and prevent the casing from being pushed fully home. The gear change shaft is inserted through the two oil seals. See photo 37.8.

One strange thing about the outer cover is that, unlike the other casings, it is screwed on with hex headed bolts rather than cross headed screws, which I found very strange. Hex headed bolts can always be tightened far tighter than cross headed screws, so you think they'd be used on the cases which need to be oil tight and not on those cases which didn't – but it's the other way round! The only possible explanation I can think of is that the clutch operating mechanism is in this housing, and that takes considerable pressure when operating the clutch, so maybe they used bolts to give added support?

I then fed the cable up through the frame at the headstock – which I think is the correct routing (see photo 37.9) and then through the cable guide on the left fork top (see photo 37.10) to the clutch lever. My clutch lever was badly scratched so I bought a new lever and repainted the original bracket. I fitted the cable by fully slackening off all the adjusters, removing the lever from the housing (see photo 37.11), then levering it

37.7 Clutch cable attached to the outer cover.

back into position and inserting the clevis pin through it. This seemed to work well. I then adjusted the clutch operating mechanism in the gearbox cover so that it bit, then turned it back half a turn and locked it with the locknut. I then fine-tuned the cable free play with the small cable adjusters on the clutch lever and half way down the cable. I adjusted the cable so that it was just slack when the clutch wasn't being used but it bit soon after the lever was pulled in – this gives maximum clutch release without fear of burning out the clutch due to overtightening. Finally I clipped the cable to the frame down tube on the adjuster screw. See photo 37.12.

My last job was to fit the oval gasket (not really necessary but it may help to prevent rattles), then the

37.8 Outer cover fitted.

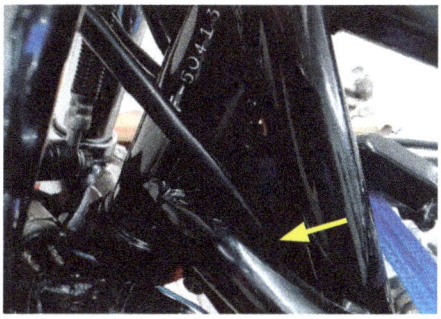

37.9 The clutch cable runs up through the gap in the frame next to the headstock.

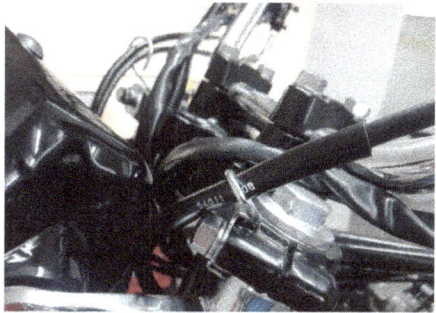

37.10 The cable goes through the guide on the top of the left fork.

HOW TO RESTORE KAWASAKI Z1, Z/KZ900 & Z/KZ1000

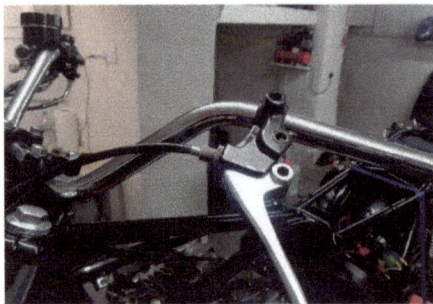

37.11 Fitting the cable to the clutch lever.

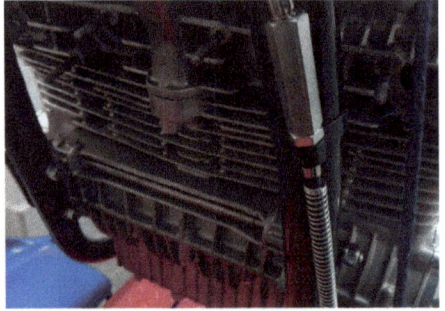

37.12 the cable is clipped to the left-hand down tube.

inspection cover to the outer cover, and it was job done (or so I thought). See photo 37.13.

It was only later in the restoration when the exhaust pipes were fitted that I realised a slight problem with the clutch cable. If you look at photo 37.14 you can see that the cable runs outside the frame, quite close to the outer exhaust downpipe. Although the cable is protected with a spring I thought it was best to move it, so I released the cable by removing the clutch lever and loosening off the metal adjusting screw on the clutch operating mechanism. I then rerouted the cable inside the frame. On refitting it I made the schoolboy error of pulling-in the clutch before I'd replaced the metal adjuster in the clutch operating mechanism. The result was that the long clutch pushrod jammed in the operating mechanism, and I had to remove the outer cover to free it. See photo 37.15. Having sorted that out the cable was now inside the frame and away from the downpipe. See photo 37.16.

LESSONS LEARNT

- Using a piece of wood (or hammer shaft) isn't the best way to lock a sprocket and isn't recommended workshop practice, but it's about the only way I know for the amateur restorer.
- The engine sprocket is done up to 100ft/lb of torque, which is F***** tight!!*
- The little pin in the gearbox shaft is the drive for the chain oiler and isn't required on later bikes.
- The oil seals in the outer gearbox cover are used as soft bearings/support for the gear change lever, not for stopping oil leaks.
- Fit the clutch actuator together so it looks like photo 37.6 **NOT** photo 37.5.
- The outer cover is held on with bolts, not cross head screws.
- The outer cover on later Z1000s don't have the housing for the chain oiler fitted. The clutch operating mechanisms were also uprated, and can be retro-fitted to earlier bikes.
- It's never over until it's over.

---

* Fairly

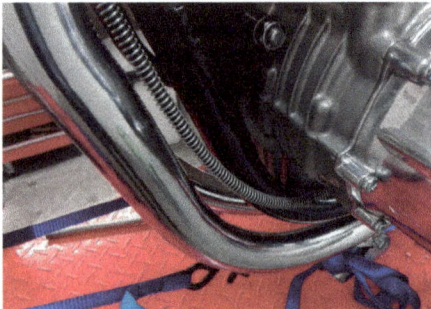

37.14 Clutch cable too near the outer downpipe.

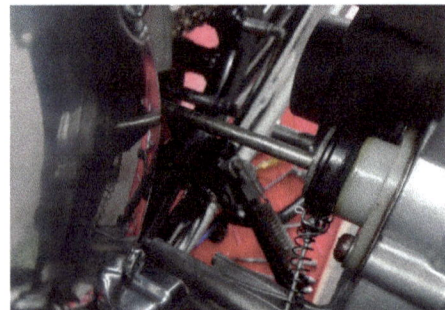

37.15 Clutch push rod jammed in the operating mechanism.

37.16 Clutch cable rerouted inside the frame.

37.13 With the clutch play adjusted the inspection cover is fitted.

Chapter 38
Refurbishing & refitting the front brakes

So to the front brakes. The original front brake system was in a poor state when I bought the bike, due mainly to a seized calliper and badly leaking front master cylinder, so it wasn't a hard decision to decide to convert the bike to twin front disc brakes, as for the European Z900 models, as I'd need to buy a new master cylinder anyway, and thought it worth buying a larger diameter master cylinder to fit twin discs. The main problem here (apart from cost) was that many of the necessary parts are currently unavailable. Ironically, all the parts required to convert earlier Z1 models to twin discs are available (when these were never produced with twin discs), but not for the later Z900/Z1000 models (which were produced with twin discs!). Those parts currently unavailable for the Z900/Z1000 are:
• Brake discs (either 6mm or 8mm).
• Brake callipers.
Note the following:
• Brake discs for a Z1/Z1A/Z1B have six mounting bolts.
• Brake discs for a Z900 have four mounting bolts.
• Brake callipers for Z1s and Z900s and early Z1000 models (A1) aren't handed, so a calliper will fit either side.

• Callipers for the later Z1000 models (A2 onward) are handed, so you need a left and a right one.
• Calliper mounting brackets for all models are handed, so you need one of each to convert to twin discs.
• Master cylinders are of larger diameter on twin disc models than single disc ones.

I had already managed to source a matched pair of the thinner, 6mm discs, and these were already fitted to the front wheel. I had also bought a second-hand calliper and right-hand mounting bracket from John Browse to add to the one I already had, because at the time they were unavailable. All other necessary parts were available to buy new.

I later learned that new right-hand calliper mounting brackets have now been remanufactured, and are available again, so that's a big bonus. If you look at photo 38.1 you can see that the shafts to hold the bracket to the calliper are longer on one side than the other, which is why the brackets are handed.

The calliper I'd bought second-hand was vapour blasted as it was in poor condition, but the powder coating company refused to paint the callipers because it had received

38.1 Calliper mounting brackets are handed.

complaints from owners whose callipers had seized because the heat used in the powder coating process had distorted the callipers. I don't think the heat was the problem – probably more a case of paint overspray that wasn't scraped off causing pistons to jam. (I had to heat the callipers to 200 degrees C when I painted them, without a problem.)

I therefore had one calliper that was vapour blasted and one still painted (as there was no point blast cleaning it if it couldn't be powder coated), and I just needed to remove the mounting brackets and the old pistons from both before refurbishing. See photo 38.2. I undid the two connecting bolts from each calliper

38.2 Brake callipers ready for refurbishment.

38.3 Calliper bracket removed from original calliper.

38.4 Trying to remove the old piston with compressed air.

38.5 Callipers ready to go to the engineers for piston removal.

and withdrew the mounting brackets and old brake pads, etc. See photo 38.3.

My next job was to try and remove the old pistons. I had already decided to fit new pistons to both callipers regardless, so wasn't bothered about damaging them when getting them out. First of all I tried to ease them out with a pair of mole grips, but the pistons were stuck fast and didn't want to know, plus it was difficult to get a good grip on the pistons, anyway. I therefore moved to plan B – compressed air – which nearly always works. I put the bleed nipples back in to seal the exit, and then inserted my compressed air nozzle in the fluid inlet hole to try and force out the pistons. Usually this is spectacularly successful in that pistons eject at high speed and shoot across the workshop! In this case, however, neither piston showed any sign of moving. Bugger. See photo 38.4.

Admitting defeat I took the callipers to the engineer to see if they could help. See photo 38.5. I'm very happy to report that they managed to remove the pistons – but only after a struggle. They had to run a tap down inside the pistons, and then screw an iron bar into that, which enabled them to slowly work out the pistons. Good on them! See photo 38.6 of the callipers as they came back from the engineer. Note how much horrible gunge there was in the callipers, and also note the threads in the pistons used to extract them. See photo 38.7 of a close-up of the gunge in one of the callipers – they badly needed cleaning!

38.6 Pistons removed by threading them – look at the gunge in the callipers!

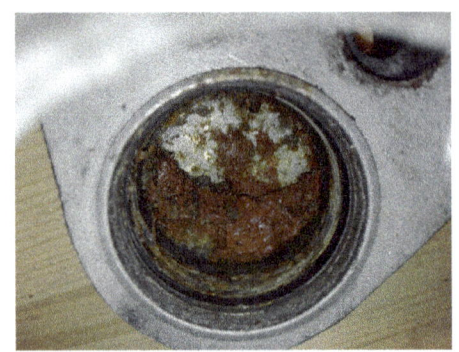
38.7 Yes, that's really thick gunge!

REFURBISHING & REFITTING THE FRONT BRAKES

I cleaned the callipers very thoroughly and used a piece of wire to clean out one of the passages as it was so blocked it wouldn't clean out with compressed air alone. See photo 38.8. When they were completely clean, I painted them and the mounting brackets with special calliper paint. To facilitate this I strung them up in the conservatory, and used that as a spray booth with appropriate dust sheets, etc. See photo 38.9. Unfortunately, what I didn't realise is just how much overspray dries in the air, and then floats around to land as a thick layer of black dust. I thought I'd done enough with the dust sheets, but the rest of the conservatory was filthy! I wasn't Mr Popular – the strong smell of aerosol throughout the house didn't go down too well, either.

I left the paint to dry for a full week before curing it in a hot oven for an hour at 200 degrees C when there was no-one else in. See photo 38.10. (I got away with this by cleaning the oven afterward to remove any odour, actually gaining Brownie points in the process!) Heating the paint to this temperature apparently hardens it fully, and makes it impervious to brake fluid – let's hope so. NB: There was very nearly a nasty incident. When I'd sprayed the callipers I'd stuffed tissue down the holes for the bleed nipples and inlet pipe to mask them, and had forgotten to take it out, but noticed it as I was just about to put the callipers in the oven. I'm not sure what would've happened otherwise, but I'm sure it wouldn't have been good!

The callipers were then ready to be reassembled with new pistons and seals. See photo 38.11. To begin with, I inserted new seals into the grooves inside the calliper faces, lubricated everything with brake fluid and inserted the new pistons, which I'm glad to say were a perfect interference fit. See photo 38.12.

After this came the dust seal. A thin metal retaining ring sits in a groove of the calliper around the piston to hold the seal in place. See photo 38.13. I put the retaining ring into the dust seal (see photo 38.14), then pushed the retaining ring into its groove, together with the dust seal. The other end of the dust seal then engages with a groove in the piston.

38.8 Thoroughly cleaning the callipers.

38.9 Callipers and brackets being painted.

38.10 Callipers being baked in the oven – yummy!

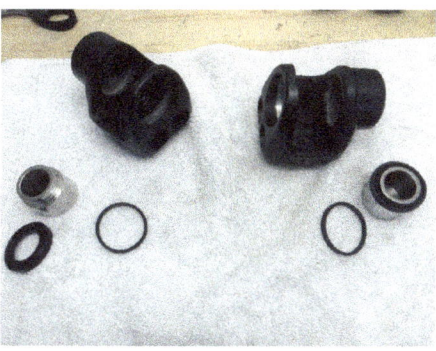
38.11 New pistons and seals ready to be fitted.

38.12 Main seal and new piston fitted.

38.13 Dust seal and its retaining ring.

38.14 Retaining ring fitted into dust seal.

38.17 New 'O' rings fitted inside the shafts.

38.19 New brake pad fitted to the mounting bracket.

See photo 38.15 of the dust seal fitted.

With the callipers sorted I turned my attention to the mounting brackets and assembled the four 'O' rings and four dust covers required per bracket. See photo 38.16. I checked that the grooves inside the shafts were nice and clean, and then inserted the 'O' rings. See photo 38.17. These were then followed by the four dust seals. See photo 38.18. The reason these seals are important is so that the calliper can slide on the mounting bracket. The mounting brackets are bolted firmly to the fork legs, but the brake callipers themselves aren't bolted to anything, which allows them to float. The callipers slide along the brackets on two bolts that run through the shafts in the mounting brackets. When the brakes are applied, the mounting bracket doesn't move, but the calliper does. If the calliper can't slide easily on the bracket the brakes won't work properly. That's why the 'O' rings are important as they allow the bolts to slide through them smoothly without rusting – and, of course, the dust seals prevent debris going down the shafts and jamming everything with dirt.

38.18 New dust seals fitted to the ends of the shafts.

38.20 Anti-squeal shim being greased before fitting.

38.15 Retaining ring seated in the calliper with the dust seal.

38.16 Preparing to refurb the calliper mounting bracket.

I then pressed one of the brake pads into the mounting brackets (see photo 38.19), and greased the small, anti-squeal shim before placing it in position on the back of the brake pad. I used a little grease as it helps prevent brake squeal – and is helpful in keeping the shim in position whilst fitting it! See photo 38.20.

I then slid the mounting bracket inside the calliper and fitted it by sliding the two bolts through the calliper and the mounting bracket. Two large, very thick washers go on the ends of the bolts before the nuts are added and everything's tightened. See photo 38.21. Apparently, the large washers aren't available any more so try not to lose them – although I think they could be fabricated if necessary.

38.21 The mounting bracket is then fitted to the calliper with two large bolts.

38.22 The other brake pad is then fitted to the calliper with its 'flying saucer' washer.

The second brake pad is then fitted to the other side of the calliper and held in place with special 'flying saucer' washers that screw into the

REFURBISHING & REFITTING THE FRONT BRAKES

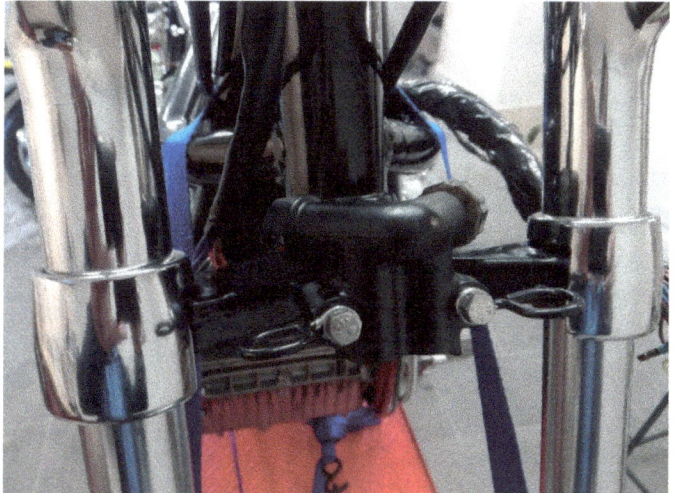

38.23 The brake junction box bolted to the bottom yoke.

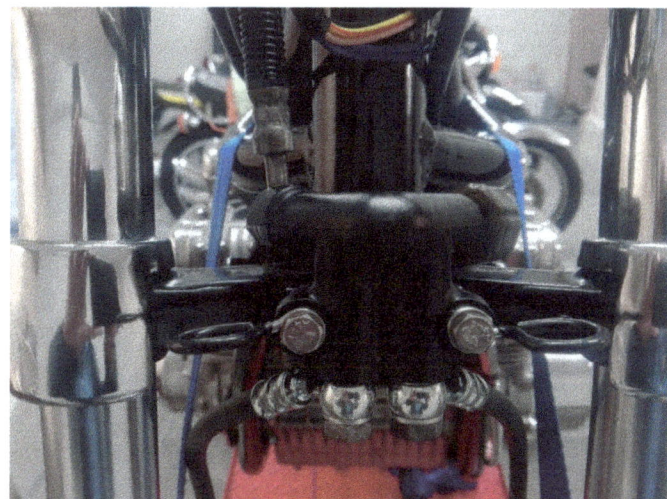

38.24 Connectors in place.

38.25 Hydraulic hoses and pipes held in the guide with a large grommet.

38.26 Original small bore master cylinder.

38.27 New large bore master cylinder.

back of the brake pad. See photo 38.22. I checked that the callipers slid along the mounting brackets without hindrance and the callipers were finished. I ensured that the pistons in both callipers were as fully retracted as possible, then slid them over the brake discs into position. I bolted the mounting brackets to the front forks using the specified torque setting, and it was job done.

Turning to the rest of the braking system, I bolted the junction box to the bottom yoke not forgetting to fit the two cable guides (one for the tacho cable and one for the speedo). See photo 38.23. I had already screwed the brake light switch into position whilst on the bench, as access is a bit limited otherwise. After this, I connected the three different hoses to the junction box using new copper washers to ensure there were no leaks. See photo 38.24.

I joined the bottom hoses to the brake pipes, and held these in place in the cable guides on the front mudguard with large rubber grommets on the ferrules of the brake hoses. See photo 38.25. The fluid pipes were then screwed into the callipers and new bleed nipples fitted.

Now, luckily, I replaced my original master cylinder (see photo 38.26) as I needed a larger one. Master cylinders are different sizes for single or twin discs and, as I was converting to twin discs, I needed the larger diameter cylinder (⅝in), so bought a lovely new one. See photo 38.27. I say luckily because

HOW TO RESTORE KAWASAKI Z1, Z/KZ900 & Z/KZ1000

this meant I didn't have to worry about restoring my old one and fitting new seals and repainting it, etc. All I had to do was buy a new one and it was job done. Aren't motorcycle mechanics simple sometimes?! (If you're of a mind to restore your own, note that master cylinders can be repaired quite easily, and new seal kits are readily available.)

With the master cylinder plumbed into the system, all that was required was to bleed the brakes. See photo 38.28. I began with the calliper furthest away from the master cylinder (the left one), not that it makes much difference in this case, and bled each in turn, repeating the process several times. To begin with the fluid simply wouldn't go into the master cylinder: it sat in the reservoir and refused to be sucked into the master cylinder, no matter how many times I pumped the brake lever.

Eventually, though, the fluid went in and the brakes were bled. The brake lever action seems fine, but I'll bleed the brakes again during the running-in period to remove any remaining air in the system.

LESSONS LEARNT
• Brake callipers and discs are currently unavailable for Z900s (although this may change), but are available for other models.
• Twin discs are thinner (6mm) than single discs (8mm).
• Getting seized pistons out of callipers is a bugger of a job.
• Brake callipers are not handed on Z1s or Z900s and can be used on either side, but they are handed on Z1000s.
• Whilst callipers aren't handed on Z1s or Z900s, their mounting brackets are.
• You don't realise how much overspray an aerosol creates until you use it in the conservatory.
• Bake your callipers at 200 degrees C for an hour for the perfect finish ... but don't forget to remove any tissue paper first!
• Check that the calliper moves smoothly on the mounting bracket.
• A larger bore master cylinder is required for twin disc conversions.
• Buying replacement parts rather than restoring existing can make a pleasant change sometimes.

38.28 Bleeding the brakes.

Chapter 39
Fitting the battery box & junction board

Kawasaki tended to move the position of its electrical systems from model to model, so what follows is specifically for a Z900, but don't be disheartened if you've got a different model: the electrics are much the same, just in different places!

I decided to refit the battery box and junction box at this stage of the restoration as I had good access to the area without the rear mudguard and chain guard in the way. There was also no airbox to worry about – although the battery box and the supporting bracket for the airbox need to be fitted first, anyway. I painted the battery box, junction box and associated brackets with aerosol as I'd forgotten to take them for blasting and powder coating with the frame, etc, and as time and money were in short supply (and these parts are 90 per cent hidden) I sprayed them with black aerosol. They came up okay – not great, but okay.

I had already decided to upgrade the regulator and rectifier units to a more modern and more efficient system, as the originals are renowned for being a bit fragile and inefficient. In my case the original regulator was fitted underneath the battery box (see photo 39.1), and the rectifier on the back of the battery box next to the junction box. See photo 39.2. Having removed them I kept them safe in case they are required for originality's sake in the future (as I did with all the parts I removed from the bike, regardless of condition). See photo 39.3.

I then bought a new, combined regulator/rectifier unit, which duly arrived – with instructions in Chinese! See photo 39.4 of the new unit and my Chinese instructions. If it had been a direct replacement it wouldn't have been a problem, but as it was an upgrade and I was replacing two multi-pin sockets with one, I was a bit fazed, so fitted it but didn't wire it up until later. As the combined unit had the same fixings as the old regulator, I decided to fit it under the battery where the old regulator had been, and where it was nicely out of the way. See photo 39.5.

I fitted the main support bracket to the front of the frame (see photo 39.6), followed by the little support bracket for the airbox, and then the battery box with the combined regulator/rectifier beneath it. I had worried that, as it was larger than the original it replaced, the new unit might not fit in the space provided, but there was room to spare. See photo 39.7.

After this I cleaned the various multi-pin connectors and mounted them on the junction box (see photo 39.8), then bolted the junction box to the side of the battery box. See photo 39.9.

Next up was the battery. I bought an AGM (Absorbed Glass Mat)

39.1 The position of the original regulator.

HOW TO RESTORE KAWASAKI Z1, Z/KZ900 & Z/KZ1000

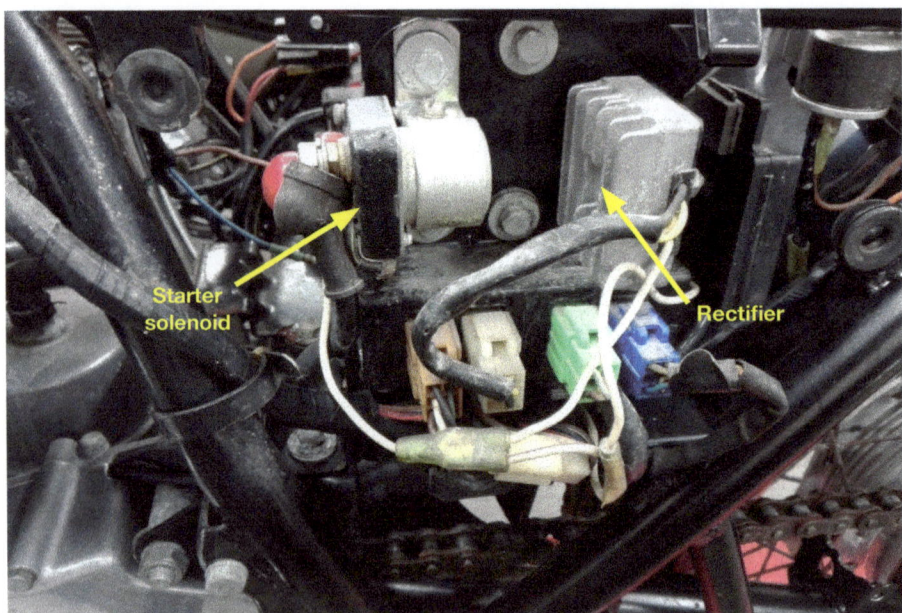

39.2 The location of the original rectifier.

39.3 The old regulator and rectifier removed from the bike.

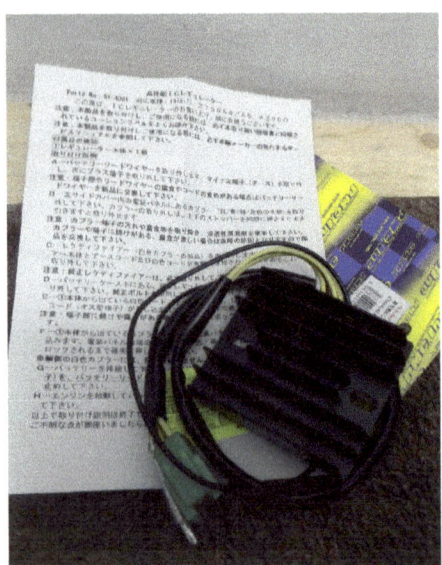

39.4 The new combined regulator and rectifier unit, with instructions – in Chinese!

39.5 New combined unit fitted underneath the battery box where the regulator used to be.

is only one problem with them – they're yellow; bright yellow.

One idiosyncrasy of the Z900 is that as Kawasaki decided to fit the world's biggest air filter and 'silencer' there was no room for the electrics where they had been on the Z1s. The battery was therefore repositioned lower down in the frame under the silencer: problem sorted, you might think. However, this means that the bottom half of the battery is beneath the side panel and in full view, and the last thing you want to see when you look at the bike is a bright yellow battery glaring at you. I therefore simply sprayed the bottom half of the battery (the visible bit) black and the problem was sorted. See photo 39.10. The battery was a perfect fit in the battery box and, with all the rubbers in place, was held tightly. I also added a piece of hard foam under the top bar for added security. See photo 39.11.

After this I bolted the starter solenoid to the left side of the junction box, which has a large cable going straight to the battery live and a large earth cable to the rear of the engine. The starter takes a huge amount of current so it needs a solenoid – a small current is sent from the starter button to the solenoid, which then provides full power to the starter motor. If the full current went through the

battery from the internet for a good price, and it arrived very quickly. I began using AGM batteries on my bikes a few years ago, and have never looked back. They hold their charge really well if left unused, and aren't damaged if they do lose charge. They don't leak acid, and are completely maintenance-free. They also work perfectly with existing charging systems so there's no wiring or other changes to worry about. Highly recommended. There

FITTING THE BATTERY BOX & JUNCTION BOARD

39.6 First mounting bar for the battery box and airbox.

39.7 Battery box and airbox support fitted.

39.8 Junction box ready for fitting.

39.9 Junction box fitted.

39.10 New AGM battery painted black.

39.11 Battery fitted.

starter button it would burn out very quickly.

The good news is that the junction box is pretty easy to wire as it mainly comprises multi-pin connectors that are handily colour-coded. I loosely draped the wiring loom into what I thought was the right area, and plugged the brown male connector on the loom into the brown female connector on the junction box. This was followed by the blue connector which was my new wiring from the alternator. That left just the green connector from my new combined regulator/rectifier. Common sense would dictate that this should go into the green connection, but there's always that element of doubt, and the white connector used to be for the old rectifier, so maybe use that one? A quick call to Z-Power confirmed that it should indeed be plugged into the green connection with the spare white wire going to the other white wires in the loom/junction box, as these are all switched live and share common wiring. The white connector, which used to connect the original rectifier, was left empty. See photo 39.12. It was only at this point that I discovered that the wiring instructions were actually on the Z-Power website, free to download in the 'free manuals/books' section.

My final job in this area was to

165

HOW TO RESTORE KAWASAKI Z1, Z/KZ900 & Z/KZ1000

add the small fuse box (added on to Z900s by Kawasaki to supplement the much criticised original single fuse on earlier machines) on its little rubber mounting to the right of the junction box, and also fit the flasher relay next to it. See photo 39.13 from later in the restoration. Note that the wiring to the flasher relay incorporates a small, in-line regulator. The first section of wiring had been completed.

LESSONS LEARNT
- Kawasaki moved electrics location at will!
- AGM (Absorbed Glass Mat) batteries are great – just spray them black if they're visible.
- Keep everything you take off the bike and don't re-use – you never know when you'll need it again or how scarce it might become (think Z900 airboxes!).
- I re-used my original wiring loom as it appeared to be in good condition throughout.
- A weak point on Z900s was always the electrics and the new combined regulator/receiver is supposedly much better – but if you're using the bike for daytime rides in the summer only, maybe you don't need it?
- I don't read Chinese (Mandarin?).
- There's a lot of info on the Z-Power website – if you look hard enough!
- Colour-coded multi-pin plugs – a Godsend!
- Solenoids – they're there for a reason.
- White or white/red wires are switched live.
- Black/white wires are earth wires (I'm beginning to learn them).
- Wiring/electrics – keep calm and wait for the secrets to slowly reveal themselves.

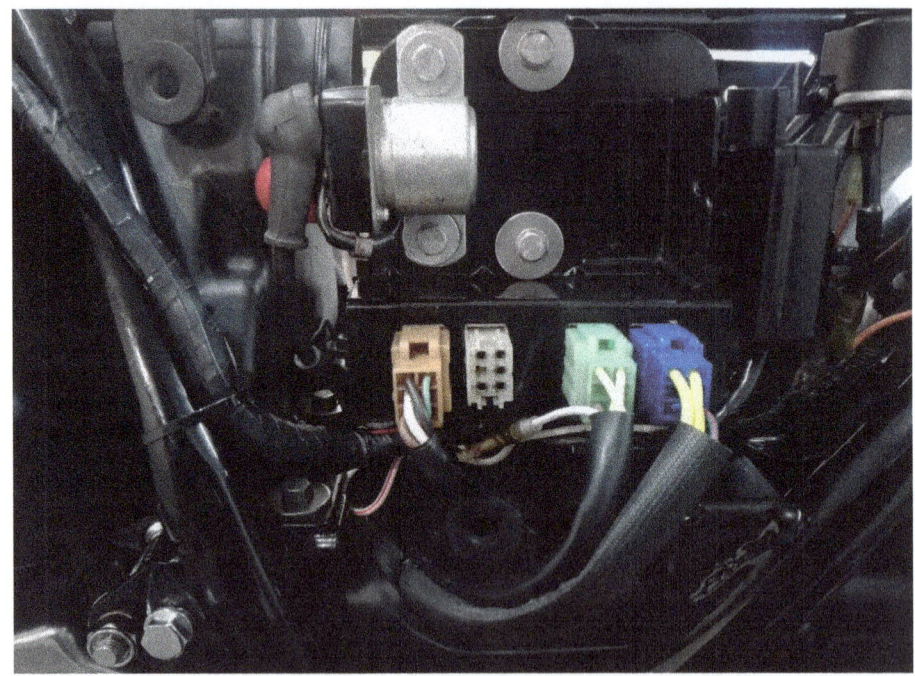

39.12 Junction box wired up.

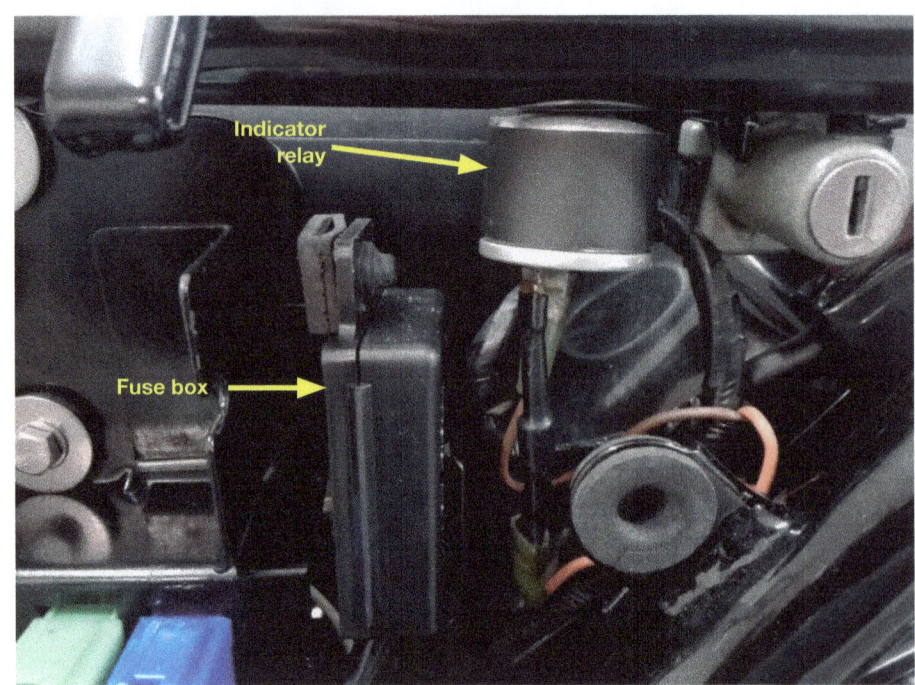

39.13 The fuse box and indicator relay.

Chapter 40
Fitting the carburettors & airbox

With the battery box sorted it was time to fit the airbox, silencer, and carburettors. Many previous owners, those for my bike included, ditched the large, complicated, and probably restrictive airbox and accompanying silencer for more sporty and sexy air filters such as K&Ns, with original airboxes lost or thrown away. The problem is that they're not made any more (I understand that some manufacturers have been approached, but they've all said they couldn't make them), and are pretty unobtainable second-hand. With many restorers wanting to restore bikes to original spec, they've become very sought-after – and subsequently very expensive. I put out a few feelers and eventually found one at John Browse Spares. The problem was the price: £270 (yes, you read that correctly) for a plastic airbox, but what price that unobtainable part? So I bought it. What can I say? Was this a foolish purchase or a wise one? To me it was worth every penny.

The same problem exists with the 'silencer' which goes on the back of the airbox, and was usually thrown out at the same time as the airbox. The good news is that some very sensible and far-sighted chap in Australia decided to do something about it, and has had them remanufactured. I therefore ordered one from Oz and it duly arrived. As with the airbox, the price was high but, taking into account manufacturing costs, and postage from Down Under, they're not too bad at £135. So, the air filter and silencer cost me over £400 (and I still had to buy a filter and new inlet hoses – thankfully, still available). Why was this restoration costing so much, I wonder?!

Before I began to fit the airbox the first thing I had to do was try and work out how the wiring loom got past the massive thing. Common sense would suggest that the loom

40.1 Working out how the wiring loom got past the airbox.

HOW TO RESTORE KAWASAKI Z1, Z/KZ900 & Z/KZ1000

somehow went between the frame and the box – but the airbox fitted snugly in the frame, and there was no way the loom would fit between the two. As the airbox wasn't on the bike originally, I had no point of reference: what to do? After some thought I posted a question on one of the Z900 Facebook groups on the internet (very, very useful – highly recommended) to see if anyone could help, and the answer soon appeared – the loom simply goes round the outside of the frame (see photo 40.1). What I didn't realise was that the side panels on a Z900 are quite large, and cover the frame and exterior wiring without problem: as my panels were away being painted I couldn't check them. Problem sorted.

My next job was to try and refurbish a rather battered and tired airbox. I dismantled it (there are gauze filters inside, together with a cover on the front to hold the inlet rubbers), and gave it a very thorough clean and spruce-up. Unfortunately, the inlet rubbers had perished and split but, luckily, although the box itself isn't available any more, the inlet rubbers are, and I bought a new set and fitted them to the front cover of the airbox. See photo 40.2. Note that the hoses are handed (they are clearly marked),

and have to be fitted in the correct location.

After that I tried to fit the front cover to the box with the gauze filters on the inside. See photo 40.3. However, after an infuriating few minutes I realised that there was no way the gauze filters would go back on with the inlet rubbers already fitted in the front cover. I therefore removed the inlet hoses and fitted the front cover and the gauzes. See photo 40.4. I fitted the inlet hoses afterwards – still a struggle though they eventually went in – and, with the short 'S'-shaped hose for the engine breather in place, the airbox was ready to be fitted. See photo 40.5. I also painted the 8 clips for the inlet manifolds and airbox hoses (see photo 40.6), which looked okay, but probably not quite the original finish.

I also fitted new inlet manifold rubbers to the cylinder head, in place of the extremely dodgy old ones that were on the bike when I bought it. See photo 40.7. Note that these manifolds have short pipes for fitting vacuum gauges, which weren't fitted to early bikes, and I don't think the early versions are available any more. After this I fitted the petrol pipes and breather pipes to the carbs as I thought this would be easier to do before the carbs were in situ, See photo 40.8.

I slotted the airbox into position, and all was ready to fit the carbs. See photo 40.9. As I'd thought, the gap between the hoses was 8cm and the carbs were 10cm deep, so I knew that getting the carbs in position wouldn't be easy. However, it was not that difficult as the inlet hoses for the airbox are made of very soft, pliable rubber, so I simply pushed and distorted them out of the way to get the carbs roughly into position, and then forced the carb flanges into the (very hard) inlet manifold rubbers. See photo 40.10. This now meant that the carbs were only 1cm wider than the available gap, and I was able to gently lever and squish the airbox hoses over the carb inlets. See photo 40.11.

With the carbs in position I began to fit the throttle cables. The first thing to note is that the two cables are different sizes, with the larger being the return cable (strangely). To begin with I screwed them into the (new) right-

40.2 New hoses fitted – they are handed.

40.3 With the hoses fitted it was impossible to fit the gauze filters behind them.

40.4 Having removed the hoses the gauze filters fitted – eventually.

40.5 Hoses refitted and airbox complete – with small oil breather hose.

40.6 Hose clips painted black.

40.7 Old and new inlet manifold rubbers.

hand switch gear (which must be done before the cables are in place). See photo 40.12. I then attached the cable ends to the throttle twist grip (see photo 40.13), and screwed together the switch gear. After this I fed the cables through the cable guide on top

FITTING THE CARBURETTORS & AIRBOX

40.8 Carbs fitted with inlet and breather tubes, ready to go on.

40.9 Inlet manifolds and airbox in place ready for the carbs – will they fit in that gap!

40.10 Carbs in place and inserted into the inlet manifolds.

40.11 Soft airbox hoses coaxed into position.

of the right front fork. See photo 40.14. Finally, I connected the other end of the cables to the carburettor butterfly. The trickiest job was trying to slide the adjusters through the brackets on top of the carburettors. I found that I had to have the two nuts on the end of the cable as far apart as possible in order for them to slide over the little lugs and into the brackets. See photo 40.15.

Next up was the silencer. See photo 40.16. This fixes to the back of the airbox and acts as an extra filter and induction noise reducer, clamping to the airbox with a large jubilee clip. See photo 40.17. You can clearly see from this that the battery has to be set low down to clear the silencer.

After this I fitted the box-shaped air filter. See photo 40.18. What

40.12 Throttle cables being screwed into the handlebar switch gear.

40.13 Inner cables being attached to throttle twist grip.

appeared to be a simple job was slightly problematic (as simple jobs tend to be) in that the filter wouldn't sit fully down in the airbox. See photo 40.19. The reason for this was that the foam seal on the front of the filter was too big, and was pushing the filter backward onto a ridge in the bottom of the airbox rather than sitting right down. I shaved some material from the seal and the filter went fully home. See photo 40.20.

HOW TO RESTORE KAWASAKI Z1, Z/KZ900 & Z/KZ1000

40.14 Cables routed through the cable guide on top of the forks.

40.15 Cables connected to the carb butterfly.

40.16 Airbox silencer.

40.17 Silencer in position.

40.18 Air filter.

40.19 Air filter inserted but won't go fully home.

My final job was to fit the new airbox cover (these are available). The cover on this model has two clips on the top, which are apparently for extended breather tubes to clip into. I'm not sure why the breather tubes are so long on these models – probably something to do with emissions? – but I obliged and bought extra-long breather tubes and attached them to the clips on the cover. Job done. See photo 40.21.

LESSONS LEARNT
• Airboxes for Z900/KZ900s aren't available any more, and second-hand ones are very hard to come by.
• Good quality reproduction silencers are available from Australia (good on ya, mate!).
• Is it worth paying £270 for an airbox? It was to me.
• Facebook groups are a real bonus as there's always someone who can help. The only problem is that you

FITTING THE CARBURETTORS & AIRBOX

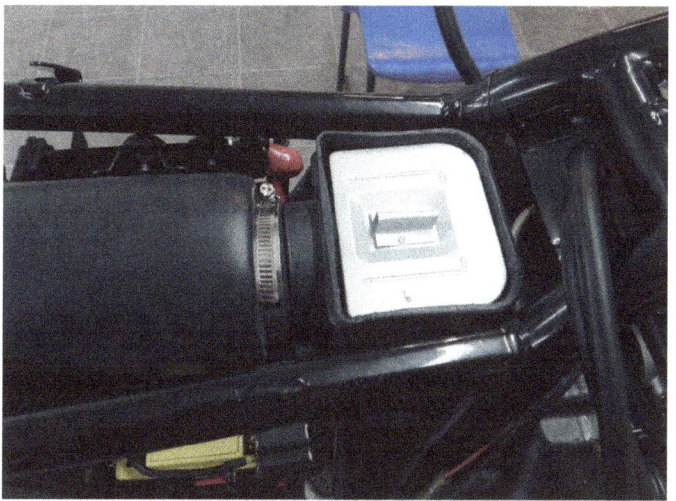

40.20 Air filter successfully fitted.

40.21 Airbox cover fitted with long carb breather tubes clipped to it.

sometimes get incorrect info from members keen to help – just be aware.
• Inlet rubbers for the airbox are available.

• The carbs do go in, between the airbox and inlet manifolds – honest!
• The two throttle cables are different sizes.
• The simple jobs can be the hardest.

• The Z900/KZ900 has extended breather tubes that clip onto the airbox cover.

Chapter 41
Fitting the rear light, mudguard & indicators

Time to fit the rear mudguard and indicators; I started with a mistake. Knowing that the plastic coating on the wires to my rear light had been damaged, exposing the wires inside, I ordered a new loom. The problem was that, when I came to fit it, I realised I had ordered the wrong part. There is a rear loom between the main loom and the rear light loom, and I had mistakenly ordered this, not the tail light loom. Words fail me. However, I decided that, rather than mess about with sending back the loom and waiting for the correct one to arrive, I'd just carry on. (Patience was never my strong point.)

I cleaned the old, damaged wiring (see photo 41.1), and applied heat-wrap to it, which is great stuff that I use all the time: slip the cover over the wire, heat it with a heat gun, and 'Hey Presto!' it tightly encloses the wire, creating a solid rubber coating that protects and insulates, and doesn't come off in six months' time like insulating tape does. As I had only black heat wrap (it does come in different colours) I wound coloured tape round the outside afterward so that I could connect the wires correctly. I wasn't too worried what the tape looked like as it wasn't meant to be permanent, and would be hidden away under the rear mudguard (even anal people like me have their limits!) See photo 41.2.

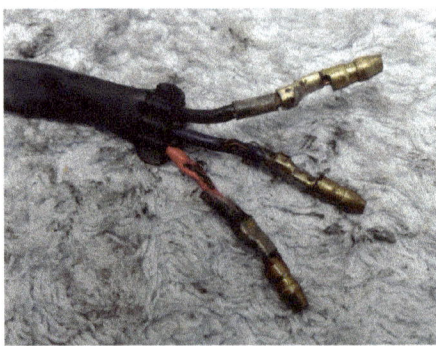

41.1 Damaged rear light wiring.

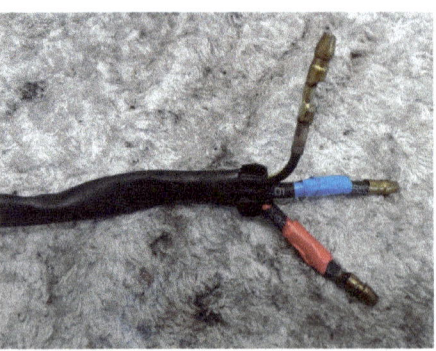

41.2 Wiring mended with heat shrinking wrap and then colour coded.

I then bolted the rear light unit to its mounting bracket using the large, horseshoe-shaped rubber pad between them, and the rather strange two-part rubbers under the Allen screws (I'm not sure if the Allen screws were used originally but there were some on the bike when I bought it, so I replaced them with stainless steel ones). See photo 41.3. I then mounted the rear light bracket to the mudguard by means of the large, square, rubber pad. See photo 41.4. With the light attached, I fed the wiring through the metal conduits underneath the mudguard and made the connections with my (new!) rear wiring loom. See photo 41.5.

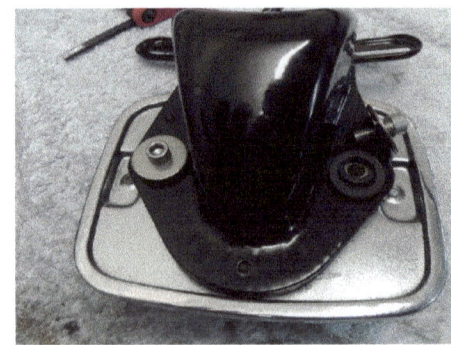

41.3 Mounting the rear light to its bracket.

FITTING THE REAR LIGHT, MUDGUARD & INDICATORS

41.4 Rubber mounting for the rear light bracket.

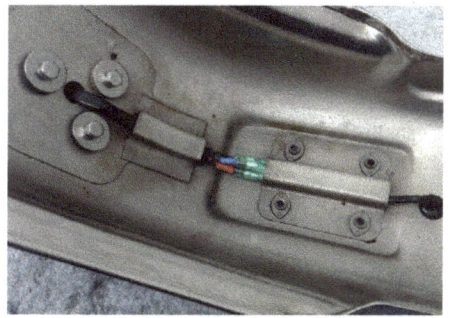

41.5 Rear light assembly bolted on and wiring fed through the shrouds.

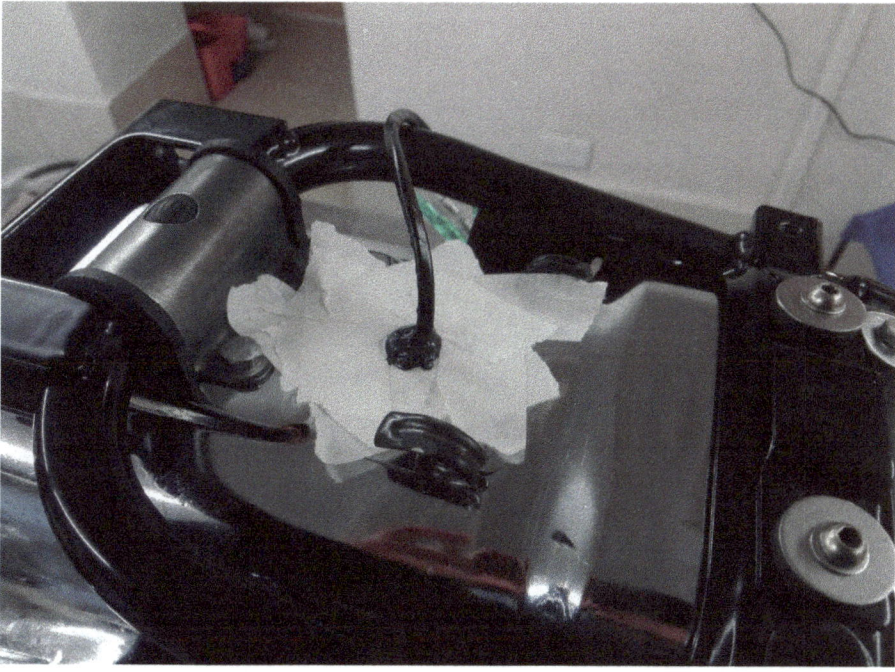

41.7 Sealing the hole in the rubber grommet round my new rear wiring harness.

I then fitted the plastic mudguard to the frame. This has small wings on the sides, which slot between small brackets on the frame to hold it in place at the front, and the mudguard is held in place at the rear by two screws. After this I fitted the metal mudguard rubber mounting brackets to the frame (see photo 41.6), and bolted on the mudguard. At this point I realised that the grommet I'd fitted where the (new!) wiring loom exited the mudguard wasn't a great fit, and water, etc, could get through, so I sealed it with some black silicone RTV sealant left over from the generator cover grommet. See photo 41.7. I also realised I'd forgotten to fit the rubber buttons on each side of the mudguard, but managed to squeeze them into place without taking off the mudguard. See photo 41.8.

I then turned my attention to

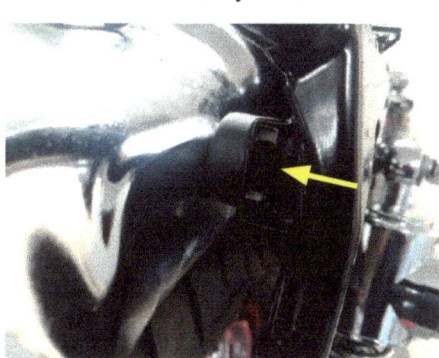

41.8 Rubber stops on each side of the mudguard.

41.6 Rubber mountings ready to receive the mudguard.

41.9 New and replacement indicators.

the indicators, realising that the new replacements had much longer threaded sections than the originals. I tried turning around the threaded section but to no avail: I had to cut them to size. See photo 41.9. I had bought an indicator fitting kit (highly recommended), which had the requisite diamond-shaped rubbers. These press into holes on the rear frame, with a second set of rubbers on the inside. The indicators then slide in, and are held with a nut on the back. See photo 41.10. I roughly connected the wires to my (new!) loom, and had to replace all of the bullet connectors as they were of a smaller diameter – very annoying to have to cut off new connectors. All replacement indicators seem to be like this with slightly smaller-than-standard bullet connectors: not sure why, but annoying. The wiring for the indicators is green to the left side and grey to the right.

I then realised that there was a spare earth lead on my (new!) rear wiring loom, and a couple of phone calls revealed that I needed earth leads on the ends of each indicator (originally missing on my bike). These were duly bought and fitted. See photo 41.11. I then made all of the connections to my (new!) rear loom as tidily as possible (see photo 41.12)

173

HOW TO RESTORE KAWASAKI Z1, Z/KZ900 & Z/KZ1000

41.10 Rear indicators fitted to the frame with diamond shaped rubber mountings.

before connecting the (new!) rear loom to the main loom via a multi-pin connector.

I then looked at the front indicators. These use the same diamond-shaped rubbers, accompanied by rubbers inside the headlamp, and an oval alloy earth connection. See photo 41.13. I knew I'd have to remove the headlamp shell later on in order to fit the instruments, so temporarily located both indicators without fully tightening them. See photo 41.14. As with the rear indicators, I replaced the small bullet connectors for larger ones (gnash, gnash), and then exchanged the replacement indicator lenses for genuine Stanley items, as they were darker and more opaque than the new ones – a small thing but it makes a difference to the look of the bike.

At this point I also refitted my seat onto the bike. Eagle-eyed readers will have already spotted that mine was not the right seat for the bike: the pattern on the top was wrong, and so was the metal base plate and seat catch. Mine was actually from an earlier model, apparently fitted in error by a recent owner. Early models had a spigot on the seat base that went into a circular latch, and weren't key-operated, but from the Z900 onward, a U-shaped bracket on the seat base was used, and the latches were key-operated. Now, I could have bought a new seat – these are available, but expensive (around £200) – but as mine was actually pretty new and in good condition, it seemed like a bit of a waste, and I wasn't too worried about total originality, anyway.

Luckily, Z-Power offers a conversion for the bracket on the seat base to fit the newer latch, which I bought and fitted to the seat base via two self-tapping screws: it worked really well. With the lock oiled and attached to the frame, the latch worked perfectly. See photo 41.15 of the bracket to convert the earlier seat base to the later latch system. The seat itself was attached to the frame with new hinge pins that slid in easily with the hinges loosened off, then tightened once the pins were in. One strange thing was that, unlike earlier models, there wasn't restraining strap or mechanism on the seat, which meant that, open, it didn't stop until it caught on the rear shock absorber bolt – not good. I think I'll make some kind of restraining strap for it.

My last job was to fit the plastic tool box behind the battery box on the right-hand side of the frame. This is held on by two small bolts. It's an important feature on a Z900/KZ900 as it contains one of the lugs for the

41.11 Fitting the earth leads to the rear of the indicator stems.

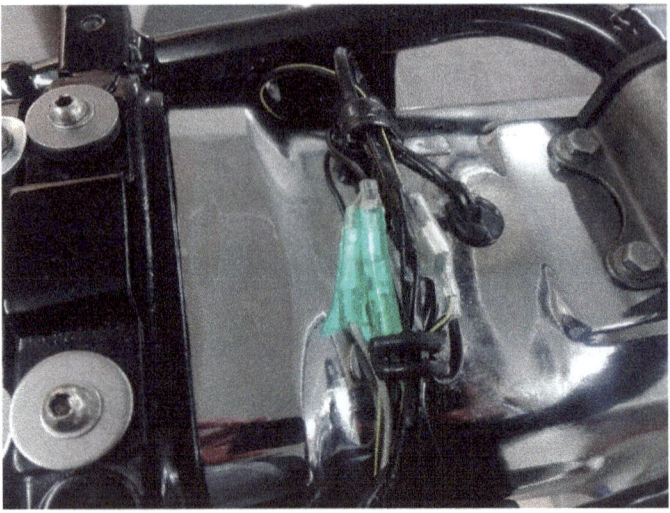

41.12 Wiring tidied up on the rear mudguard.

FITTING THE REAR LIGHT, MUDGUARD & INDICATORS

41.13 Front indicators fitted with alloy earth connectors on the ends.

right-hand side panel, so must be fitted.

LESSONS LEARNT
- Heat wrap wiring covers – brilliant!
- There are earth leads to the rear of all indicators.
- Replacement indicators are generic and have small bullet connectors; the threaded sections are too long; all of the leads are black, and the lenses are a bit pale – otherwise marvellous!
- Original Stanley indicator lenses are quite dark and thick compared with replacement items.
- Indicators are wired green to the left and grey to the right. I remember this by using the Yorkshire saying: 'It's a right grey day.'
- When ordering new parts, order the right ones! Unlike my rear light wiring loom, which wasn't.
- Patience is a virtue.

Note: European models generally have a strap in the middle of the seat, and also sport longer rear mudguards – in case you're in search of originality.

41.14 Front indicators and headlamp temporarily fitted.

41.15 Bracket conversion for my earlier seat base.

Chapter 42
Fitting the instrument panel

Time to refurbish, assemble and mount the instruments on the top yoke. My old instrument wiring was in poor condition (see photo 42.1), so I bought a new instrument loom. The thing about this was that (as with many other replacement parts) it wasn't exactly the same as my original one – very much like it and it worked, but still different; probably from a later model. Now, I'm not knocking this as at least there are new parts out there that will fit, but it does make everything that little bit more difficult. In the case of the instrument wiring loom, for instance, it meant three things –

• The bulb holders in the instruments were larger than the originals, leading to problems with fitting them.
• The bulb holders were different for the instrument warning lights and had to be squeezed in to fit in the binnacle.
• The bulbs were different so the (expensive) LED bayonet bulbs I'd bought in advance didn't fit.

Nothing in the above was insurmountable, but did make things a little trickier. Be aware of what are direct replacements for parts and what are items (usually from later models) that will fit and do the job, but which are that little bit different to the originals and may require adjusting to fit.

42.1 The original wiring had seen better days.

42.2 Dismantling the old units with broken bracket.

FITTING THE INSTRUMENT PANEL

I dismantled the original instruments to assess the damage (caused by the 'incident' on the way home from buying the bike), and to decide on the best course of action. See photo 42.2. The instruments, unlike the original wiring, didn't look to be in too bad condition, although the mounting bracket was fractured and the bottom cover of the tacho was badly damaged, so both required replacing. See photo 42.3. Unfortunately, the 'incident' had also grazed the waist ring of the tacho (see photo 42.4), and although I think it would still have worked okay, it looked unsightly. I could have sent the tacho to have the waist ring repaired, but the companies I spoke to would only refurbish the whole clock at a cost of around £70, not just replace the waist ring. And if I was to have the tacho refurbished I thought I'd have to have the speedo done to match, so a total cost of £140. However, new replacement speedos and tachos were available from Z-Power for around £120 a pair with a free mounting bracket, so in the end it seemed easier to buy new instruments; so that's what I did.

I bolted the new tacho and speedo to the new bracket, ready to connect the wiring (see photo 42.5), but then I realised that the pre-fitted illumination lights in the instruments didn't fit with the new wiring loom, which had its own illumination bulbs attached. See photo 42.6. I therefore removed the instruments from the bracket, removed the bulbs and bulb holders that came with the instruments, and inserted those from the new wiring loom instead. See photo 42.7. Unfortunately, the rubber bulb holders on the new wiring loom were considerably bigger than the originals, and had to be very forcibly inserted into the back of the instruments – I hoped I'd never have to take them out again as I knew it wouldn't be easy. At this point I realised that I'd not inserted the wires through the back of the brackets first, and the bulbs would therefore have to be removed before rerouting the wires.

42.5 New speedo and tacho attached to bracket with new wiring loom ready.

42.3 The original units look okay.

42.6 Discovering that the new loom doesn't connect to the new tacho and speedo illumination wires.

42.4 Damage to the tacho waist ring caused in the 'incident' on the way home.

HOW TO RESTORE KAWASAKI Z1, Z/KZ900 & Z/KZ1000

42.7 Tacho and speedo removed from bracket and illumination bulbs from new loom inserted – but not through the bracket.

42.8 Old illumination bulbs inserted and connected to new loom; warning lights inserted – just!

42.9 Back screwed onto instrument panel – but before ignition switch is fitted.

42.11 Instrument panel finally assembled correctly.

42.10 Ignition switch now fitted – but not its mounting bracket!

I tried to remove the oversized rubber bulb holders from the rear of the instruments but they didn't want to come back out (as I'd thought). Although I did eventually persuade them to let go, I destroyed the metal connections inside them in the process and they were scrap. Not only that, but three of the four bulbs came out of their holders as I tried to remove them, were now rattling around inside the instruments, and didn't want to come out! I eventually removed them with the aid of my small telescopic magnet. Coaxing them back out of the small holes in the bottom of the clocks was like an infuriating parlour game!

As a result, I cut off the new (but now destroyed) bulb holders from the wiring loom, added new connectors, and connected them to the bulbs and holders that had come with the instruments. See photo 42.8. A simple job that had taken a couple of hours. Frustrating!

After this I referred to the wiring diagram in the back of the manual to check which warning light was which, and then fitted these to the instrument mounting bracket. Once again, the rubber bulb holders were slightly different to the originals, and whilst this time they weren't such a tight fit, they did have little rubber tails on them that the originals didn't, that interfered with the bulb holder next to them and meant that the bottom cover didn't want to go on. Ho-hum. Eventually, I tamed the extra rubber bits and squished them sufficiently to fit the bottom cover.

FITTING THE INSTRUMENT PANEL

42.12 Fitting the lower trims to the instruments.

42.13 Assembling the cone shaped mounting bushes, nuts and washers ready to mount the instruments on the top yoke. Headlamp shell and front indicators removed in readiness.

Basking in the glow of victory I soon realised that I needed to fit the ignition switch before the bottom cover (see photo 42.9) ... I removed the bottom cover, inserted the ignition switch and replaced the cover before realising that I needed to insert the switch's mounting bracket as well (see photo 42.10). I removed the bottom cover, inserted the ignition switch's mounting bracket and replaced the bottom cover for the final time: hurrah! I then fitted the top cover which is simply held in place by the bezel on the ignition switch, and it was job done! See photo 42.11 of the instrument binnacle assembled (finally!).

After succeeding in the face of adversity I fitted new covers to the bottoms of the clocks, which was quite straightforward apart from there being too much wiring to the bulbs, but this could quite easily be hidden under the covers – I just had to make sure not to trap any wires. See photo 42.12. Chrome bottom covers are also available – but too blingy for my liking.

With the instrument panel now complete, I readied the four, cone-shaped mounting rubbers (see photo 42.13), and the panel was then bolted to the top yoke, having first removed the headlamp for access, (see photo 42.14), and the clocks and idiot lights were fitted – although not yet wired. See photo 42.15.

LESSONS LEARNT

• Pattern or replacement parts are a blessing, but are often slightly different to the originals. They'll fit, but in a different way.
• LED bulb replacements can be a good idea but, as yet, there isn't a headlamp conversion for the Z900, and stop/tail light conversions are quite complicated due to the 'brake failure warning light.' Warning light bulbs are easy to change to LEDs – unless your new wiring loom has different bloody fittings!
• I'm still reliving the moment I saw the bike go off the trailer in the rear view mirror – my own personal horror film ... and I'm still paying for it!
• Replace or restore? At last there's a choice. It depends what you want to achieve and how much things cost, I guess.
• Learning to assemble parts in the correct order comes with experience. As a first-time restorer of a particular model you're bound to get it wrong from time-to-time. Shrug and learn from it – and keep repeating Robert M Persig's mantra!

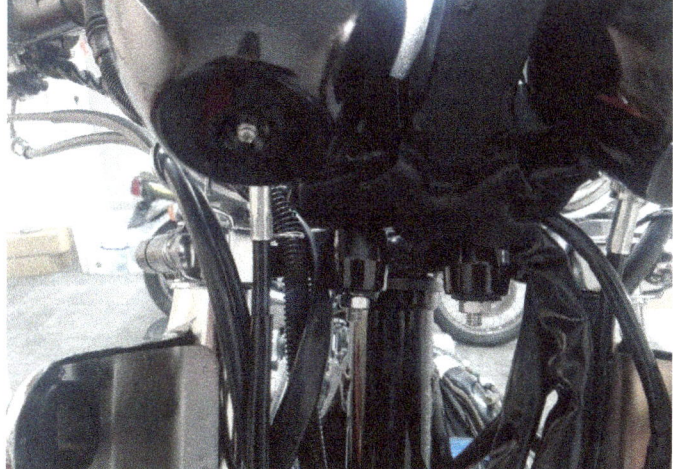

42.14 Instrument panel being bolted on to the top yoke.

42.15 Instruments fitted but not yet wired up.

Chapter 43
Assembling & wiring the headlamp

With the instrument panel fitted it was time to sort out the headlamp. My original headlamp had suffered serious damage when the bike made a break for freedom from the trailer, so I bought second-hand chrome rims which I'd had rechromed. The headlamp nacelle had somehow survived the worst of the carnage, so I had that blasted and powder coated. See photo 43.1 of the nacelle as it was originally before being painted, with the original buzzer for the indicators fitted. Most owners disconnected these quite early on as they're rather annoying, and for that reason I decided not to refit mine.

The nacelle fits very simply to the front fork shrouds via the indicator stalks. See photo 43.2 of the stalks, and note the oval-shaped earth plates that also serve as big washers to hold the headlamp firmly. I didn't fully tighten the nuts as I knew the man at the MoT* station would want to align the headlamp aim (It's still four months until bikes over 40 years old no longer require an MoT, and I needed one to get the bike registered in the UK). The wires from the main loom were then pulled through the back of the headlamp, ready for the lamp to be fitted. See photo 43.3.

With the headlamp nacelle in place I began work on the headlamp lens and rims. I saw that the lens of my original Stanley unit had some deep scratches in it from the 'incident' with the trailer, and, after some misgivings, I thought I'd better replace it. The bad news is that this period item is a sealed beam unit, and Stanley items are no longer available, and there are no direct replacements. The good news is that it is a standard 7in unit, as fitted to many other vehicles at the time, such as Minis and Land Rovers. After a bit of searching on the internet I found one to fit a Mini that was of a slightly higher wattage than the original. It duly arrived and it looked okay, but, as ever, was a slightly different shape to the original, with a slightly raised profile and a sidelight bulb fitted, but it would do. See photo 43.4 of the original Stanley one on the left, and replacement unit on the right. (It's

---

* MoT: Ministry of Transport – the annual safety test currently required in the UK for any vehicle over three years old. From May 2018 the test will no longer be required for vehicles over 40 years old (historic vehicles). I assume that, after this date, historic vehicles imported from abroad won't have to have an MoT before they can be registered, but not entirely sure.

43.1 My original headlamp nacelle with warning buzzer for the indicators fitted.

43.2 Fitting the nacelle to the front fork shrouds with the indicator stems and earth plates.

ASSEMBLING & WIRING THE HEADLAMP

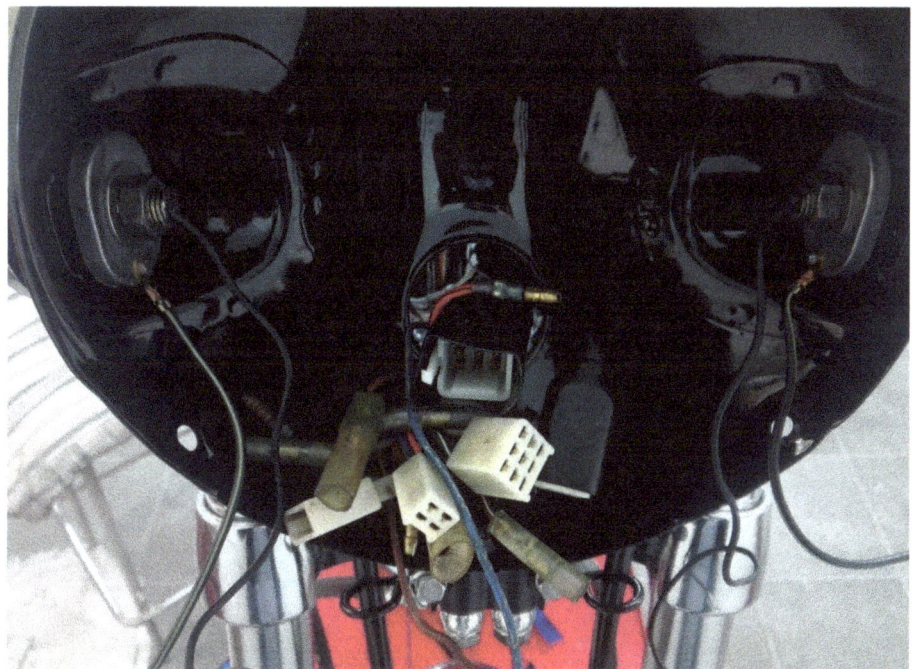

43.3 Headlamp nacelle ready to be wired up before the headlamp rim is attached via two small screws through the holes visible near the bottom.

43.8 The inner rim and backplate are screwed together with two small screws.

43.4 The original Stanley sealed beam on the left and my replacement one for a Mini on the right.

43.6 The backplate in position on the lamp.

43.9 The outer rim is attached to the backplate with two shouldered bolts – at the 3 and 9 o'clock positions in the photo.

43.10 The headlamp beam adjusting screw.

43.5 The three brackets on the lamp align with the notches on the backplate – in only one position.

43.7 The tongue from the inner rim inserted in the backplate.

difficult to see in the photo but the lens on the original is scratched in the 5 o'clock position) Also look at photo 43.8 where you can see the raised glass of the new lamp.

The first part of assembly was to fit the back plate to the headlight. Notches in the back plate locate with three brackets on the headlight to ensure it is in the correct position. See photos 43.5 and 43.6 of the plate on the lamp. The inner rim is then fitted to the front of the lamp by inserting a tongue into it from the back plate (see photo 43.7), and then mated to the back plate with two small screws. See photo 43.8. After this the outer rim is fitted to the back plate by two shouldered bolts. See photo 43.9.

The final part of the assembly was to fit the spring-loaded headlamp adjuster screw. See photo 43.10. This is inserted through the front of the outer rim, and adjusts the aim of the headlight beam. See photo 43.11.

With the headlight assembled it was time to tackle the wiring in the headlight and fit the headlamp lens to the nacelle. Now, thankfully, Kawasaki used multi-pin connectors for the most part, so the main wiring is taken care of by two large, multi-pin connectors from the main loom to

181

HOW TO RESTORE KAWASAKI Z1, Z/KZ900 & Z/KZ1000

43.11 The headlight beam adjuster in position.

43.12 Headlamp wiring – not too bad.

the instrument binnacle. These can be seen in the centre rear of photo 43.12. That was 90 per cent of the wiring sorted, leaving only a few extra wires. Good news.

The headlamp connector has three wires on it – red/black, red/yellow, and black/yellow (earth) – which plug into the three wires of the same colour from the loom (seen near the bottom in photo 43.12). The indicators are wired, with grey being the right indicator and green the left (remember: 'It's a right grey day'). The wires from them to the indicators were black on my bike, as they are generic replacements, which always seem to be black, no matter what. These can be seen to the top and centre rear of photo 43.12. The earth wires (black/yellow) from the indicator mounting brackets join all the other earth wires in a black/yellow connector from the loom. That's it – headlamp wiring done.

Note that there are some extra wires which weren't used, as seen in the bottom right of photo 43.12. I think these were for the hazard lights and indicator warning buzzer, which I've removed, so they're no longer required and were simply left. Also note that there are four wires from the main loom that don't go into the headlamp: two for the horn and two for the front brake light switch. The horn wires are black and green with spade terminals, and the brake light switch wires are brown and blue with female bullet connectors. In both cases it doesn't matter which way round the wires connect.

The final thing to note is the rubber grommet that sits in the top of the headlamp nacelle. This is actually a hole for a 'speed warning

43.13 Hole for the speed warning light in the headlamp (plugged up) and bizarre hole for rubber key holder in instrument panel on Z1s.

light' for the Japanese market. Almost unbelievably, Z1s were never sold in Japan as its laws restricted motorcycle size to 750cc. In Japan the Z2 – a 750cc version of the Z1 – could be purchased,. Not only that but all vehicles had to have a 'speed warning light' fitted which lit up when they were going above a certain speed (30mph, I think), and this hole is where the warning light was fitted. Amazing, but true. I think the laws regarding engine size were later relaxed, and by the time the Z900 came out, it could have been available in Japan, but I'm not sure.

Anyway, Z900 headlamps are made with a hole in the top for this reason. Bizarrely, Z1s also have a hole in the instrument panel for a little rubber bung (an optional extra) to hold a spare key! What were they thinking? See photo 43.13.

LESSONS LEARNT
- Stanley headlamps aren't available new, though other 7in sealed beam units are, albeit with a slightly different profile.
- The sealed beam unit assembles onto the rims and back plate in a very logical way, which ensures the headlight is fitted correctly, and is easily adjusted.
- Headlamp wiring is (thankfully) pretty straightforward and logical.
- The hole in the top of the headlamp is intended to house a speed warning light.
- The hole in the top of Z1/Z1A/Z1B instrument panels is made to take a rubber bung with a slot in it to hold a spare key (!) These were available as an optional extra. Not quite sure of Kawasaki's thinking on this one!
- Z1s were never sold in Japan.

Chapter 44
Ignition, handlebar & rear brake wiring

Time to sort out the rest of the wiring, starting with the ignition system. To my surprise the bike was already fitted with Dyna S electronic ignition, which was a real bonus. True, it had been poorly wired, and that needed tidying up, but other than that it appeared fine. I looked on the internet and found a copy of the original fitting instructions which helped me understand the wiring. There are three wires coming out of the unit: one wire is the live feed coming into the unit, and the other two wires go out to the ignition coils.

To begin with I thoroughly inspected the ignition coils, as I'd given them only a cursory once-over when I'd removed them, and discovered that although the coils might still be okay, the HT leads certainly weren't: there were weaknesses in several of the wires under the outer sheathing. See photo 44.1. Having stripped away the sheathing, the true extent of the damage to the HT leads underneath was evident. See photo 44.2. As the HT leads are hard-wired into the ignition coils, it meant that new items were required.

The coils fire two cylinders each. One coil fires cylinders 1 and 4, and

44.1 Signs of HT lead being damaged underneath rubber sheath.

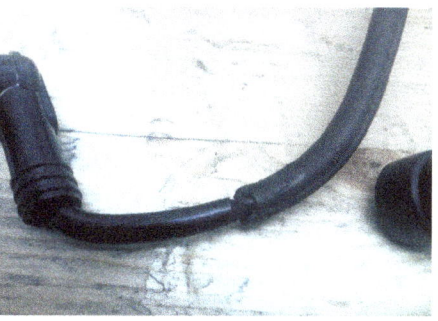
44.2 Extent of damage revealed.

the other fires cylinders 2 and 3.

The new coils duly arrived, but the wiring was different to my originals and, again, there were no instructions. This was further complicated by having the electronic ignition fitted which also had different wiring to the original. I knew that one wire on the coil would be live from the ignition switch and the other would be from the electronic ignition to trigger the spark, but which was which?

My original coils had one yellow/red wire (live) and one green or black wire from the electronic ignition (green was for 2 and 3 coil, and black was for 1 and 4 coil), but both the replacement coils had one black and one yellow wire. Which of these was the live and which triggered from the electronic ignition? It seemed obvious that the yellow was the live and the black the triggered – but was it? What if it was the other way round with the blacks live and the yellows triggered? And what would happen if I did connect the coils the wrong way round – would they be damaged? I rang Z-Power but they weren't entirely sure themselves.

Eventually, I looked at the back of the original coils and established that the yellow/red live wire went to the right-hand terminal. See photo 44.3. I compared this with the new coils and found that the yellow wires on these also went to the right-hand terminal: the yellow was almost certainly the live and the black wires

HOW TO RESTORE KAWASAKI Z1, Z/KZ900 & Z/KZ1000

44.3 The wiring for the original coils.

connected to the electronic ignition, so that's how I wired them. I just had to make sure that I had the correct wire from the electronic ignition going to the correct coil, as both my coils had the same black wires (instead of one green and one black on the originals), and I didn't want to mix them up. I used the rather bodged original wiring in the first instance just to get my head round it. See photo 44.4.

Having established that the system was working okay – sparks at the plugs! – I tidied the wiring a bit, removing the horrible red wires originally used for the live feed replacing them with proper connections. I also marked one of the two black wires to the ignition coils in order to prevent them getting mixed up if they were ever removed. See photo 44.4A.

I then timed the ignition statically to get it roughly right so that the engine would run – I used a strobe to time it accurately later on when the engine was running. To begin with I rotated the engine until the timing marks stamped 1 and 4 appeared on the advance and retard mechanism through the peephole in the electronic ignition mounting plate (there are another set of marks stamped 2 and 3), and aligned the mark on the crankcase, not with the 'F' mark but with the mark about ½in further round clockwise from the 'F' mark. This is the fully advanced timing mark. See photo 44.5. I then connected a bulb to the wire between the electronic ignition to 1 and 4 coil and earth. After this, I turned the advance and retard unit clockwise by hand to the fully advanced position, and adjusted the electronic ignition plate until the bulb (one of the expensive LED ones from the instrument panel that I couldn't use!) just lit. See photo 44.6. The ignition timing was now roughly set.

After this I found the two multi-pin connectors for the handlebar switches and connected them – thank heaven for multi-pin connectors! A couple of extra black and blue wires from the right-hand switch were also connected. See photo 44.7. There was then a spare multi-pin connector on the loom left over. By pulling back the tape to see the colour of the

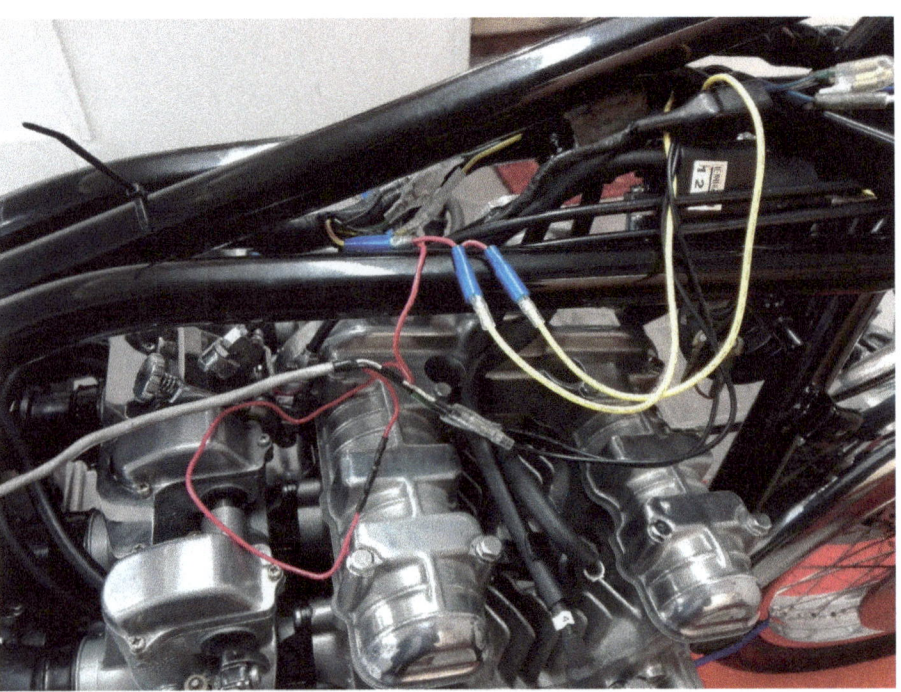
44.4 New coils with yellow wires as live feed and black wires going to the triggers from the Dyna S electronic ignition. New sparkplug caps and lead numbers fitted.

44.4A Old red wires removed and wiring tidied.

44.5 Timing set to fully advanced mark.

IGNITION, HANDLEBAR & REAR BRAKE WIRING

44.6 Timing set so bulb just illuminates when advance mechanism turned (clockwise) to full advance.

44.8 Redundant multi-pin connector for the hazard warning switch. Just tied out of the way.

44.9 Old right-hand handlebar switch.

44.10 New left-hand handlebar switch.

44.7 Multi-pin connectors for loom to handlebar switchgear.

wires, I established that it was the now redundant hazard warning light connector. Comparing the colour of the wires against the wiring diagram confirmed this. See photo 44.8. I then looked at the handlebar switches; the right-hand side one was in a bad way from where brake fluid had leaked all over it. See photo 44.9. To be honest I could have refurbished the original switch as it was probably not as bad as it looked but, as replacement switches were available at a very reasonable price, I bought some – so much easier! I also replaced the left-hand switch as although it was okay I thought it would look odd compared with the new right-hand one. See photo 44.10.

I used the coloured wiring diagram in the back of the Kawasaki manual to check for the colour coding of wires, as although it's not that clear, it's a darn sight clearer than the black and white diagram in the Haynes manual which comes without a key, so you've absolutely no idea what colour the wires are – bloody marvellous!

I then turned my attention to the strange-looking object which was just sitting there connected to nothing that I'd found next to the coils when I'd dismantled the bike. See photo 44.11. After consulting the wiring diagram again, I realised that it was the brake light failure switch. Kawasaki was innovative in fitting such a modern feature to its bikes – many years before many others had even front brake lights, let alone a light to tell you whether or not the brake light was working.

I also realised that the three wires I'd found which had simply been cut off next to the loom should have been connected to the switch. See a rather blurred photo 44.12 of the cut wires. I can only surmise that because the wiring to the rear light had chafed on the rear mudguard and gone through to the wire, a previous owner had cut the wires to the brake light failure switch in an effort to prevent the strange electrical problems that must have been caused by this – but I doubt if it worked! Anyway, I reconnected the switch to its wires (using spade connectors as I'd run out of bullet connectors by this time). See photo 44.13. I then used a cable tie to hold it securely to the frame – and the damn thing worked perfectly! Result. (This switch is currently unavailable, and it would have been annoying not to have the warning light working.)

I then connected the horn with the black and brown wires from the main loom. See photo 44.14. The main thing to note is that the little cross-head screw to the left adjusts the horn's sound. I can't tell you how many people I've met who have told me their horn is kaput, to then be stunned when it suddenly sounds loud and clear just by turning that little screw. In my case the horn worked, but feebly. After a little adjustment to the screw it sounded loud and clear. Sometimes simple things like this are all it takes.

I wasn't using the hazard lights so I had already removed the hazard relay (separate to the indicator relay) and its regulator that usually sit above the battery. See photo 44.15. As usual, I kept them safe in case they were ever needed – you never know. I also sealed the wiring that went to them to preclude the possibility of short circuits, etc, being caused by loose wires. At the same time I fitted a new rear brake light switch. The original one fitted poorly, and it was only after a while that I realised it wasn't original but a very poor quality after-market replacement, so I bought a new one. See photo 44.16. If you look at photo 44.17 you can see the new brake light switch fitted, and above that the heat wrap covering the redundant wires to the hazard relay and its regulator. Also note the empty

44.11 Brake light failure switch as found.

44.12 Out-of-focus photo showing where the wiring for the brake light failure switch had been cut off.

44.13 Brake light warning switch reconnected.

44.14 Horn in situ with small adjusting screw on the left.

44.15 Redundant hazard warning relay and its regulator.

44.16 Old aftermarket rear brake light switch and proper aftermarket replacement.

IGNITION, HANDLEBAR & REAR BRAKE WIRING

44.17 Brake light switch fitted with wiring for the hazard relay sealed off. Redundant brackets for the hazard relay and regulator above the battery.

brackets above the battery, which is where the relay and regulator used to be attached.

The wiring was just about sorted.

LESSONS LEARNT
• Check the HT leads on older coils to ensure they're not broken internally.
• Thank God for multi-pin connectors.
• Why don't replacement electrical parts come with a wiring diagram or instructions?
• The internet is a blessing when looking for old wiring diagrams, etc.
• If you think logically and take your time then the wiring isn't that bad – thank heavens for colour coding!
• Set the ignition timing with a bulb to begin with, then time it accurately with a strobe later.
• If you don't want to use the hazard warning lights just leave them out.
• How can a manual have a black and white wiring diagram with no key? For example, some wires are marked as SL – what colour is that? Other wires are marked as BL, is that Black or Blue? Don't get me wrong, I think Haynes manuals are really useful, but in this case it was definitely lacking.

Chapter 45
Fitting the exhaust system

Time to fit the brand new exhaust system! To my mind there's only one exhaust system to fit to a Z900 and that's the original 4-into-4 setup. It's so iconic, and looks so wonderful that even though some 4-into-1 systems are great and look sporty, etc, there's no substitute for the real thing. They can also be fitted to Z1000s with the addition of a small bracket on the rear exhaust mountings. I think the worst thing Kawasaki ever did was to fit a 4-into-2 exhaust to the Z1000: it made an exceptional bike look ordinary. I can understand why it did so – the original systems were prone to rot through quite quickly, so Kawasaki was faced with a barrage of warranty claims, and decided enough was enough. In the long run, though, Kawasaki lost out as the magic of the model was diminished. The King of Motorcycles was now just another knight amongst many others, and Kawasaki has been trying to recreate that magic ever since. As I write the Z900RS has just launched: a retro machine painted in Z1 colours, intended to recreate the glory days. Despite this, the bike that Kawasaki will always be known for is the Z1.

Each to their own, but I just love the original pipes. The big day finally arrived and the big parcel was delivered! See photo 45.1. I removed my new (and very expensive) exhausts, made by Doremi in Japan, from the packaging and they looked good. I'm not sure if Doremi is the original manufacturer but the pipes look identical to the originals (apart from the stamping on the two upper silencers, of course). The original downpipes didn't turn blue as they

45.1 The exhaust system has arrived!

45.2 Exhaust fitting kit.

FITTING THE EXHAUST SYSTEM

were double-skinned, and I was very glad to discover that these repro ones were double-skinned, too – great stuff (I hate it when downpipes turn blue).

In readiness to fit the exhausts I assembled the mounting kit – some original and some new. See photo 45.2. The first thing I did was to insert the four top hat bushes into the brackets on the rear frame hangers. See photo 45.3. I then prepared to fit the first exhaust and realised that the exhaust clamps are handed.

45.3 Top-hat bushes in place on the rear frame hanger.

45.4 Exhaust clamps are handed.

45.5 Exhausts are numbered.

See photo 45.4, which shows that different sections of the clamps have fins missing in order to clear the frame downtubes. I selected the first exhaust to be fitted – number two. Note that the exhausts are numbered underneath to ensure correct fitting. See photo 45.5.

I then selected all of the parts I needed to fit the exhaust to the cylinder head. See photo 45.6. The first to go on were the copper gaskets. I put a little grease on one side to stick them to the head whilst the pipe was fitted – otherwise it would've been a really hard job trying to hold them in place. The gaskets are slightly curved on one side, and I fitted this side towards the head as the surface area of the head is greater than that of the exhaust, and I wanted to get the best seal possible. With the gasket in place I slid the collar over the pipe (do this before fitting the pipe!) and

45.6 Ready to mount the first exhaust pipe.

offered up the pipe to the head. When it was in position I loosely inserted the bolt through the silencer bracket and into the rear frame hanger, and the exhaust stayed where it was. I could then take the two metal collets and fit them round the downpipe, flange outward, before sliding the clamp back up the downpipe and onto the manifold studs. All I had to do then was put on the two nuts and tighten them – though not fully until all of the exhausts were in place. The first exhaust was fitted. See photo 45.7.

I then fitted the small balance tube over the spigot on the silencer ready to accept the next silencer on top of it. See photo 45.8. The tube was quite a tight fit, and I wondered how I'd get the top silencer to fit into it before realising that the spigot on the top silencer is of much smaller diameter than the bottom one, and easily slips into the tube. I also centred the balance tube clamp on the centre line of the silencer as it can't be rotated afterward. Next, I fitted the second silencer (silencer number 1 in this case) in the same manner as the first. In order to do so I had to briefly remove the bolt from the rear of the first silencer; I was worried the entire thing would come off, but it held its position just by hanging off the cylinder head mounting. Even so, I slotted home the bolt as quickly as

45.7 First pipe in position with rear bolt loosely inserted.

HOW TO RESTORE KAWASAKI Z1, Z/KZ900 & Z/KZ1000

45.8 Balancer tube fitted to lower silencer.

45.9 Second exhaust fitted on top of the first.

possible! The second silencer was now in position. See photo 45.9.

All that remained to do was tighten the exhaust balance tube between the silencers at the back, and tighten the mounting bolt on the rear frame using the thin, self-locking nut supplied (thin so it misses the chain on the drive side).

I repeated the process on the other side of the bike, and very quickly the exhausts were all fitted. Once they were all in place, I went back and fully tightened the nuts on the exhaust manifold. The final job was to fit two rubber stoppers to the underside of 1 and 2 silencers for the side stand and main stand to sit against. I now had a bike that was really beginning to look good! Love those exhausts. See photo 45.10.

LESSONS LEARNT
• Kawasaki decided not to fit the 4-into-4 exhaust system to the Z1000 due to excessive warranty claims – a shortsighted decision in my opinion.
• The replacement exhausts are very expensive (over £1000) but worth every penny – quality items.
• Exhaust manifold clamps are handed.
• Slide the exhaust clamps onto the pipes before fitting them.
• Use a few blobs of grease on the copper gaskets to old them in place on the cylinder head during fitting.
• You know you're getting somewhere when the exhausts are on.

45.10 Exhaust system fitted – fantastic!

Chapter 46
Preparing the tank for painting

I really don't know what was in the petrol tank when I bought he bike – whether it was just really, really old fuel that had metamorphosed, or whether someone had added some evil liquid or other in an effort to start it, I'm not sure. What I do know, however, is that, whatever it was, it was the most evil-smelling, foul, brown liquid I've ever come across. When I opened the petrol cap for the first time and took a sniff to try and work out what was in there, I very nearly passed out. I managed to pour away most of it, and then set about chemically cleaning the inside of the tank in preparation for sealing it. I have to say that it wasn't until the end of this process using some heavy-duty chemical cleaners, that the horrible smell finally went. Not nice.

My first job was to remove the locking petrol cap from the tank, which I did by driving out the locking pin with a thin drift. See photo 46.1. After this, I set about cleaning the inside of the tank using my preferred method of strong chemicals. Some people put nuts and bolts in and shake the tank, but I find that chemicals will work just as well – and with less effort.

The chemicals are available from DIY stores, but easier to buy on-line these days as they're becoming harder to buy over-the-counter due to some complete idiots going round attacking people with acid.

To begin with I used a strong dilution of *caustic soda* to remove the gunge from the bottom of the tank. See photo 46.2. In order to do

46.1 Removing the fuel filler cap.

46.2 Initial cleaning with caustic soda.

this I filled the tank three-quarters full with water, then added the caustic soda crystals, whereupon the tank immediately became hot due to the chemical reaction, and scum appeared on the surface. I agitated the tank a bit with my rubber-gloved hand over the filler cap, and left the chemicals to do their stuff for 24 hours. Note that you should never put the caustic soda in first and then add the water as the chemical reaction can be so violent as to boil out of the tank. Note also my heavy-duty rubber gloves – this stuff is not to be messed with.

After 24 hours I carefully emptied the tank and dried it out with a heat gun set on low. See photo 46.3. To my surprise there were still some traces of the horrible gunge in the tank – what was that stuff? I went on to phase two of the cleaning process and attacked the rust inside the tank with a strong dilution of *spirits of salt*, usually used for cleaning drains when caustic soda has failed. *Spirits of salt* is basically hydrochloric acid – a really mean so-and-so.

Once again I added water first before adding some of the hydrochloric acid, then agitated it a bit before adding more acid and then the whole bottle before topping up with water. This time I left it for about an hour only, agitating it every so often, before emptying it. See photo 46.4. Note that I carried out this operation outside as the fumes are pretty noxious. I then emptied the contents and neutralised the acid in the tank with a little bleach (otherwise it'll keep working and etching if you allow it to), before thoroughly drying the tank, once again with my heat gun. The inside of the tank was now clean and rust-free – and finally clear of the horrible gunge! See photo 46.5.

I then prepared to seal the tank with POR 15 sealant. I know that sealing a tank is a divisive issue, and some say not to do it. I seal tanks because I think it stops them rusting through when stood for long periods of time. I also use and swear by POR 15, which doesn't peel off or dissolve and is methanol-proof. The horror stories I hear about sealant coming off in a tank are usually because the tank wasn't prepared properly beforehand – no sealant will work if applied to rust or gunge that's still in the tank. Anyway, I've always sealed tanks, and still do – but be aware that many will disagree with me on this.

I left the old petrol tap in place as a bung, although I knew that the sealant would block it permanently, but this didn't matter as mine was so full of that horrible gunge that it needed replacing, anyway. I then stirred the POR 15 sealant, and then stirred some more, and then some more. This sealant tends to form a thick sludge at the bottom of the tin, and you need to get that thoroughly mixed into the rest of the paint for it to work properly. I then poured the sealant into the tank and rotated the tank to ensure complete coverage inside. After a few minutes I poured out the excess sealant and left the tank to dry – which takes at least

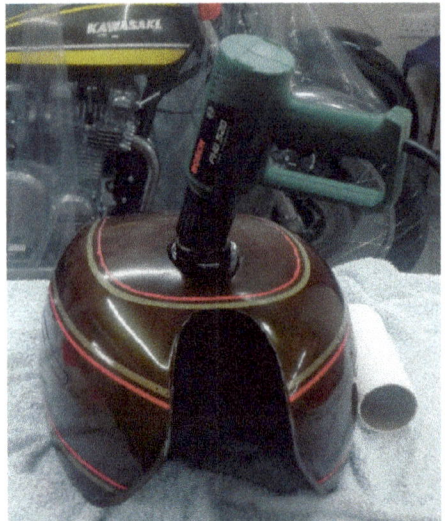
46.3 Drying tank with the aid of a heat gun.

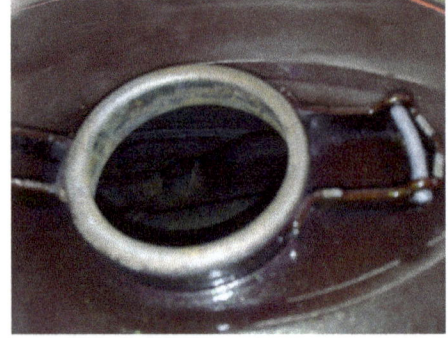
46.5 Inside now clean.

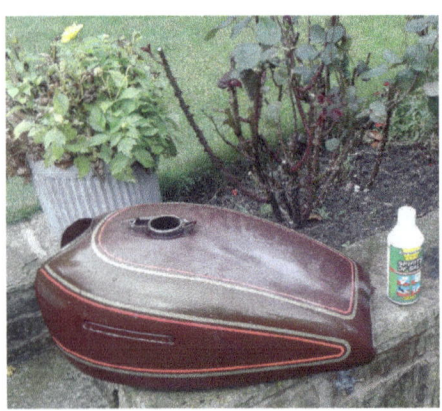
46.4 Second cleaning with Spirits of Salt.

46.6 Sealing the tank with POR 15.

PREPARING THE TANK FOR PAINTING

46.7 Tank and panels ready to go to the painter's.

three days. See photo 46.6.

One major word of warning: POR 15 is resistant to every solvent I know, so if you accidentally spill or splash some on the outside of the tank you must wipe it off immediately (while it's still wet) or it'll never come off. The only recourse in that situation is to have your tank repainted. In my case it didn't matter, as I was having my tank repainted anyway, but if you're sealing a tank that's already been painted then be very careful!

The tank was now sealed to my satisfaction, and it and all of the panels were ready to be taken to Mark Hutchinson in Pontefract to be painted. See photo 46.7. Note the marks on the tank where I spilt some *caustic soda*, didn't clean it up quickly enough, and it attacked the paintwork. Also note how faded the right-hand side panel is – probably from the sun.

Now, for reasons best known to myself, I decided to paint the tank in green metallic (candy) rather than the original brown metallic; not only that, but to paint it in the style of a Z1A (heresy! heresy!). I just love the colour and style of the metallic green and yellow Z1A so that's what I decided to do. By now, you will have realised that I'm not someone who wants everything original: I have my own style and I'm happy with it. Do I want the original carburettor airbox? Yes. The original exhaust system? Yes. But I also want it painted in the style of a Z1A because I think it looks good. That's my preference. End of.

I therefore took my tank and panels to Mark Hutchinson, an excellent painter who specialises in Z900s. When I arrived at his workshop he showed me around and insisted on allowing me to see and compare the various paint jobs from various bikes. In photo 46.8 you can see the candy brown and orange, and candy green and yellow tanks from a Z1A; in photo 46.9 the candy super red and candy super blue tanks for a Z1B, and in photo 46.10 the diamond dark green tank for a Z900 awaiting repainting. Great to have so many tanks together to compare.

He also explained that the candy (metallic) finish only really comes into its own in the sunshine, and in an effort to mimic this (it being a dull and overcast October day) I used the flash to at least give some idea of the depth that can be achieved by a good painter. See photo 46.11. Mark then lined up all the different tailpieces from the Z1 to the Z900 showing the different pinstriping. See photo 46.12. You can also see from this that the Z900 tailpiece is a slightly different shape to that of earlier Z1s – more curved.

Mark also told me that my tank had already been repainted at some point, and that a decent job had been done, which was good news. I spent a happy hour or so wandering around his Aladdin's Cave of a workshop (he's probably got around five Z900s in various states of restoration), and chatting about all-things Z900. See photo 46.13 of some of his collection of Z900 petrol tanks. I eventually tore myself away, leaving my tank with Mark, and looking forward to the day when I could return and collect the finished bodywork.

In the meantime, I set to work reassembling the petrol cap. I had taken the cap to be rechromed, but they had made a mess of it. The cap is Mazak*, and they clearly

---

*Mazak (known as Zamak in the States) is a zinc aluminium alloy used on classic cars and bikes for such as door handles and petrol caps as it's light and easy to cast.

46.8 Z1A Candy brown and candy yellow tanks.

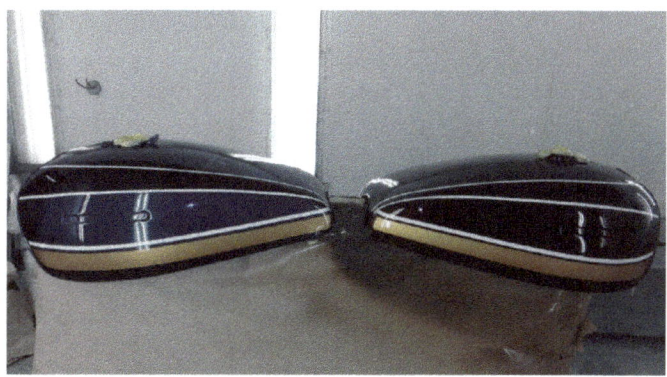

46.9 Z1B Candy super blue and candy super red tanks.

193

HOW TO RESTORE KAWASAKI Z1, Z/KZ900 & Z/KZ1000

46.10 **Z900** Diamond dark green tank.

46.11 You need sunlight to bring out the beautiful metallic finish.

46.15 Preparing to fit the keyhole cover.

46.12 Rear panels, left to right **Z1, Z1A, Z1B, Z900**.

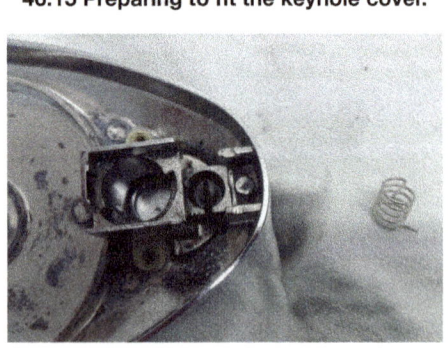

46.16 Keyhole cover inserted ready for the spring.

46.13 *Tanks*? You want *Tanks*? We got Tanks!

46.14 Poorly finished fuel cap, polished through to the copper in an effort to remove the corrosion – fail.

46.17 Keyhole cover spring in place.

don't chrome Mazak, but instead of admitting that they gave me a load of nonsense and said it just needed more polishing, the result being that they polished right through the existing chrome to the copper coating below. They had never rechromed it in the first place, and just tried to polish out the corrosion, which was clearly far too deep for this to be effective. Why not just say that they don't chrome Mazak rather than stringing me along with some load of codswallop? See photo 46.14. I had to take it to my usual plater, who agreed to rechrome and finish it properly for me at short notice as a favour, and because it was only one small part. They ground away the unsightly corrosion and rechromed the cap properly. (See photo 46.25 of the re-rechromed and polished cap.)

With the cap now properly chromed I began reassembly of the key cover and catch assembly, starting with the key cover. This slots into the fuel cap, and is held under tension by a hair spring. See photo 46.15. I inserted the key cover with its slot ready to take the spring. I carefully opened the slot a little to ensure it was wide enough for the spring, see photo 46.16, and then fitted the spring, which was tricky. In the end, rather than trying to tension the spring, whilst at the same time shoving the arm of the spring into the jaws of the cover (practically impossible), I unseated the key

PREPARING THE TANK FOR PAINTING

46.18 Locking assembly.

46.22 Seal mechanism ready for assembly.

46.19 The two barrels and spring inserted.

46.20 The latch in place with small spring behind it.

46.21 Lock mechanism fitted.

Next up was the catch mechanism which I laid out in order of assembly, as usual. See photo 46.18. The first thing that struck me was that the barrel was in two pieces. Why? I realised that any key will fit the lock, not just your ignition key, as the key-way is just a blank slot. In order to prevent the cap being unlocked with, say, a screwdriver, the barrel is made in two pieces so that the top half just turns without releasing the catch. Only if something goes right into the barrels (like a key, for instance!) will the catch release. Be aware, though, that any key will open the cap.

I fitted the two parts of the barrel and held them in place with the long, thin spring. See photo 46.19. I then fitted the actual catch on top of these with its little spring behind it. See photo 46.20. Finally, I screwed the little cage over this and it was job done. See photo 46.21.

After this I had to fit the actual cap assembly. Again, I laid out the parts in order of assembly – see photo 46.22 – then screwed them all together, leaving the seal off the cap as I realised I needed a new seal to replace the old one, which was hardened and split. See photo 46.23. A new seal was ordered and fitted on arrival. See photo 46.24. The cap was now finished. See photo 46.25.

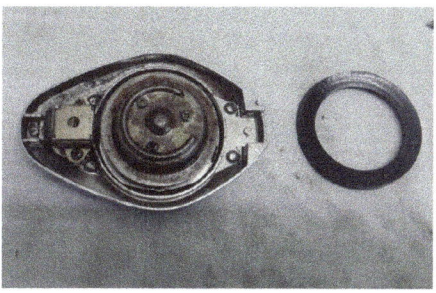

46.23 Seal mechanism in place, awaiting new seal.

46.24 The cap with the new seal in place.

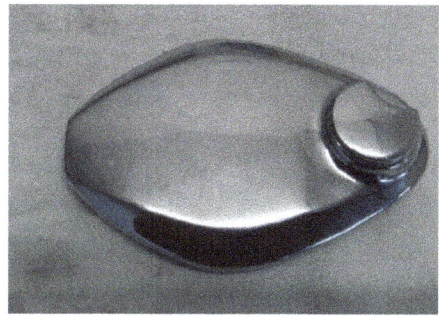

46.25 Finished (re-rechromed) petrol cap.

cover slightly so that it would turn fully round to where the arm of the spring was, and then pushed in the arm of the spring before moving the cover back to its proper position and reseating it, tensioning the spring at the same time. Eventually it was job done. See photo 46.17.

LESSONS LEARNT
- Cleaning the inside of petrol tanks is never easy and there are several different methods.
- I use strong chemicals: caustic soda followed by spirits of salt (hydrochloric acid) – works for me.
- Sealing the inside of petrol tanks is controversial. I've used POR15 from Frost Automotive for many years without problem.
- If you're a chroming company and you don't chrome Mazak then just say so from the start.
- The catch inside the petrol cap is very fiddly – and can be opened with any key.

Chapter 47
Painting & refitting the tank & bodywork

It was finally time to collect the newly-painted tank and panels from Mark Hutchinson – exciting! I had a long chat with Mark about what exactly is involved in painting a Z900 tank and panels. The most important thing to establish is that there are no paint codes for Z900s! They are painted in several coats of several different finishes, and how these are applied, how thickly, and how many coats, will determine the final colour.

To begin with tanks are taken to be vapour blasted back to bare metal before any necessary repairs are made to the tank – dents and pinholes, etc. After this they are given a coat of etch primer which is then flattened with 800 wet and dry (always used wet), before being sprayed with a high-build primer and again flattened with 800 wet and dry. Next, the tanks are sprayed with a black guide coat and again flattened with 800 wet and dry (a guide coat helps highlight any minute imperfections or unevenness in the paint thus far). Sanding reveals high spots (the black is sanded away) or low spots (the black remains after sanding). These high and low spots can then be carefully flattened with wet and dry. The tank is next de-greased and is then ready for final painting. See photo 47.1 of a tank being flattened after a guide coat has been added. Note that this a replacement Z1/Z1A/Z1B petrol tank that has the fitting holes for both the small emblems (Z1) and the larger emblems (Z1A & Z1B) – the shape of the tank was the same on all Z1s. Z900 and Z1000 tanks are both slightly different shapes.

Z1/Z1A/Z1B tanks and tailpieces are then painted white. After this any pinstripes or lighter coloured areas required (on a green and yellow tank that'd be the yellow; on an orange and brown tank that'd be the orange, etc) are marked out and masked over with masking tape. Note that this doesn't apply to side panels as they don't have pinstripes. The tanks and tailpieces are then sprayed black,

47.1 Black guide coat being flattened down over the grey primer

PAINTING & REFITTING THE TANK & BODYWORK

the masking tape is removed, and you end up with a tank or tailpiece that looks like the finished article in terms of pattern or stripes, but is just black and white in colour, forming the background to the semi-transparent colours that will be sprayed over them to give the final finish.

Also note that all the lighter colours and pinstriping on a Z1 are painted as above. After this Kawasaki increasingly used decals, and by the time the Z900s were produced, only decals were used for pinstripes. So on a Z900 the tank and panels are all sprayed completely black as there are no painted pinstripes, only decals to be added later. Z1As have painted lighter colours, as per the Z1s, but the white stripes are decals. Z1Bs also had some of the lighter colours painted but the white and gold stripes were now decals and Z900s/Z1000s used only decals.

So, Z1/Z1A/Z1B tank and panels are now painted black and white; Z900/Z1000 are black only. They are then sprayed with two or three coats of silver flake (which gives the paint its metallic finish). How much silver flake is added at this point will affect the final colour.

After this the tank and panels are ready for their final colour, which is Candy. Candy is a tinted lacquer that is coloured but transparent, so it's a bit like a plastic sweet wrapper or lighting gel in the theatre: you look through it and everything changes colour according to the colour of the sweet wrapper. (Which is probably why the lacquer is called 'Candy'?) In the case of our tanks, a different coloured lacquer is used to create various finishes – green or red for the Z1 or Z1A tanks, for example. As with the silver flake, several coats of lacquer are applied and, as with sweet wrappers, the more coats, the darker the colour.

The effect of the coloured candy lacquer is to change the final colour according to the base coat (black or white): if the lacquer was green the black parts turn dark green and the white parts turn yellow; if the lacquer was red the black parts turn a reddish brown and the white parts turn orange.

After the lacquer has been applied any decal pinstripes are added (none on Z1s), and the panels are finished with a protective clear lacquer. Job done. You can tell which pinstripes are paint and which decals by running your finger over them – the decals are slightly raised from the rest of the paintwork. That's it, paintwork finished.

The important thing to note is that the paintwork is made up of many different coats, especially the silver flake and the candy lacquer, and these affect final colour. To this end, virtually every bike is slightly different in colour: how many coats of flake or candy lacquer are applied; the pressure the spray gun's running at; ambient temperature, the type of spray gun used – all will affect final colour. There is no such thing as a definitive colour for Zeds; they're a combination of colours. If you want to raise Mark's blood pressure just ask him what the paint code is for a Zed!

If you look at photo 47.2 of an original Z1 tank, you can see that that where the lacquer has been scratched it's white underneath; it's only the silver flake and lacquer that give it its orange colour. Similarly, if you look at photo 47.3 of an old tailpiece, you can see where the lacquer has faded in the light and exposed the silver flake underneath. If you look at photo 47.4 you can see a selection of tailpieces with stripes: some are painted (white then silver flake, then candy lacquer), and some are decals.

Anyway, my tank and panels were finally finished (there was a three month waiting list), and were ready to fit at last. See photo 47.5. Note that I had decided to have my bike painted in green and yellow Z1A colours as I love that colour and style combination. It's not standard but it's what I wanted.

I started by fitting the tailpiece, and inserted the four rubber mountings into the holes in the tail – two under the tail and two on the arms above the rear shocks. These

47.2 Candy lacquer has been scratched to reveal the white underneath.

47.3 Candy lacquer has faded to reveal the flake underneath.

47.4 Stripes were originally all painted and slowly changed until they were all decals.

HOW TO RESTORE KAWASAKI Z1, Z/KZ900 & Z/KZ1000

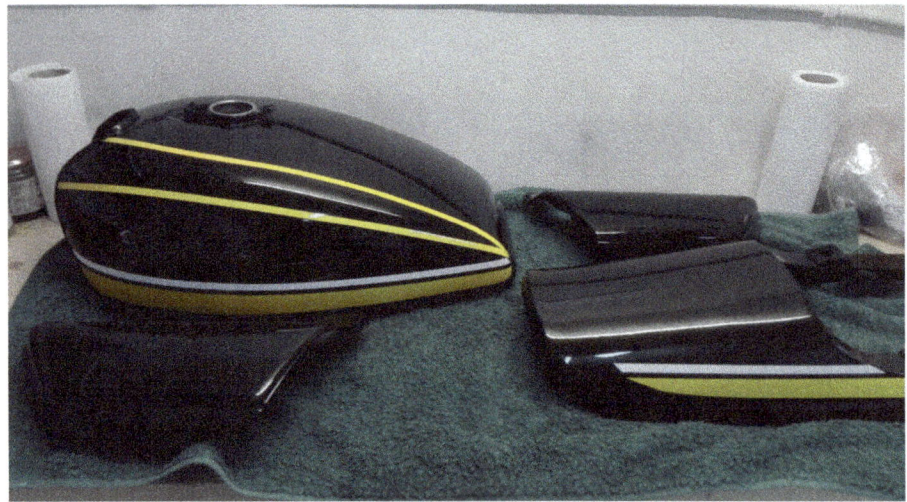

47.5 My tank and panels painted and ready for fitting! At last!

47.6 One of the four rubber bobbins used to mount the tail piece.

rubber bobbins are quite clever as they push through the holes, but their sides are not vertical: they have a small waist and larger top, so are kind of V-shaped. See photo 47.6. They are then secured on the top by large circular rubbers that are also V-shaped internally (see photo 47.7), and fit over the top of the rubber bobbins. See photo 47.8. Because of their shape, they hold each other tightly in place. The tail was then fitted to the bike with short bolts and penny washers. See photo 47.9.

Next up were the side panel

emblems. See photo 47.10. I used Z900 emblems, not KZ900 as I prefer the former. I was thinking of fitting the earlier 'Double Overhead Camshaft' emblems to the panels, not to try and make mine look like an earlier bike, but because they look good. However, I discovered that the earlier emblems have different mounting holes, and it was bit late to change them, so I stuck with the Z900 items (the holes for the KZ900 and Z900 emblems are the same). I pushed the spigots on the emblems through their holes and secured them with the little circular clip washers that I fitted with the aid of a small extended socket and a hammer. See photo 47.11. The main thing to note here is not to push the emblems in without supporting the panels from behind – if you're not careful you could easily crack a panel.

Next up I refitted the fuel cap. I cleared out the hole on the tank bracket ready to take the fitting pin (see photo 47.12) before fitting the cap by gently tapping the fitting pin through it and the bracket. See photo 47.13. I then prepared to fit my new tank emblems (see photo 47.14) by first screwing the screws into the mounting holes on the side of the tank to check that the threads were

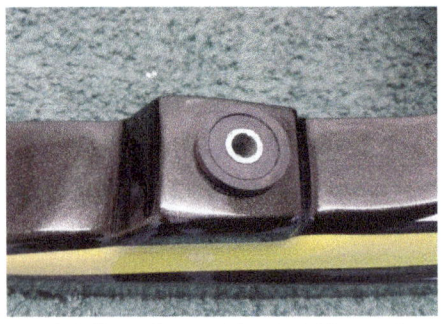

47.7 The chamfered rubber collars that go on the bobbins.

47.8 One of the rubber bobbins and collars in place.

47.9 Tail piece fitted.

PAINTING & REFITTING THE TANK & BODYWORK

47.10 New emblems for the side panels. I chose Z900.

47.14 New tank emblems ready to be fitted.

47.17 Preparing to fit the new petrol tap.

47.11 The emblems held in place by circular spring washers, fitted with a small extended socket.

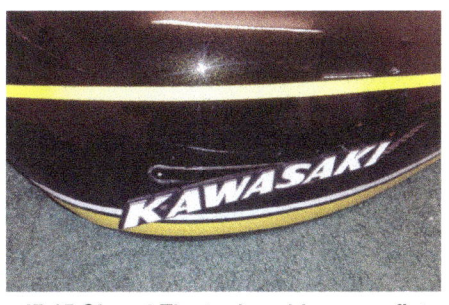

47.15 Oh, no! The tank emblems are flat and need to be carefully bent to shape.

47.18 Fitting the petrol pipes before fitting the tap.

47.12 Clearing excess paint from the petrol cap mounting.

47.16 Tank emblem fitted.

47.13 Petrol cap fitted with long pin.

clear of paint, etc. I then began to screw the emblems to the tank, only to discover that the emblems were flat and would need to be carefully bent to fit – horrors! (I'm not great with stuff like that). See photo 47.15. Luckily, it turned out to be not as bad a job as I'd imagined, and after some judicious bending the emblems were in place. See photo 47.16.

The last job before fitting the tank was to fit the new fuel tap. See photo 47.17. I cleaned the threads on the tap before bolting it on. However, when it came to fitting the fuel pipes to the tap with the tank on the bike I thought again: it's a nightmare trying to get the pipes on the back of the tap. I removed the tap and fitted the pipes first – see photo 47.18 – and

47.19 Tank fitted!

HOW TO RESTORE KAWASAKI Z1, Z/KZ900 & Z/KZ1000

then refitted the tap to the tank. The secret here is that the adaptor that screws to the tank also screws into the fuel tap – with a left-hand thread. (See the adaptor still on the tank in photo 47.18.) If you offer up the tap to the adaptor and then screw the adaptor onto the tank, it also screws the tap into the adaptor at the bottom by virtue of it being a left-hand thread, and tightens that, too. Clever. I have since decided that the easiest way to remove the tank in future would be to slightly loosen the petrol tap sufficient for it to turn round without leaking, and then remove the fuel pipes from the front, rather than from the back of the tap. (I have since tried this and it worked fine – as the least worse option – but my fuel pipes were long enough to allow me to do that.) The tank was now fitted. See photo 47.19.

All that remained was to clip on the side panels – I applied a little WD40 to the lugs to make it easier to remove them in the future without risk of cracking them. That was it, the bike was finally complete. Hurrah! See photo 47.20.

LESSONS LEARNT
- There is no such thing as a paint code for paintwork on a Z.
- Tanks and panels are painted black and white to begin with – the white will become the lighter colour and the black will become the darker colour.
- After the black and white, several coats of silver flake are added to give a metallic finish.
- After the silver flake, several coats of candy lacquer are added to give the final colour.
- Some pinstripes are just lacquered white lines and some are decals, depending on model.
- The mounting for the tailpiece is clever V-shaped rubbers and collars.
- Don't press on unsupported side panels.
- New tank emblems are flat, not curved.
- Petrol taps have a clever right- and left-handed thread adaptor for fitting to the tank.
- Whichever way you do it, removing the petrol pipes to remove the tank isn't easy.
- I was trembling fitting the last few panels I was so excited!

For general info, here's a list of the various colour combinations available on different models:

Z1 Candy brown and orange, Candy green and yellow.
Z1A Candy brown and orange, Candy green and yellow.
Z1B Candy super red and candy super blue.
Z900 Diamond dark green, diamond brown.
KZ900 LTD Classic red.
Z1000 A1 Diamond wine red, Diamond sky blue.
Z1000 A2 Luminous green, luminous red (callipers behind forks).
Z1000 LTD various colours including black, blue and red.
Z1000 A3/A4 luminous navy blue, luminous dark red.

(Note that whilst the colour combinations may be the same between different models, paintwork designs changed.)

47.20 It's finished!

Chapter 48
Teething troubles: no oil pressure & misfiring

The bike was finished: hurrah! The teething problems were now upon us: boo! I was very happy (and very surprised) to discover that all of the electrics worked on the bike – even the stop light failure warning light! The only minor problem was that the left indicator warning light wasn't working, and it turned out that the bulb had become dislodged during fitting. Access was easy by simply unscrewing the bezel from the ignition switch – a 30-second fix.

I also checked that the starter motor was working fine and turned over the engine a few times – which is where my problems began ... Having chugged the engine a few times on the starter I noticed that the oil pressure warning light hadn't gone out. Hmmm. I was only turning the engine on the starter, but surely I should get oil pressure? I could see through the sight glass in the clutch cover that the oil level went down on the starter, so clearly oil was being sucked up ... a faulty pressure switch, maybe?

After a little thought (and some panic) I removed the inspection cap from the end of the oil gallery and found that it was bone dry – absolutely no sign of oil at all. Bad news. See photo 48.1. I thought that maybe there was an air lock somewhere in the system, so turned over the engine on the starter with the inspection cap off. No joy. Maybe a little more encouragement was needed?

With panic levels rising, I turned over the engine continuously for about a minute until the new and fully charged battery was drained. (Why is it that, at times like these, you find yourself pushing the starter button as hard as possible – as if that's going to make any difference!). No oil. No sign of oil. And not only that, it was now evening and I had to leave the bike (with the battery on charge) until the next day. I had rather troubled sleep that night.

The next day I thought I would try and start the engine and see if the corresponding increase in power and pressure would solve the problem, so rigged up a couple of funnels as a temporary fuel tank. (At this point I was still waiting for the tank and panels to come back from the paint shop.) See photo 48.2. The good news was that the bike started on the first touch of the button, normally something to celebrate, but on this occasion I hardly registered it. All I knew was that there was still no oil; no oil at all. Damn.

I tried to quell my rising sense of panic and frustration and think

48.1 Inspection cap removed from the oil gallery – bone dry, no sign of oil at all – bad news.

48.2 Temporary fuel tanks – I don't think it'll catch on.

201

HOW TO RESTORE KAWASAKI Z1, Z/KZ900 & Z/KZ1000

48.3 Draining the oil from the oil filter housing.

48.4 Oil all over the engine – hurrah!

logically, deciding to try and trace the oil flow from source, one step at a time. I knew that the first place the oil went to from the pump was the oil filter, so I removed the small oil filter drain plug (not the main drain plug) and drained the oil from the filter housing. See photo 48.3. (The oil filter sits in its own housing so has its own, separate drain plug.) With the oil from the filter drained, I briefly tried the engine – and oil poured out of the drain hole! Hurrah!

I now knew that the pump was definitely working (thank God), and that oil was passing from the pump into the oil filter. There was clearly a problem between the oil filter and the main oil gallery: maybe the little 'O' ring in the passageway from the oil filer to the gallery, between the two crankcases, had come unseated during assembly and blocked the passageway? That would mean a complete engine rebuild, right back to splitting the crankcases. I tried not to think about it.

Thankfully, Kawasaki, in its wisdom, had put another inspection cap in the system just below the oil pressure switch, so I removed this – which was a complete bugger to get to with the carbs, etc. I then gingerly tried the engine again with my heart in my mouth – the last real throw of the dice – and suddenly, seconds later, oil came pouring out! Hurrah! I have never been so glad to see oil pouring out of an engine in my life! See photo 48.4.

I replaced both inspection caps and the oil drain plug for the oil filter,

and started the bike again: almost immediately the oil pressure warning light went out. I had oil pressure! Oil was flowing round the engine! Hoo-flipping-ray! What a relief!

So, what had happened? As I'd surmised, there was a massive air lock in the main oil feed passages, but how come? I posted my experience on one of the Facebook groups dedicated to the Z900s, and Neil Conway replied with what appeared to be the cause of this problem. Apparently, some oil pressure switches do not have a small bleed valve fitted to allow air through, although most do. If there's no bleed valve the switch won't allow any air through, and an air lock stays where it is. I'm sure this is what happened to mine. I might replace the switch in the future as the air lock can recur if air enters the system again – which can happen under hard, sustained acceleration (no oil to the pump as it's all at the back of the sump!). Anyway, problem solved and understood.*

With oil pressure now achieved I decided to run the engine a little more, and go through the usual checks and adjustments before the

---

* I have to report that having ridden the bike 25 miles the oil pressure suddenly disappeared again. I took the oil filter, etc, off to check everything, and when I reassembled it, oil pressure was restored and has been fine ever since. I can only think that there was still some air in the system which collected under the oil pressure switch and prevented oil flow again. Weird, but everything is good now.

tank, etc, arrived so that everything would be ready. Taking the bike off the lift it looked like a bike again! For some reason, looking at it on the ground made it appear a hundred times better than when on the lift. Strange, but true. I wheeled it to the edge of the garage to reduce exhaust fumes inside, and started it.

I revved the engine a few times and all seemed okay – but not good. After checking I realised that the

48.5 Good temperature on No 1 cylinder.

48.6 Much lower temperature on No 2 cylinder.

TEETHING TROUBLES: NO OIL PRESSURE & MISFIRING

engine was running on three cylinders only; number 2 cylinder (inside left) was misfiring. I knew this because I briefly (!) felt each exhaust pipe and discovered that number 2 was much colder than the others. To confirm my suspicions I checked the temperatures with my heat sensor gun. See photo 48.5 of the normal temperature on number 1 cylinder as the engine warmed up, and photo 48.6 of the much lower temperature on number 2 cylinder. Bugger.

I checked for a spark with a spare plug – all okay – damn! (It's at times like this that you want it not to work). I whipped out the plug and swapped it for my spare. No joy; still the same poor running, or not running at all, I wasn't quite sure which. Bugger again. See photo 48.7 – I tried a lot of different plugs! I took out the plug again and ran the engine, and saw that the valves were going up and down – so not a stuck valve. Hmmm. The carburettor? I hoped not: I knew I'd cleaned them thoroughly and built them well.

I put the plug back in and ran the engine again before taking out the plug again – it appeared wet. So, petrol apparently getting through okay. I ran the bike again and checked the exhaust pressure coming out of the silencers. To my surprise, number 2 exhaust was a far higher pressure than the others – even though number 2 wasn't firing! Aha! I thought, the exhaust valve isn't seating properly and is leaking, which is why there's more pressure: the piston's pushing all the compression out of the exhaust valve.

At this point I should have checked the compression, but forgot to. I wheeled the bike back inside and removed the cam cover to check the rocker clearances. See photo 48.8. I checked for any clearance on the exhaust valve on number 2 cylinder and found that it was tight on the tappet, even when fully closed. I couldn't get even my smallest feeler gauge (2 thou) through. See photo 48.9.

Belatedly, I checked the compression just off the kick-start (with the cam cover off you don't want to turn it over on the starter as oil will go everywhere). The pressure in number 1 cylinder was over 4 bar but under 3 bar in number 2 cylinder. See photos 48.10 and 48.11. (Remember, I was testing compression by just kicking over

48.7 Checking the plugs – several times!

48.8 Cam cover removed.

48.9 Cam is tight on the exhaust valve when fully closed.

203

HOW TO RESTORE KAWASAKI Z1, Z/KZ900 & Z/KZ1000

48.10 Pressure on No 1 cylinder.

48.11 Pressure on No 2 cylinder.

the bike, so a low reading was to be expected. Compression readings should be taken when the engine is warm/hot, with the engine turned over on the starter (or with the engine running) and with WOT – Wide Open Throttle. This is required to suck as much air into the cylinder as possible, which is then compressed and gives a proper reading.) I replaced the shim with a much smaller one, measured the gap and ordered the correct size shim, which was, of course, considerably thinner than the one in

48.12 Fitting a new, thinner shim to reinstate the gap between camshaft and tappet bucket.

there. See photo 48.12. The correct tappet clearance was now reinstated.

What had happened? Somehow, that valve hadn't seated properly during the rebuild. Despite tapping it after fitting with a hammer, and turning over the engine by hand when the cams were in, the valve hadn't seen fit to seat itself, and it was only after starting and running the engine for a short while that it did so, closing the tappet gap to below nothing, so the valve was slightly open at all times. I've had something similar happen before. I decided that it was this that had caused the valve not to close fully, leading to no compression – and therefore no ignition.

I refitted the cam cover and restarted the engine … still the same problem: number 2 cylinder wasn't firing. Bugger.

LESSONS LEARNT
• When trying to find the cause of a cylinder not firing there are only three potential sources – ignition, fuel or mechanical – so the procedure is to slowly work through, eliminating each in turn.
• Although there had definitely been a problem with the exhaust valve on number 2 cylinder, it hadn't been bad enough to cause the problem (or were there two problems?).
• Mechanical problems had now been discounted – the compression reading on all cylinders was good and almost identical.
• So maybe an ignition problem? Unlikely, as I'd already checked for a spark and had swapped plugs, but I have known sparks to suddenly disappear when under compression, so not to be ruled out. A carburettor/fuel problem, then?
• Look on the bright side: if this problem had not occurred, I may not have discovered the problem with the exhaust valve on number 2 cylinder until I checked the valve clearances a few hundred miles down the road, by which time it may have done some damage – maybe burning out the valve. So a blessing in disguise then?!
• Time to look at the ignition and fuel systems.

Chapter 49

Teething troubles II: the misfire continues

With the engine still misfiring and mechanical problems ruled out, it was time to look elsewhere. Considering this logically –
• I'd rebuilt the carbs and cleaned them thoroughly. There are no real moving parts in them apart from the throttle valve, so nothing to go wrong, really. The spark plug also looked wet suggesting that fuel was getting through.
• I was getting a good spark.
• The electronic ignition system was old and an unknown quantity, and may have a fault.
• The ignition coils were brand new but, as such, were untried and untested – maybe one was duff?

I decided, on balance, that my best course of action was to look at the ignition system next (even if only to rule it out), as it was easier to check than taking off the carbs again – which I really didn't want to do!

I decided to swap round the ignition coils and HT leads to see if the problem moved with them, swapping the input wires from the electronic ignition to the coils. At the same time I also swapped the HT leads from each coil to the plugs. The coil that was firing numbers 1 and 4 cylinders was now firing numbers 2 and 3 cylinders, and vice-versa. See photo 49.1. I started the engine again and … number 2 cylinder was still not firing. I therefore knew, by a process of elimination, that this was a carburettor/fuel problem.

I reinstated the ignition to how it had been, bit the bullet and removed the carburettors from the engine. All looked okay with nothing obvious. See photo 49.2. The inlet manifolds were brand new with no signs of

49.1 Ignition leads and ignition coils swapped round.

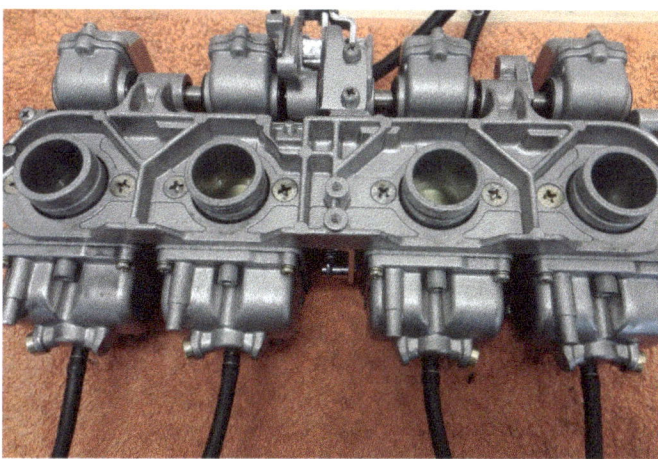
49.2 Carbs removed from engine – all looks okay.

CLASSIC MOTORCYCLE RESTORATION

damage, so I discounted an air leak. Something was definitely amiss with carb number 2 – but what?

I removed the float bowl from number 2 carb and checked all of the jets for any sign of a blockage (see photo 49.3) but all appeared clear. I removed the jets and starter pipe for good measure and gave them a good clean, but there was no sign of anything wrong. I then removed the floats and checked that they did actually float (see photo 49.4): as I thought, they were fine. I blew down through the float needle to check that fuel could pass through and it seemed okay, but I took off the float bowl of carb number 1 to compare it. See photo 49.5. The float needles on both carbs operated identically. Damn. I had found no 'smoking gun,' nothing that was definitely the cause of the problem. There's noting worse than taking everything apart, and not finding anything obviously wrong, because you know damn well that when you put it back together again, it still won't work! And so it proved.

I replaced the carbs on the engine (reconnecting the fiddly

49.5 Removing the float bowl from No 1 cylinder to compare float needles.

49.3 Float bowl removed to check for blockages in the jets etc.

49.6 Swapping pairs of carburettors round.

49.4 Checking that the floats do, in fact, float.

throttle cables, of course), and started the engine: number 2 cylinder still wasn't firing. No surprise there. I decided that the best course of action was to devise a way of checking whether or not the misfire moved with the carb, in a similar fashion to how I had checked the ignition.

I removed the carbs from the engine (again), and removed them from the gantry. See photo 49.6. I then swapped around the pairs of carbs so that the two on the left were now on the right, and vice-versa. You

have to swap the carbs in pairs as they're connected: there's nothing to prevent them working like this, it's just that the air screws are now facing the middle, and are fairly inaccessible. See photo 49.7.

Not wanting to create a lot of work for myself, I half-assembled the carbs, not refitting the choke or the carb tops, and when I put them back on the engine (just as difficult as ever) I connected one throttle cable only, omitting the return cable, and didn't seat the inlets on the carbs. See

TEETHING TROUBLES II: THE MISFIRE CONTINUES

49.7 Carbs swapped round on the gantry – air screws on the wrong sides.

49.8 Carbs temporarily refitted on opposite sides to check whether cylinder No 2 or No 4 wasn't running.

photo 49.8. The carbs should run fine like this, at least temporarily. I started the engine and … number 2 cylinder was now running fine, but number 4 cylinder wasn't ... The problem was definitely due to a fault with number 2 carburettor.

I removed the carbs (again), and completely stripped carb number 2. The only thing I could think of was that the very tiny passageway from the pilot jet to the carb venturi was blocked. I had cleaned this when I'd first rebuilt the carbs, of course, but not with foaming carb cleaner that could be seen foaming out of the hole, so couldn't be certain it wasn't blocked. See photo 49.9.

I therefore cleaned out that airway with everything I could: carb cleaner, a cut off wire from a wire brush pushed down the hole with small mole grips, and a lot of compressed air. Several beads of silica from the vapour blasting process came out of the hole: maybe these had caused the problem?

I reassembled the carbs on the gantry (again), and fitted them back on the bike (again). I started the bike … number 2 cylinder was running fine! The tiny little airway had been blocked, which was the reason why the carb wouldn't work. To be honest I'd thought about that little airway before. I knew I'd cleaned it (clearly, not very well) and was of the opinion that, even if it was blocked, it wouldn't affect the carb that much that it wouldn't run at all, at any engine speed. Not so – that airway is

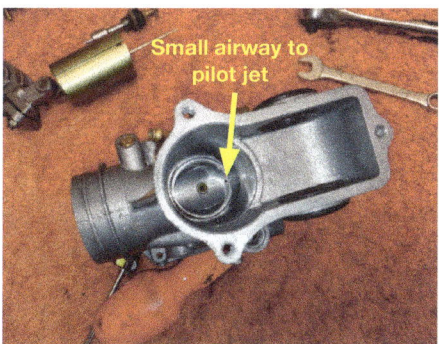

49.9 Carbs off again and triple checking that the small air passageway to the pilot jet wasn't blocked.

clearly vital to the proper functioning of the carbs.

LESSON LEARNT

I think that's how you have to look at a problem like this – what you've learnt from it. I knew that the airway was important and, being so small, susceptible to becoming blocked, but I never thought for a minute that it would prevent the carb from working at all. I also learnt that I need to take my own advice – always use foaming carb cleaner. If I had done this I'd not have encountered the problem in the first place ... but nor would I have learnt a vital lesson, either. (Although I did subsequently discover, when working on my Z1A carbs, that if you stick the nozzle on the carb cleaner up the hole for the pilot jet, carb cleaner will spurt out of the little airway in the venturi if it's clear).
• Work through problems methodically, one-by-one.
• Try to eliminate potential causes one at a time – don't jump to conclusions.
• You can run the bike with the carbs on the wrong sides and not fully fitted.
• The minute airway in the venturi is very important.
• Note that earlier on I thought the plug looked wet, suggesting fuel was getting through. I think now that maybe this was in fact oil, as the combustion chambers had oil in following the rebuild, which burnt off when the engine started – apart from No. 2 cylinder of course, which wasn't firing. Just a reminder that faults can be sneaky and give you the wrong clues!
• Don't tell everyone else to clean their carbs thoroughly and then not do it yourself.
• Don't tell everyone else to use foaming carb cleaner and then use non-foaming carb cleaner yourself.
• It's not a problem, it's an opportunity to learn something new!

I encountered another small problem a little later, when I realised that the bike carburettors were flooding and leaking petrol when the bike was standing. I traced this to a leaking (new) petrol tap. The tap didn't actually leak petrol, it didn't shut off properly, so it was like leaving the fuel tap on, which was flooding the carbs. It was a new tap but clearly faulty. I contacted the supplier and a new tap was despatched. Problem sorted.

Chapter 50
Tools & equipment

Here are some of the tools and equipment I'd recommend when rebuilding a bike.

CONSUMABLES

With reference to photo 50.1: general purpose grease for bearings outside the engine, and for threads and such; solvent cleaner for cleaning off Wellseal; carb and brake cleaner, almost as pungent as the solvent cleaner but great on brakes and carburettors; white spirit for cleaning greasy parts; dashboard wipes for any rubber parts – brings them up nicely; workshop tissue (or in my case kitchen towel); buy it by the van-load – essential; engine oil – in this case only relatively cheap stuff for running in; 10 grade front fork oil; disposable rubber gloves – I don't always wear them but, for the really dirty jobs, they're great (my hands got really bad a few years ago due to high-power garage soap, so I look after them more now – still haven't got any fingerprints!); WD40, what can I say, probably the most used of everything in the workshop – not only great for lubricating and electrical connections, but also very good for cleaning greasy parts; brake fluid; ACF-50 used for preventing parts from going rusty. I used this under the mudguards, etc, and every winter I cover my bikes with it to prevent corrosion whilst they're laid up; engine assembly lubricant, really essential for lubricating engine parts during assembly so they're not too damaged on initial start-up before the oil circulates – just imagine what would have happened in my case with the air lock if I'd not used it; RTV sealant for the alternator grommet and for sealing anything else; Wellseal, the only gasket cement that I ever use, period; Tipp-Ex, good for highlighting the timing marks on the ignition for the strobe; freezer bags

50.1 Consumables.

TOOLS & EQUIPMENT

of various sizes and a marker pen for bagging and tagging all your parts – makes the job so much easier; Loctite thread seal and bearing seal (medium strength), essential for locking threads and preventing bearings from spinning in their housings; Solvol Autosol for polishing chrome and alloy – still not found anything better.

GENERAL WORKSHOP TOOLS

As a rule, buy only good quality tools: they're expensive, but will do the job properly, be a joy to work with, and last a lifetime.

Possibly the best workshop tool I have ever bought has been my bike lift. It makes working on bikes soooo much easier and enjoyable - and they're not too expensive these days. Downsides are that they are very heavy, take up a lot of room in the workshop (space is always at a premium), and it's not easy getting the bikes on and off of it safely – but still bloody marvellous!

With reference to photo 50.2: a mini socket set and a full-size socket set with a variety of extensions, etc: absolutely essential; two sets of metric spanners (so you can hold one nut whilst turning the other); a wide selection of cross-head screwdrivers. I also bought a set of JIS (Japanese Industry Standard) screwdrivers, specifically designed to fit the cross-head screws on a Japanese engine: I found that they fitted the screw heads on the bike far better than normal screwdrivers, but I had to order them from the USA. When they finally arrived (after the normal customs duty malarkey), they were smaller than I expected, but because they fitted the cross-head screws on the engine so perfectly I could tighten the screws far better with the quite small JIS screwdrivers than larger standard Phillips ones – highly recommended; Stanley knife; engine brushes for cleaning out thread holes and oil ways – essential; a selection of wire brushes for cleaning parts; a copper and hide-headed mallet, absolutely essential for 'persuading' parts to go in – double check which way round the head is before using(!); a set of drifts from very small to long and large, for drifting out parts from the floats on carburettors to the swinging arm spindle; a full set of circlip pliers – some open out,

50.2 General workshop tools.

some open in, some have thick tips and others thin – buy a full set as otherwise the one you haven't got will be the one you want; magnifying glass for checking carb jets, etc; a full set of metric Allen keys; assorted pliers and wire cutters; an adjustable spanner and mole grips – they're always needed at some point; a selection of hammers; a telescopic magnet – I can't tell you how useful and essential this tool is; a small inspection light on a flexible stem – really useful for looking into oilways, etc – essential; a set of metric feeler gauges, and a set of Imperial gauges helps, too; a selection of old toothbrushes and small wire brushes for cleaning those small parts.

SPECIAL TOOLS

With reference to photo 50.3: a Vernier calliper gauge for measuring wear on parts, etc; my new cordless impact wrench: don't know how I ever managed without it for removing very tight or seized nuts and bolts in an instant: highly recommended;

50.3 Special tools.

HOW TO RESTORE KAWASAKI Z1, Z/KZ900 & Z/KZ1000

50.4 More special tools.

a measuring jug – how else are you going to measure 169cc of fork fluid?; a compression tester, very useful for checking that all is well with the head and valves; a stroboscopic ignition timer for spot-on timing; a stud removal tool – completely useless in my case; don't know if there are better ones on the market; a set of Allen keys to fit a socket set, when normal Allen keys aren't enough (like for the bottom of the front forks); a normal impact driver, essential; a pair of wire-strippers and crimps for making electrical connections. I always use crimped bullets and they work okay – I'm totally rubbish at soldering; a temperature gun that can read temperatures from afar – really useful on downpipes, etc; a fork seal removal tool; a chain link extractor (and one to insert links if you so wish);

taps for running threads on casings, etc, after blast cleaning – essential; a 'C' spanner for adjusting shocks and also adjusting the lower steering stem nut.

Some other special tools are also highly recommended. With reference to photo 50.4: a good grease gun – mine was my father's, and is still going well today; a rotor removal tool – it looks pretty simple, but it worked well; a set of vacuum gauges: good for checking that the carbs are working properly, though they can give incorrect readings and, as ever, won't tell you what the problem is if the readings vary – an excellent tool for raising blood pressure; a tool to prise shims from their tappet buckets – essential – and the more I used it, the easier it became; a set of JIS (Japanese Industry Standard) screwdrivers (again!); a three-legged honing tool – if your cylinder bores don't need reboring, they will almost certainly need and benefit from being honed; a compression tester to check levels of compression in the cylinders; a stroboscopic timing light to set the ignition timing bang on; a good quality torque wrench – again, mine was my father's, it's of good quality, and gives torque settings you can trust; a gas blowtorch for heating parts such as alloy casings before fitting bearings, etc; clutch locking tools – they do work when you've engaged your brain; a vice – I now manage by having a movable vice that clamps to the bench if I really need it, which means it's out of the way most of the time but there when needed – and you will need it; a tool to lap in the valve guides if the valves are new or the seats have been recut. (I also use the one that fits to a drill, not in the picture). Another essential special tool I forgot to include in the photos is a valve spring compressor for removing and replacing valves from the cylinder head.

SPARE ESSENTIALS

Little bits and bobs are always required throughout the rebuild which, if you haven't got, can hold up the job massively, so it's good to have a selection of these to hand. With reference to photo 50.5: a set of different size circlips; a wide selection of stainless steel nuts and bolts

50.5 Essential spares.

TOOLS & EQUIPMENT

bought in bulk from various suppliers; a set of split pins; a set of different size small springs; a set of fibre washers; a set of rubber grommets; a selection of very small washers; a set of stainless steel 'R' pins; a set of copper washers; a set of neoprene 'O' rings. All of the foregoing are really helpful throughout any rebuild, and often a godsend.

As always, though, chances are that no matter how big the selection you have, the one item that you want isn't there!

MANUALS
You can't really have enough of these. Hopefully, this restoration manual will cover most of what you need, but it's always worth having as much info as possible to hand. With reference to photo 50.6, the other two manuals I'd recommend are the *Haynes Manual* and the *Kawasaki Workshop Manual*. I bought the Haynes publication from a bookseller and the Kawasaki one (which is really comprehensive – no surprise there!) – from eBay, although I think you may also be able to download it – highly recommended. Also, Kawasaki manuals for different models are generally available, so you should be able to get one for your exact model. There is also the *Clymer Manual*, but I've used these in the past and not found them that helpful (even worse than the *Haynes Manuals* which aren't that great themselves) so didn't bother buying one this time (which probably means it's absolutely excellent!)

One other essential item is a *Kawasaki Parts Catalogue*, available to download rather than buy as a hard copy. I downloaded mine from the Z-Power website and used it all the time. The only problem I encountered was that next to many parts it says NLA (no longer available), and the first time I read it I nearly had a heart attack as so many parts were marked as NLA. However, most parts marked as NLA in the parts catalogues actually are available, it's just that they're old catalogues, published before many items were remanufactured.

50.6 Manuals.

50.7 Originality guides.

OTHER PUBLICATIONS
With reference to photo 50.7, other publications that I found very useful when rebuilding the bike (some giving background info; others more technical, such as for the Z900s) are two excellent originality guides, essential reading for rivet counters everywhere; *Original Kawasaki* by the very respected restorer Dave Marsden, which covers all of the differences between the 900 models, and then there's *Kawasaki Z1 & Z2* by John Brookes, which covers the differences and original fittings in minute detail (which bolt heads were used, etc; great to look through and wonder at the detail therein). NB John Brookes' book has limited availability: try specialist parts suppliers, or order through his website: kawasakiz1z2partsbook.webs.com

Apart from the foregoing, there are some very interesting books on the history of the Z900: two books by Dave Sheehan – *The Kawasaki Z1 Story* (Veloce) and *Superbikes and the 70s* – both good reads. And don't forget the *Kawasaki Owner's Manuals* which contain some really useful information about day-to-day servicing. Reprints are generally available.

LESSONS LEARNT
- Buy quality tools whenever possible – they're a joy to work with, will last forever, and fit properly.
- Buy a bike lift: you won't regret it.
- You need good manuals – and you need to read them, too.
- There are lots of consumables and spare essentials you can buy – especially if you've got a thing for those little boxes!
- Special tools are often essential and make the job so much easier.

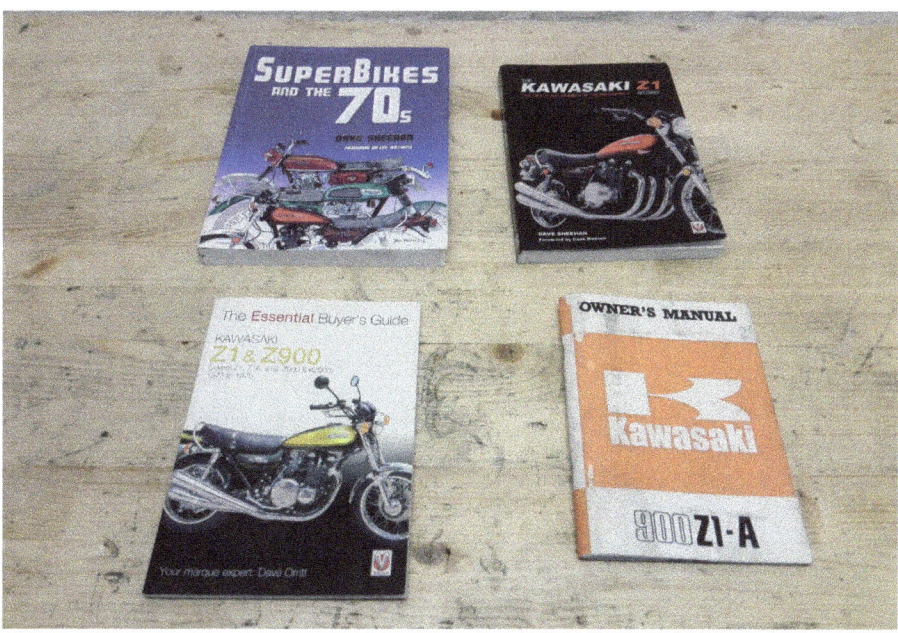

50.8 Other recommended books.

Chapter 51
Summing it all up

I have always loved the Z900. I am generally a British biker, through-and-through, and the only Japanese bike I've ever really wanted was a Z900. I bought my Z1A already restored (although, as with my KZ900, the front cam chain guide was broken and I ended up rebuilding the whole engine) and I bought the KZ900 to restore for this manual. I've rebuilt many bikes over the years, but I'd never restored a Japanese machine, so it was an exciting project.

I would really have liked to restore a Z1/Z1A/Z1B but the prices of these, even in an unrestored state, are very high, and continue to climb. I think I maybe could have found one at a reasonable price with a little more digging, but I needed a bike relatively quickly so I could proceed with the restoration and this manual. I think I paid over the odds for my bike – £6000 in March 2017 – but I needed a bike to restore so that was what I paid. Maybe I should have haggled more?

I trailered the bike home and, whilst doing so, it came off the trailer (yes, it still hurts), which badly damaged the headlight, indicators, front brake master cylinder, tacho, front mudguard, and front forks. Not great, but it could have been so much worse.

Having finally got the bike home, I was unable to begin work on it for a while as, although I was desperate to start (and had agreed a completion date with my publisher), life got in the way in the form of a new kitchen/dining room that I was installing. Not only did this take longer than expected/hoped, it also took a lot of my very low cash reserves (having spent £6000 on the bike there wasn't much left anyway!). I knew that this would create problems later with what was going to be an expensive restoration.

Whilst unable to start on the restoration proper, I used the time to track down elusive parts so that I had them ready for when I could start. I sourced a second-hand airbox and a new silencer (missing from my bike and currently unavailable new), and a second-hand calliper and disc to convert to twin discs, plus a second-hand set of forks, and a second-hand headlamp. I also bought expensive new front fork shrouds from America as I mistakenly thought that they were generally no longer available.

I finally got properly to grips with dismantling the bike in September 2017, and worked as hard as I could to get the various parts to various finishers, as I knew the waiting list for work was quite long. I managed to get parts to the blast cleaner/powder coater and chrome plater by the beginning of October, and my tank and panels, etc, to the painter by mid-October. In the case of the tank, this was just as well because there was what turned out to be a four-month waiting list.

Whilst some parts were away being blasted and chromed, etc, I was able to use the time to clean and check engine internals. The bike was showing 22,000 miles on the odometer, which I think was correct. To my surprise, I found the engine to be in amazingly good condition throughout – a real credit to Kawasaki. I decided not to have a rebore or even change the piston rings as all seemed to be fine. The only parts I needed to replace were the exhaust valve guides and valve springs, and the camshaft bushes, plus, of course, the broken cam chain guide, the Achilles heel of the engine. The exact same part broke on my Z1A in exactly the same manner (snapped off top and bottom).

When the crankcases came back from being blasted disaster struck when I put them in the dishwasher with a dishwasher tablet, and they came out iron grey. In the end I had to

SUMMING IT ALL UP

take them back and have them blast cleaned again. Lesson learnt. When the cases came back, I found that all of the threads needed to be run down with a tap as they were very rough: something had happened to them during the blasting/cleaning process. I've never had this happen before but you couldn't run a bolt down them at all, they were very bad. I also found it very hard to remove the silica beads from the cases, and especially from parts such as the carbs with their complex passageways. If I can find an alternative to vapour blasting I'll try it next time.

The main thing I discovered when rebuilding the engine was just how well it was designed. Just about everything in the engine was still working perfectly, with no sign of wear or damage. The crankshaft, including the big ends and main bearings, were fine, as was the clutch, pistons, bores, and camshafts, etc. Just about everything was in pretty much pristine condition because it was so well-designed. The only item that really let it down was the cam chain guide, which was completely broken on both bikes. To be honest, though, if that's all you've really got to watch for then it can't be bad!

I also replaced the camshaft bearings, as they looked a bit worn, and had to replace the exhaust valve guides as they were definitely worn. Other than that I just honed the cylinder bores, replaced all of the seals, and put it back together again. I must say I was very impressed.

I was also pleasantly surprised by how easy it was to work on the engine. At first sight it's a very complicated 900cc, 4-cylinder, double over head camshaft engine with horizontally split crankcases and 'complexity' in abundance. But it's so well built and with so many prompts to help you avoid mistakes it's just great to work on. (Just about every part of the engine is marked as to where it fits and which way round it goes, which is normally a conundrum for a first-time restorer, but not with this one.) Even the double over head camshafts and cam chain system that I had never worked on before provided no real problems, and were very easy to install.

As for the cycle parts, these had fared less well due mainly to age, wear and tear, and general abuse by previous owners. Everything was okay, though a bit tatty. Parts that really needed replacement or refurbishment (rather than those I replaced because they were a bit tired) were the front master cylinder and brake calliper, the head races, the wheel bearings, and the swinging arm bushes (all of which were completely worn out), and some of the electrics. Note that it is impossible to grease the head races or wheel bearings without dismantling, so these are often neglected and in need of replacement after 40 years plus. Apart from this the bike was in very good shape for a 42-year-old, and had survived the attentions of previous owners, including being sportified with a 4-into-1 exhaust and K&N air filters.

I was also impressed, and pleasantly surprised, by the availability of virtually all parts, and the very good service that suppliers provided. It's also good to know that, because so many were made, even if a part's not available you can generally find one from somewhere (Googling a part number can work wonders!)

Due to the Z900 being so fast and so bullet-proof, it was raced a lot back in the day, and still is now. Because of this there's a whole world of uprated parts out there, with everything from big bore conversions and uprated cams and carbs to brakes and wheels suspension. If you want to make a fast road or race bike you can upgrade to your heart's content – as long as you've a fat wallet!

So, what has it all cost? The answer to that is – a lot. Because I wanted to build a really nice bike I had everything cleaned and vapour blasted and chromed or replaced, and that cost. I could have done it cheaper but I didn't want to. I wanted a completely restored bike to my own specification, so that's what I did. The restoration cost around £6500, making a total of £12,500 with the original purchase price. Ouch! Worth every penny in my book, though. Some of my bigger costs were: blasting/powder coating £580; tank and panel painting £550; new exhaust system £1100; chrome plating £450; twin disc conversion approximately £425; wheel building, including a new rim and two new tyres, £420; new airbox and silencer £400; new front forks £175.

I'm also very happy to report that my gamble of not replacing parts regardless seems to have paid off, and the bike runs like a dream. There's not a hint of smoke from the exhausts, and the engine has a really satisfying 'whirr' to it that tells you it's right. All of the electrics work; the brakes are good, and, of course, it looks absolutely stunning! I had the bike MoTd and applied to DVLA to have the bike registered in the UK – about a six week wait! Just as well it was only February. By May 2018 the bike had been registered on a 'P' plate and I've since had many wonderful rides out on it. It has fully lived up to expectation.

See photos 51.1 to 51.19 of the bike from the start of the rebuild to the end.

I'm really happy with the restoration and the way the bike's turned out, and hope that I get to keep it for many years. In turn, I really hope you've found this manual useful, and that it helps you to complete your own restoration!

Keep the faith!

51.1 The bike as bought.

HOW TO RESTORE KAWASAKI Z1, Z/KZ900 & Z/KZ1000

51.2 It was okay but very neglected and dirty.

51.3 Halfway through dismantling.

51.4 The bike fully dismantled.

51.5 The engine back in the frame.

SUMMING IT ALL UP

51.6 The bike half assembled.

51.7 Bike nearly finished.

51.8 to 51.19 (below and following pages): Bike finished.

HOW TO RESTORE KAWASAKI Z1, Z/KZ900 & Z/KZ1000

SUMMING IT ALL UP

Chapter 52

Parts, services, clubs & UK registration

PARTS SUPPLIERS

Z-Power
01942 262864
www.z-power.co.uk
A great parts supplier that stocks a very wide range. Delivery is very quick and advice is available. It can be difficult to find parts on the website so if you can't see it, give them a ring.

Z1 Enterprises
www.z1enterprises.com
Parts supplier in the US – also supplies some upgraded parts.

Wemoto.com
www.wemoto.com
01273 597072
An on-line based parts supplier based in the UK. Clear website.

Partzilla
www.partzilla.com
An on-line based parts supplier in the US, with a good, clear website and worldwide shipping service.

Johnny's vintage motorcycles, USA
www.johnnysvintagemotorcycle.com
Parts supplier – also does a good video on YouTube of the differences between a Z1 and a Z900.
Webike, Japan
Supplier of standard and uprated parts
japan.webike.net

John Browse
01978 355 556
Supplier of hard-to-find and no longer available parts

Motorsport
Motorsport.com
Supplier of some racing upgrades.

Schnitz Racing
Schnitzracing.com
Supplier of some racing upgrades.

Andrews Motorsports
Andrewsmotorsports.com
Supplier of engine tuning parts: eg adjustable camshaft sprockets.

CHROME PLATING, VAPOUR BLASTING AND POWDER COATING

Agbrigg chrome platers
agbriggchrome.mycylex.co.uk
07815419885
An okay chrome plating company – but don't ask them to do Mazak!

Prestige Plating
01709 577004
A very good chrome plating company that provides an excellent finish – but there's a long waiting time – about five months.

Two Brothers blasting and powder coating
0114 249 1995
A good vapour blasting and powder coating company in Sheffield.

Paintwork
Mark Hutchinson
01977 700011
Top-notch painter – long waiting time. Pontefract.

Dream Machine Paintwork
0115 973 6615
High quality classic and custom paintwork. Nottingham.

Paintworkz USA
www.paintworkz.com

OTHER SPECIALISTS

Z-Clocks
www.z-clocks.co.uk
Speedo and tacho refurbishment.

Manhattan Motorcycles
0114 258 2161
A good motorcycle shop in Sheffield.

PARTS, SERVICES, CLUBS & UK REGISTRATION

Black Cat Wheel Builders
mi6712.wixsite.com/blackcatwheels
Provides a very good wheel building service.

D&K Motorcycles/Two Wheel Spares
Suppliers of bikes for restoration and second-hand spares. Staffordshire

DK Classic motorcycles – on eBay

Two Wheel Spares – on eBay
(Also has a separate website for new(ish) bikes – confusing)

OWNERS' CLUBS

Z1 Owners' Club, UK
www.z1ownersclub.co.uk
Also on Facebook,

Z1 Owners' Club, USA
www.z1ownersclub.com
With a forum for technical Q & As.
Also on Facebook.

Australian Owners' Club
www.zowners.com.au.

FACEBOOK PAGES

An increasing number of pages on Facebook are dedicated to all-things Z1, etc. Always worth a look as new ones and specialised ones are always being added. Here are a few –

Z1 Historical.
Kawasaki Z1 Owners.
Z1 Owners UK.
Z1 Owners Club USA.
Z1 Owners.

REGISTERING A BIKE IN THE UK

At the time of writing I'm in the process of registering the bike in the UK. The process is currently as follows –
• Have proof that VAT and import duties gave been paid using the NOVA system (Notification Of Vehicle Arrivals). In my case this was done by the company I bought the bike from, which provided me with the confirmation letter.
• Get the bike insured using the frame number.
• Get the bike MoTd (I think this will still be required for new registrations for all bikes, even those that are normally MoT exempt).
• Either ring Kawasaki Customer Services (01628 856643) and ask for proof of the date of manufacture using the engine and frame number (there is a charge of £50 for this service); or contact the Vintage Japanese Motorcycle Owners' Club (VJMC) and they will provide the same service for £35 to non-members.
• Photocopy of your plastic driving licence or similar to prove your address.
• Obtain form V55/5 from the DVLA – and the guidance notes on how to complete it, form V355/5.
• Send all of these forms to DVLA (originals, not photocopies, apart from the driving licence),
• Keep fingers crossed,
• DVLA should then contact you to give approval and charge you £55 to register the bike with a new registration number, and send you a new log book (registration certificate to those of you under 40).

ACKNOWLEDGEMENTS

There are so many people I have to thank for their help and encouragement in the restoration of my bike and the writing of this manual. To name but a few they are as follows: Dave, Phil and Trev at Z-Power, Dave Orrit, Mark Hutchinson, Nigel Prescott, and Ian Padley. And of course thanks to Christine for putting up with all the noise and disruption and fumes associated with restoring a bike, together with a grumpy and distant husband (when your head's full of crankcase parts it's hard to communicate), and for not seeing me for much of the time (or was that a bonus?).

FACEBOOK PAGE

Finally, I have set up a Facebook page dedicated to updates and supplements to this manual.
The page is called Kawasaki Z1/Z900/Z1000 Restoration Manual Updates, and is designed to inform readers about new information and parts, etc, for our bikes that become available after the book is published. Feel free to join the group for the new information it has, and to make your own comments and suggestions. I look forward to welcoming you to the group.

YOUTUBE CHANNEL

The author has a YouTube channel dedicated to the dismantling, repair and reassembly of classic motorcycles, including the Z1s. The name of the channel is CHRIS ROOKE, and it is well worth watching and subscribing to.

ALSO AVAILABLE FROM VELOCE:

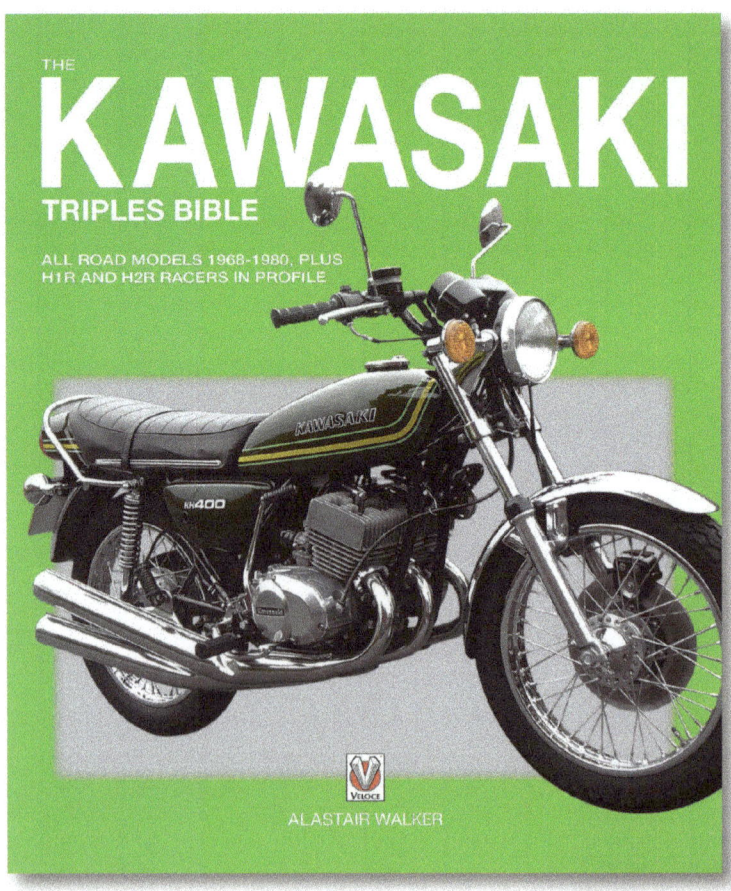

Now in paperback! *The Kawasaki Triples Bible* covers the entire production of three-cylinder two-strokes from '68 to '80. A year-by-year breakdown of bike specs and information covering all models, makes this an invaluable resource for any collector, restorer, or fan of these fabulous two-stroke motorcycles.

ISBN: 978-1-845849-81-8
Paperback • 25x20.7cm • 160 pages
• 183 colour and b&w pictures

Many books have been published about Japanese motorcycles, but none has focused exclusively on the Japanese motorcycle-based chopper, bobber, trike and quad customfa bike scene ... until now. Featuring stunning photography, this is a great book for Japanese bike fans, and fans of the custom bike scene in general.

ISBN: 978-1-845845-30-8
Hardback • 25x25cm
• 128 pages • 275 colour pictures

For more information and price details, visit our website at www.veloce.co.uk
email: info@veloce.co.uk • Tel: +44(0)1305 260068

The Kawasaki Z1 Story tells how the smallest of Japan's Big Four motorcycle manufacturers nearly beat the world's biggest to become the first to the market with a Four, and how Honda's CB750 debut almost spelled the end for the Z-1 … before Kawasaki stunned everybody with something bigger, faster, and better!

ISBN: 978-1-845848-07-1
Paperback • 21x14.8cm
• 256 pages • 135 pictures

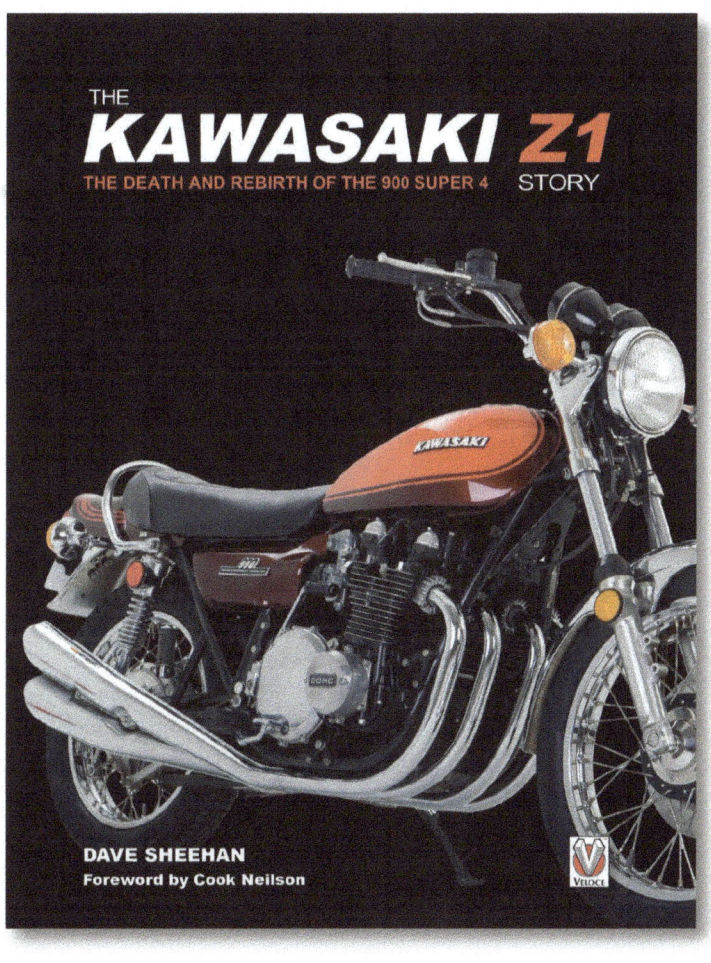

Having this book in your pocket is just like having a real marque expert at your side. Benefit from David Orritt's years of ownership, learn how to spot a bad bike quickly and how to assess a promising bike like a professional. Get the right bike at the right price!

ISBN: 978-1-845845-23-0
Paperback • 19.5x13.9cm
• 64 pages • 93 colour pictures

For more information and price details, visit our website at www.veloce.co.uk
email: info@veloce.co.uk • Tel: +44(0)1305 260068

MORE ENTHUSIAST'S RESTORATION MANUALS:

This book gives enthusiasts of the single overhead camshaft Honda Four a step-by-step guide to a full restoration. Whether it be the small but luxurious CB350/4 right through to the groundbreaking CB750/4. This guide covers dismantling the motorcycle and its components, restoring and sourcing parts, paint spraying, decals and polishing. The chapters cover, Engine, frame, forks, fuel, exhaust, seat, brakes, tyres, electrics, up to the rebuild and on to safe setup and general maintenance and finally onto riding safely and storage.

ISBN: 978-1-845847-46-3
Paperback • 27x20.7cm • 176 pages • 682 colour pictures

Whether a CX500, luxurious CS650 Silver Wing, or CX650 Turbo, this book provides a step-by-step guide to a full restoration. From dismantling, sourcing and restoring parts, to spray painting, decals and polishing. From the rebuild itself, to general maintenance and riding safety, this is the only restoration manual you'll need.

ISBN: 978-1-845847-73-9
Paperback • 27x20.7cm • 176 pages • 759 colour pictures

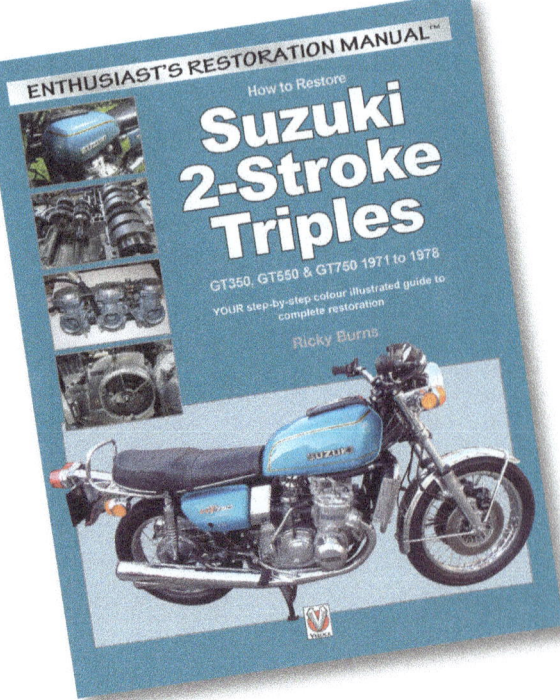

Whether it be an entry level GT380, or a ground-breaking water-cooled GT750, this step-by-step full restoration guide covers it, from dismantling, sourcing parts, spraying and decals, to polishing, safe set-up and general maintenance. Even riding safely and storage are covered, making this a must-have guide for all Suzuki Triple enthusiasts.

ISBN: 978-1-845848-20-0
Paperback • 27x20.7cm • 176 pages • 586 colour pictures

For more information and price details, visit our website at www.veloce.co.uk
email: info@veloce.co.uk • Tel: +44(0)1305 260068

Index

Airbox 167, 168, 171
Airbox silencer 167, 170, 171
Air filter 170, 171
Alloy polishing 74-77

Battery 25, 30, 163, 164
Battery box 163
Brake callipers 157-161
Brake discs 93, 157
Brake light failure switch 30, 185
Brake master cylinder 161, 162
Buying a bike 11-16

Cam chain 51, 84
Cam chain guides 49, 51, 54, 105, 115, 116
Cam cover 38
Camshafts 51, 52, 113-115
Carburettor problems 203-207
Carburettors 27, 127-139, 167-170
Chroming 71
Clutch 42, 43, 44, 140-142
Clutch cable 26, 155, 156
Clutch operating mechanism 154
Crankcases 55-57, 60, 72, 73, 83-88,
Crankshaft 59, 78, 79, 83, 84
Cylinder barrels 54, 104-107
Cylinder head 51, 52, 107-112

Date stamps 10, 33, 70
Dismantling (planning) 20, 21, 22
Draining the oil 37

Electronic ignition 38, 183-185
Engine breather 38, 115
Engine removal 55, 56, 57
Engine remounting 88
Engine replacement 101, 102
Exhaust 32, 33, 188-190

Facebook groups 219
Foot pegs 33
Fork yokes 62, 63
Front brake 25, 28, 157-162
Front forks 61-65, 89-91, 98, 99
Front mudguard 62, 99
Front wheel 61, 66, 67, 69, 70, 92-96, 99, 100
Fuse box 166

Gasket removal 70
Gear change mechanism 47, 119, 120
Gear selector drum 58, 59, 83-85, 119
Gearbox cover 27, 46, 120, 121, 154
Gearbox sprocket 45, 46, 153
Generator 40, 41, 124, 125
Grab rail 24

Handlebars 25, 26
Hazard lights 31, 186, 187
Head races 63, 97, 98
Headlamp 25, 180-182

Ignition coils 30, 183
Ignition switch 178

Indicators 25, 29, 30, 166, 173, 174
Inlet manifolds 27, 28, 168
Inner timing case 39
Instruments 25, 26, 176-179

Junction box 29, 30, 163, 165

Kick-start 33, 44, 58, 80, 85, 87

Main stand 97

Oil cooler 37, 38
Oil filter 48, 87, 88
Oil pressure problem 201, 202
Oil pressure release valve 59, 85, 115, 116
Oil pressure switch 28, 38, 115, 116
Oil pump 48, 49, 80, 81, 82, 86, 87
Owners' clubs 219

Paint colours 200
Parts suppliers 218
Petrol filler cap 193-195, 199
Petrol tank 191-193, 196-200
Petrol tap 199, 200
Pistons 54, 103-107
Publications 211

Rear brake 33, 95, 96, 149, 151
Rear brake light switch 186, 187
Rear chain 34, 36, 151, 152
Rear cowling 24, 197, 198
Rear light 172, 173
Rear mudguard 24, 173
Rear shock absorbers 146, 147
Rear sprocket 35, 36, 148, 150
Rear wheel 34, 35, 67, 68, 70, 92-96, 148-152
Rear wheel hub shock absorbers 149
Rebuilding (planning) 69
Rectifier 29, 30, 164
Registering a bike in the UK 219
Regulator 29, 30, 163, 164
Regulator/rectifier 164, 165
Rotor 40, 41, 122

Seat 23, 174
SHIMS 116-118
Side panels 198, 199
Side stand 36
Specialist services 218
Speedo 176-179
Speedo drive 93
Starter motor 40, 122, 123, 125
Starter solenoid 164
Steering lock 97
Sump 48-50, 86-88
Swinging arm 35, 143-147
Switch gear 26, 27, 185

Tacho 176-179
Tank 23
Tappets 53, 116-118
Ten Golden Rules 17-19
Throttle cable 25, 169
Tool box 174
Tools 208-211
Transmission 58, 59, 79, 80, 84, 85
Tuning carburettors 137-139
Tyres 93

Unobtainable parts 9
Unsprung weight 93

Valve guides 109
Valve timing 38, 39, 113-115
Valves 109, 110
Vapour blasting 70-73

Wiring harness 29
Wiring loom 166-168

Yokes 98, 99

Z1 7, 8, 182
Z1A 7, 8, 182
Z1B 8, 9, 182
Z2 182
Z900 8, 9
Z1000 8, 9